ZIM

ZIM
A BASEBALL LIFE

Don Zimmer

with Bill Madden

KINGSTON, NEW YORK   **TOTAL SPORTS PUBLISHING**   NEW YORK, NEW YORK

For information about permission to reproduce selections from this book, please write to:

Permissions
Total Sports Publishing
100 Enterprise Drive
Kingston, NY 12401
www.TotalSportsPublishing.com

Cover design: Todd Radom
Cover Photographs: Neil Leifer
Interior design: Ann Sullivan

Library of Congress Cataloging-in-Publication Data

Zimmer, Don, 1931-
    Zim: a baseball life / by Don Zimmer with Bill Madden.
        p. cm.
    Includes index.
    ISBN 1-930844-19-0
  1. Zimmer, Don, 1931- 2. Baseball players—United States—Biography. 3. Baseball coaches—United States—Biography. I. Madden, Bill. II. Title.

GV865.Z56 A3 2001
796.357'092—dc21
[B]
                                                        2001017000

Printed in Canada

This book is for the hundreds and hundreds of friends I've made in baseball, but most importantly for my best friend, Soot Bauerle Zimmer. My baseball friends have said she is a saint, and that's an understatement for having to put up with me for half a century. They say I've had a baseball life. This woman is my life.

—D.Z.

For Lil, my No. 1 fan, on whom baseball is no longer lost.

—C.W. M.

CONTENTS

PROLOGUE

It had taken him nearly six weeks to make the call. After contemplating the pain in his knee and the aftereffects of a severe case of the flu (brought on by a half-dozen cross-country trips at the end of the season), he decided he would come back for his 53rd year in baseball. On this day, Don Zimmer found himself strolling among the images of the game's immortals in the Hall of Fame. Outside, the grounds were covered with a fresh coating of snow, temperatures hovering in the 20s, and all those summers in Brooklyn, Los Angeles, Cincinnati, Washington, Tokyo, San Diego, Boston, Texas, Chicago, Denver, and the Bronx never seemed so far away. It was, as Zimmer observed, about the unlikeliest place he could ever expect to be at any time in his life, let alone three weeks before Christmas and six weeks before his 70th birthday.

"I still can't figure out why you want a .235 hitter like me here," he said to Hall of Fame President Dale Petroskey, who merely smiled and replied, "Because you're as much a part of this game as any of the people enshrined here."

It seems they wanted his uniform to be displayed as part of a special Subway Series exhibit—a request Zimmer could only find amusing. "Imagine," he said, "all these guys on these great Yankee teams of Joe Torre, and I'm the first one going to the Hall of Fame!"

As he would soon discover, however, they wanted much more than just his uniform. They wanted the man and, most especially, his memories.

To the baby boomer generation, he was our unlikely baseball tour guide—this squat, bald, impish man with a face like lumpy oatmeal; the self-made journeyman with whom we could all so easily identify. It was his journey that took us from the innocence of our gum-card-collecting youth to our $150 seats at the World Series five decades later. And all the while, he could maintain the pixyish smile of a man who knew that the real meaning of the baseball life was fun.

As Petroskey and the Hall of Fame historians would later attest, it was Zimmer, and Zimmer alone, who could provide that bridge—uninterrupted—from the infancy of integrated baseball to the era of the $250 million contract. Now it was a game in which Hispanics made up nearly 25 percent of its population. Only Zimmer was there when a young Puerto Rican outfielder named Roberto Clemente was being squirreled away in the Brooklyn Dodger farm system, and when another Puerto Rican outfielder, Bernie Williams, would haul in an $87.5 million contract from the New York Yankees. And when a thirty-something refugee pitcher they called "El Duque" joined the Yankees in 1998 after reportedly fleeing Castro's Cuba on a rickety boat, Zimmer had been the only one who could speak from experience to him of having played on those same Havana ballfields before the revolutionists arrived.

Yes, as Petroskey knew, only Zimmer could tell them what it was like to be both Jackie Robinson's teammate and Derek Jeter's mentor.

Like Forrest Gump, he was right there, in the middle of it all, as baseball evolved from a sleepy-time, all-white, mom-and-pop pastime whose boundaries did not extend farther west than the Mississippi River, to a global, corporate colossus.

You could only wonder how much of this was sifting through his mind as he strolled through the great hall of plaques in the heart of the museum. So many former teammates—Robinson, Reese, Snider, Campanella, Koufax, Drysdale. The fiercely contested opponents of youth who became kindred friends—Berra, Musial, Ashburn, and Roberts.

"Robin Roberts lives near me in the Tampa area," Zimmer said, grinning, "and I was at a breakfast with him the day before I came up here. I couldn't resist telling him I was going to the Hall of Fame. He told me to say hello to his plaque. So that's what I'm doing."

"Ashburn, now there was a dandy. We were teammates twice, on a bad Cubs team and an even worse Mets team. Oh, the fun I had with him, especially years later when he was a broadcaster with the Phillies and I was either coaching or managing the Cubs. He'd always have me on his pregame show. We told our stories and we'd both be laughing so hard we could barely get through the show."

But when he got to Pee Wee Reese's plaque, he paused, his face stiffening. His clear blue eyes began to water and for a solemn moment Zimmer was unable to contain his emotion.

"Captain," he said softly. "God, how I miss him."

Not far away from Reese's plaque were the ones of Snider, Campy, and Robinson.

"I hope I live to see the day when Gil Hodges has a plaque here too," Zimmer said. "I don't know what the criteria are, but in my mind if Gil Hodges isn't a Hall of Famer, I don't know who is. There was a man."

He moved on, past the cubicle that contained the great black stars of the '50s and '60s—Hank Aaron, Willie Mays, and Frank Robinson.

"I only played with Frank," he said. "Fiercest competitor you could ever find. Aaron was just one great ballplayer. People only talk about his home runs. He doesn't get the credit he deserves as an out-fielder. He could throw and field with Clemente or Kaline. Mays, what can you say? Wasn't no way he couldn't beat you. He was simply the best there ever was. That's just my opinion."

He had stories about all of them, of course. Stories he would gladly retell for the Hall archivists. Hell, he'd been telling them for seven decades, to all the new generations of baseball players if they wanted to hear them. They did.

"What was Pee Wee Reese like?" Jeter would ask him, echoing the question of yesteryear, "What did you do in the war, Daddy?"

And Zimmer would reply in mock disdain, "You don't want to know. Do you think I'm gonna tell you he wasn't as good as you?"

And then he would proceed to regale the young Yankee short-stop with his Brooklyn war stories. He would tell him how Reese was a totally different shortstop than Jeter in that he didn't have the size, the speed, or the power. What he had was indefinable leadership. It was a different game back then. Shortstops weren't expected to hit home runs. Pitchers weren't afraid to pitch inside, and they finished what they started. Guys played hurt for fear of losing their jobs. Worked offseasons, too, to make ends meet.

"I don't begrudge anything today's players get," Zimmer said. "It astounds me that owners would pay as much for one player as they have for the entire ballclub. I can't relate to that, but I accept it as how the game has changed. One way it *hasn't* changed, though, is that money doesn't necessarily buy championships. I live in Tampa and I watched the team there spend a ton of money before the 2000 sea-son. Then they went out and won 69 games. You spend all that money, you expect to win. Maybe that's what makes Steinbrenner different. He gets accused of spending a lot of money and he does. But he wins. Must be because he spends it on the right players."

Zimmer knew from the money too. Any one of his individual World Series shares from the Yankee championships of '96, '98, '99, and 2000 was more than he earned his entire playing career. But despite the cold, corporate, money-driven enterprise baseball has become, the fun, he insisted, still hasn't gone out of it for him.

"Maybe," he said, "it might have, had I not been around this Yan-kee team with Joe Torre these last five years. There's nothing more fun than winning, and these guys have been special."

So after coming to this sacred baseball place at the behest of its keepers, he was more assured than ever that coming back for another season was the right thing for him to do. He remained Joe Torre's indispensable sidekick and the last link to Pee Wee Reese's Brooklyn. And he would remain true to both.

BILL MADDEN
COOPERSTOWN, N.Y.
DECEMBER 2000

FOREWORD

Quite simply, Don Zimmer has a feel for the game like nobody else. He sits next to me in the dugout for every game, offering sound advice and entertaining us with incredible stories.

Zim has managed four different teams (San Diego, Boston, Texas, and the Chicago Cubs). He has also coached for the Yankees two other times before he joined the team in 1996, so I knew his experience plus his time in New York would be valuable for me. He's old school, yet to watch him communicate with the young players says a lot about his love for the game and the way it's played.

Zim's experience was invaluable on our way to four World Series championships. During a game, it's "we can steal on this guy" or "let's hit and run here." We would agree and disagree, but we never stopped communicating to find a way to win. Zim and I make a good combo—sort of like fire and ice. I guess I don't have to tell you who's who.

Passion is a word that describes my bench coach very well. He's got that fire in his belly. I thought I was going to lose Zim to retirement in 1999 when, during spring training, he had knee surgery and I was diagnosed with prostate cancer. I asked George Steinbrenner if he would be okay with Zim taking over during my absence. The workload of managing, a bad knee, and the Yankees—with all the pressure to win—took its toll. At first, Zim (out of respect) tried to handle the team in the same manner as I would. I told him to just be himself, but he felt very responsible, and the fire burned bright and intense.

I've managed for more than 15 years, and hired friends to be coaches. In Zim's case, I hired a coach who has become one of my closest friends. Picking Zim as my bench coach may have been the best decision I have ever made. I check with him for approval on everything except what wine to order at dinner. Although I must say, he's come a long way. To slip in beside Don Zimmer in the dugout, you would understand why I've come to love this man. Four World Series in five years—I'd say we're a pretty good daily double. Also, the friendship that my wife Ali and I share with both Don and Soot is terrific.

Zim: A Baseball Life is a warm, funny, sentimental journey through seven decades of baseball. Zim has seen it all, and now he tells it all as our personal historian of the game over the last half century. I've been so fortunate to be the beneficiary of all this knowledge sitting right next to me. Now, in the pages that follow, everyone else will find out exactly what I mean.

JOE TORRE
DECEMBER 2000

ACKNOWLEDGMENTS

The author would like to acknowledge and thank the following people for their contributions to this book:

Soot Zimmer, for having both the foresight and the tireless devotion to compile the two dozen scrapbooks and all the priceless photographs of her husband's career which helped provide the basis for this book.

Rick Cerrone, Arthur Richman, Jason Zillo, Billy O'Sullivan, Matt McKendry, and Rikki Dileo of the New York Yankees public relations department for researching background information on Don Zimmer's coaching career with the Yankees.

Josh Weintraub, segment producer for The Late Show with David Letterman, for providing additional anecdotal material obtained from Mr. Zimmer from his appearances on the program.

Art Berke, a cherished friend who provided the author the vast resources of *Sports Illustrated*, which were invaluable in filling in details of Mr. Zimmer's life.

Moss Klein, Marty Appel, and Bob Raissman for assisting in the research for this book.

Jeff Idelson and the Baseball Hall of Fame for the hospitality they showed Mr. Zimmer and their assistance in other research for this book.

David Fisher and Tom Connor, who believed so deeply in this project and provided the relentless encouragement to see it to fruition.

RLR Associates Ltd., particularly Jonathan Diamond and Jennifer Unter, for making it happen.

Jed Thorn, for his capable line editing of this book.

And lastly, Robert Wilson, a writer's editor, who was a delight to work with. To quote Bogie's "Rick" to Claude Rains' Captain Renault: "This could be the beginning of a beautiful friendship."

ZIM

1

Who Am I and How Did I Get Here?

I thought of calling this book "Confessions of a .235 Lifetime Hitter," if only because my own grandchildren have told me that the thing I'll be most remembered for after 52 years in baseball is wearing an army helmet in the dugout. Not for being a central figure in one of the most brilliant managing moves in World Series history, or for being one of the four $125,000 "premium" expansion players selected by the original Mets in 1961, or even for managing two of baseball's most storied franchises, the Boston Red Sox and Chicago Cubs, in two of their most exciting seasons.

Nope, my grandkids tell me, that army helmet—which a national TV audience of 30 million people saw me wearing in the Yankee dugout the night after I got beaned in the head by a foul ball—has forever given me my special niche in baseball history.

I suppose that's only appropriate since the most defining moments of my career have involved my head. In this latest and hopefully last one, it was the fifth inning of the first game of the 1999 Division Series between the Yankees and Texas Rangers. I was sitting next to Joe Torre in the Yankee dugout in my capacity as bench coach. Chuck Knoblauch, the Yankees' leadoff man, was at the plate and he took a funny swing at the pitch. I was half-looking out on the field and half-watching Knoblauch and I didn't see the ball until it was about two feet from my face. I ducked my head and—smack!—I felt the ball hit me on the side of my face. The next thing I knew I was laying on the floor of the dugout, numb and woozy. Then I saw blood and I got panicked. I yelled, "Get this jacket off!"

They cut the jacket off me, carried me back into the clubhouse and laid me on the trainer's table. I was bleeding like a hog and didn't really know how badly I was hurt. I knew I had been whacked in the head but I didn't know where. That's what scared me, knowing all the things that have happened to my head.

As I lay there, I looked up and Yogi Berra and George Steinbrenner were standing over me. It was then that they told me the ball had hit me between the neck and ear and had nicked the ear which accounted for all the blood. George was especially concerned and I heard him say they're going to have to put a Plexiglass shield in front of the dugout "because we can't have guys getting hurt like this."

They told me my wife, Jean, who I have always affectionately called Soot, was out in the hallway, and they led her into the clubhouse. I told her, "Have someone take you back to your seat in the stands, grab yourself a hotdog and enjoy the rest of the game."

After she left, all I could think was, *This would have been a helluva way to end my career in baseball, especially since this was the way it all started.*

I grew up in Cincinnati, Ohio, and attended Western Hills High School. My coach there, Paul Nohr, was one of the greatest high school baseball coaches ever. Nearly a dozen of his players, including Pete Rose, Russ Nixon, Clyde Vollmer, Herman Wehmeier, Ed Brinkman, and Art Mahaffey, went on to the big leagues, and four of them—Rose, Nixon, Jim Frey, and myself—all managed in the big leagues. That's quite a legacy.

The summer before my senior year at Western Hills, my American Legion team won the national championship. The finals were held at Gilmore Stadium in Los Angeles and we got to meet Babe Ruth, who was at the game doing some promotional work for American Legion baseball. Ruth gave a speech after the final game—I'll never forget how hoarse his voice was; he died a year later—and they finally had to quiet the crowd down after about two or three minutes so he could talk. He said he had traveled all over the country watching American Legion baseball and the best team won. You can imagine how that made us all feel. Then he signed a ball for every one of us.

When we returned in triumph to Cincinnati, it seemed like the whole town came out to the railroad station to greet us. I lived on a dead-end street with no traffic and we played ball there just about every day. That summer, the ball we used was the one Ruth signed for me. What did I know? We played with it until we knocked the cover off it and then we put black tape all over it. The last time I saw it, it was in some sewer. Only a few years ago did I realize Babe Ruth signed balls are worth anywhere from $5,000–$10,000 in good shape.

As a reward for winning the championship, the townspeople gave us a trip to New York and tickets for the first two games of the 1947 World Series between the Yankees and Dodgers.

I'll never forget that first day I set foot inside Yankee Stadium and saw Jackie Robinson at first base for the Dodgers. I think of that every time I walk into Yankee Stadium. That was Jackie's rookie season, and little did I know a few years later I'd be calling him a teammate and, even more importantly, a friend.

During my senior year, in which I made all-Ohio as quarterback for our football team and played shortstop on the baseball team, I was offered numerous scholarships to play both sports in college. I got invited along with one of my best friends, Glenn Sample (who was a tough lineman), to fly down to the University of Kentucky for the weekend where the legendary coach, Bear Bryant, had invited us. I had never been in an airplane. Sample was planning to go to college. I wasn't, but for a chance to get my first plane ride, I made the trip with him. I roomed with Babe Parilli, one of the all-time great quarterbacks who went from Kentucky to a long career in the pros. They had us throw passes and do some running in our T-shirts and shorts, and afterward Bryant offered us full four-year scholarships.

I told him I was only interested in playing baseball, and he understood. Years later, when I was managing Knoxville in the Southern Association, Bryant's son was the general manager of the Birmingham team in the league. On our first trip to Birmingham, the visiting clubhouse man came to me and said, "There's a guy outside with a hat who wants to see you." It was Bryant. A few years after that, he came to visit me again in Boston when I was managing the Red Sox and one of his former 'Bama quarterbacks, Butch Hobson, was my third baseman.

I often thought about how funny it was to become friends with Bryant, even though I never played for him. I just wanted to play baseball and the sooner I got my career underway the better. Naturally, my first preference was to play for my hometown team, the Reds, and they kept telling me how much they wanted me. Their local scout, Buzz Boyle, invited me out to Crosley Field on a number of occasions and I got to know all the Reds players at the time, as well as their manager, Johnny Neun.

At the same time, Cliff Alexander, the football coach at our rival Woodward High, was a bird dog scout for the Dodgers, and one day he came to me and told me he'd like to take me to Brooklyn for a tryout. I told the Reds about it and Johnny Neun got half-hot and called my dad and said, "We've been recruiting him, you can't let him go to Brooklyn!" My dad assured him I wouldn't sign in New York.

When I got to Brooklyn and reported to Ebbets Field, George Sisler, the Hall of Fame first baseman, was conducting the tryout as the director of minor league operations for the Dodgers. Mind you, Sisler was a legend, a lifetime .340 hitter, and when I got up to bat for the first time, he was leaning on the cage behind me, a real imposing figure. The last thing I wanted to do was to swing and miss. So I choked up on the bat and started spraying the ball all over the field. After that first round, Cliff Alexander came over and said to me: "Where did you come up with that new style of hitting?" I told him I just wanted to make contact for Sisler. He looked at me and shook his head. "When we come back here tomorrow," he said, "go back to your old swing. I told him you were a power hitter and he's wondering where the power is."

Well, the next day I hit three or four balls out of the ballpark and Branch Rickey, the Dodger president, was there to watch it. After the tryout, he said, "We'll offer you $2,500 to sign a contract with us." Because my dad had promised the Reds I wouldn't sign anything in New York, I went home to Cincinnati and told the Reds of the Dodger offer. They said to me: "We can't offer you that, but we'll give you $2,000 and start you off in Class-B ball instead of Class D where the Dodgers will start you." They came up with the weakest excuse for not giving me the same money, saying "We're not sure if your arm is big league caliber." They'd been courting me two years, watching me play quarterback and shortstop, and if there's one thing they knew about me it was that my arm was my best attribute.

So I had no trouble saying no to my hometown team and sign-ing with the Dodgers. As promised, they started me out at their lowest rung, a Class-D farm team in Cambridge, Maryland. I'd like to say I wasted no time in making the Reds look bad, but it didn't quite work out that way. In fact, my first experience in professional baseball was probably more embarrassing to the Dodgers.

I reported to Cambridge in 1949 with a salary of $150 per month—$2,550 for the whole season. I bought a used green Ford coupe with a stick shift for $700 and, yeah, I thought I was a real hot potato.

In only my fourth game I made Eastern Shore League history. It was the last year of the league's existence and I probably did as much as anyone to hasten its shutdown. We played in a very primi-tive old ballpark in which the infield was full of bumps and ruts. In this particular game, I was playing shortstop and our pitcher was a guy named Zeke Zeisz, who was the only veteran on the team.

The first ground ball to me hit a rut and struck me in the shoul-der before continuing on into left field. The next ball to come my way hit me in the neck and also wound up in left field. Now, there was a pop fly hit into shallow left. I went out and the left fielder came in. But when the left fielder gave up on the ball, it came down and bounced off my glove. I couldn't believe what was happening to me, but I shrugged it off, chalking it up to the field conditions and circumstances beyond my control.

The next inning, another hard ground ball was hit to me at short and this time I fielded it cleanly. Unfortunately, in my elation of finally catching something that came my way, I threw the ball across the diamond two feet over the first baseman's head and off the front of an outhouse that was behind first base. You've heard the old expres-sion "He went from the penthouse to the shithouse"? Well that pretty much describes my introduction to professional baseball.

After the game, I was walking off the field behind Zeisz and our third baseman, Hank Parker. I heard Zeisz say, "What the hell kind of shortstop is that guy? He can't play a lick!" Parker replied, "He was playing high school ball six days ago. Give the kid a break!" I never forgot that vote of confidence.

Meanwhile, I had arranged to have the newspapers sent home to my father in Cincinnati, and a couple of days later I got a phone call from him. All he said was: "Well, it didn't take you long to break a record. Six errors in one game? According to the paper, nobody ever did that before in that league!"

I finished my first pro season with numbers that hardly gave hint of a future in the big leagues—a .227 batting average, four homers in 304 at bats, and 27 errors. I half-expected the Dodgers to release me, but the next year they sent me to Hornell, New York, a little railroad town in the PONY League, another Class-D affiliate. We played in a tiny little ballpark right next to the railroad and it was filled every night. I don't know if it was the enthusiastic crowds or just the year's experience, but I had a real breakout season there. I hit .315 and led the league in runs scored with 146 and homers with 23. I also knocked in 122 runs in 123 games and stole home 10 times! We had a big Cuban left fielder named Oscar Sierra who couldn't run a lick but hit nothing but line drives. I'd get on base, steal second and third, and Sierra would knock me in. I stole 63 bases all told. Charlie Neal, who would later go with me to the big leagues, was also on that team, playing second and third.

The next year I reported to Vero Beach looking forward to seeing if I could make a higher level. There were over 700 players in spring training as the Dodgers had 23 farm teams back then. They sent me to Elmira of the Class-A Eastern League. The jump from Class D to Class A was one of the biggest ever made by a player in the Dodger organization. This was when they began talking about me as the Dodgers' shortstop successor to Pee Wee Reese.

I was in pretty select company. At that time, the Dodgers had six other shortstops in their organization—Eddie Miksis, Tommy Brown, Rocky Bridges, Billy Hunter, Chico Carrasquel, and Jim Pendleton—who all wound up in the big leagues. I might add, none of them—including me—was ever able to replace Pee Wee. There's a reason Pee Wee's in the Hall of Fame. He was a great shortstop for a long, long time.

Over the winter, between the 1950 and '51 seasons, my older brother Harold, who we called Junior, asked me if I could get him a tryout with the Dodgers. Harold was a pretty good hitter and might have been a better ballplayer than I was. He just didn't really have a position. So I made a call to the Dodgers' farm director, Fresco Thompson, who agreed to pay Harold's expenses to Vero Beach for spring training. When he got there, he quickly showed them he had a good bat, and the Dodgers signed him to a contract.

I had wanted Harold to go to Hornell, after the great experience I'd had there the year before, but for some reason he was intent on going to the Dodgers' other Class-D team in Hazard, Kentucky, in the Mountain States League, managed by a fellow named Max Macon. Macon had played about 200 games in the major leagues as an outfielder and pitcher in the '40s for the Dodgers and Braves before embarking on a minor league managing career. The word among most of the Dodger farmhands was that he wasn't a particularly good guy to play for and not many of them liked him. In addition, Macon was an icon in Hazard (if there is such a thing as an icon in Hazard), having won the Mountain States League batting title the year before with a .392 average.

It was obvious Macon, who was only a couple of years removed from the major leagues, was a man playing among children in this Class-D league comprised mostly of teenagers fresh off the high school sandlots. Nevertheless, the folks of Hazard showered him with gifts after the season, and as my brother was to find out, this was a little perk old Max wasn't about to have threatened.

A few weeks into the 1951 season for Hazard, my brother was hitting .336 with nine homers in 37 games. Macon was beginning to feel threatened by his presence and one day slapped Harold with a $25 fine for missing a sign or something. In those days $25 was like a month's meal money. When Harold appealed to Macon about the fine being excessive and more than he could possibly pay, he was told, "That's too bad, you're gonna pay it." That's when my brother pinned Macon up against the wall. The next day, Harold was sent to Ponca City, Oklahoma, where he finished up the season. He might have continued on and even made the big leagues, but the whole Max Macon experience soured my brother toward professional baseball and he just quit. That winter, however, he told me about a pitcher he'd met in Hazard who, he said, would be pitching in the majors the next year.

"You must be nuts," I said. "You're talking about somebody going from Class-D ball to the majors! Nobody does that!"

"This guy will," Harold said. "You mark my words. He's that good!"

The pitcher he was talking about was Johnny Podres, who was 21–3 at Hazard and led the league in strikeouts (228 in 200 innings) and ERA (1.67). For 1952, the Dodgers moved Podres all the way up to Triple A at Montreal and, sure enough, by the end of the season he was in Brooklyn. To stay, I might add.

I had another good season at Elmira, the highlight being getting married to Jean Bauerle, my high school sweetheart, at home plate. It was a real baseball ceremony, with my teammates holding bats over our heads as we took our vows, and if Soot didn't know before what kind of life she was getting herself into, she certainly knew now.

My progression through the Dodger minor league system toward Brooklyn was fast and steady. I hit .319 at Mobile in 1952, prompting the Dodgers to send me to St. Paul, their Triple-A affiliate, for the 1953 season. I was only 22 years old and one step away from the big leagues.

Actually, there was a time that spring when I thought I might even start the season with the Dodgers. I had had a helluva spring and Charlie Dressen, the Dodger manager, really took a liking to me, especially after I stole third base in a Grapefruit League game against the Reds when the Cincinnati pitcher, Kent Peterson, never bothered to check me at second base. "That's the way to do it!" I heard Charlie yelling on the bench.

I got to go north with the Dodgers as they barnstormed their way through the South, playing exhibition games in Jacksonville, Knoxville, and Louisville. Finally, when we got to Washington, Charlie called me to his room and said, "Kid, you deserved to make the team, but we're going to send you to St. Paul where you can play every day. If something happens to Pee Wee, I promise you'll be here."

And after the year I was having at St. Paul, I really believed it was just a matter of time before the Dodgers would call me up. Little did I know, I was going to be closer to death than the big leagues in a couple of weeks. By the first week of July, I was hitting .300 and battling Wally Post, a future slugger for the Reds, and Al Smith, who went on to a fine career with the Indians, White Sox, and Orioles, for the American Association home run title. We were finishing up a homestand against the Yankees' Kansas City farm team and I hit three homers against a lefthander named Bob Wiesler. That put me up by five over Post and Smith as we went on the road.

The first stop was Columbus where we had a twi-night double-header against the Cardinals' top farm team. A big righthander named Jim Kirk was pitching the first game for Columbus. I remember as I came up the first time against him there was a bunch of trees in center field that didn't have many leaves on them and it was tough picking up the ball. The first pitch from Kirk was a ball up close to my head and I turned to the catcher and said, "I didn't see that ball too good, did you?" His reply was that between the trees in center field and the twilight it was hard to see. Sure enough, the next pitch hit me right square in the left side of the head and I went down like a KO'd boxer.

The next thing I knew, Clay Bryant, our manager, was standing over me. I said to him, "Am I bleeding?" And he said, "No, Zim, just lie still, you're okay." But I was anything but okay. The ball had fractured my skull and that led to blood clots forming on my brain which required spinal taps every two or three days afterward in order to monitor my condition. Bryant's reassuring words were all I remembered until I woke up in White Cross Hospital six days later.

My wife and my parents were standing there at my bedside, looking down at me and, to me, it looked like three each of them. I was seeing triple! Then I tried to say something and found out I couldn't speak either! My wife began to explain to me what had happened. Like I said, my skull had been fractured and there had been a blood clot on the left side. After first thinking I'd have a quick and full recovery, the doctors realized it was a lot worse. I had been hit on the side of the brain that was my speech center. They had to drill three holes in the left side of my skull to relieve the pressure, but when my condition didn't improve, a couple of days later they drilled another hole in the right side of my skull. People think I've got a metal plate in my head—that's always been the story—but the fact is they filled those holes up with what they call tantalum buttons that act kind of like corks in a bottle. I can therefore truthfully state that all of those players who played for me through the years and thought I sometimes managed like I had a hole in my head were wrong. I actually have four holes in my head!

The doctor would come in every day and test my reflexes with a rubber mallet and a needle to my foot. Day after day, I didn't feel anything when he moved the needle to the right side of my foot, and I was really scared. My father, who owned a wholesale fruit and vegetable company in Cincinnati, made the trip to Columbus every day to offer me encouragement. Finally, I began to regain some feeling, and each day Soot, who was now pregnant with our daughter, Donna, would help me walk around the hospital corridors. To help restore my eyesight, the doctors fit my head with a brace so I couldn't turn it and had me do eye exercises, identifying objects by moving them back and forth in front of my eyes. After a few weeks of that, my sight was almost back to normal, but I had developed a stutter in my speech. The doctors also had me taking anti-convulsion pills. In the meantime, my weight had dropped from 170 to 124. All I could think about was what was going to happen to my career.

Then one day, the Dodgers' front office chiefs, general manager Buzzie Bavasi and farm director Fresco Thompson, came to the hospital to check out my condition and offer their encouragement. They told me not to worry about playing baseball anymore. There would always be a job in the Dodger organization for me. That was the last thing I wanted to hear. I was only 22 years old and I was in the midst of my best season ever. I couldn't think about not playing anymore. Just the suggestion from them that I might not ever play again gave me the incentive to prove everybody wrong.

After I was released from the hospital, they held a special day for me in St. Paul in September and I received dozens of telegrams from well-wishers. Two of them in particular were special and I still have them. The first one was from the Columbus Redbirds team and it read: "Congratulations to a great player on this your day. St. Paul will be missing its greatest shortstop next year when you're playing for the Dodgers." The second one read simply: "Please accept my heartiest congratulations. I know your courage will continue to make your baseball career a bright one." It was signed, Jim Kirk.

You can be sure I thought back on all of this when I was lying on that trainer's table in the Yankee clubhouse all these years later after getting beaned by Knoblauch's line drive. Happily, my recovery from this one was considerably faster. I was back in the dugout a couple of innings later and the first thing I said to Joe was, "What the hell was wrong with you? Why didn't you catch that ball? You've got hands like meat hooks!"

Joe just looked at me and laughed. When I came into the Yankee clubhouse the next day after this latest beaning, there was this big hatbox in my locker. I opened it up and there is this old army helmet. It wasn't a replica. It was the real thing. Well, I looked around the clubhouse trying to decide who the culprit was who put this thing here. First, I thought it was Mel Stottlemyre, our pitching coach, who's a big prankster. Then I figured it was probably Jeter who's always doing things to me, like rubbing my head. So I put the helmet on and walked over to Jeter's locker and said, "Did you give me this thing? Well, I'm wearing it now!" Jeter laughed and said, "No sir. Not me." Then George walked into the clubhouse and saw me standing there with the helmet on my head and started laughing. "Well," he said, "I guess the helmet's cheaper than Plexiglass. But you don't have the guts to wear that thing in the dugout."

That's all I had to hear. When we went out to the dugout for the start of the game, I sat the helmet down between Joe and myself. We got the Rangers out in the top of the first and Knoblauch walked past me to the bat rack to lead off for us. As he passed in front of me, I said, "Do you have any objections if I wear this since you popped me last night?" "Hell no," he said.

Well, as I said, it seems like everybody in America saw me wearing that helmet, and after the game, both my son, Tommy, and my daughter called and asked me for it. Since then, people have offered me thousands of dollars for it. How crazy is this game? Sixty years after ruining that Babe Ruth ball, I get whacked in the head and make an old army helmet worth almost as much!

I later found out the person who sent it to me was not Stottlemyre or Jeter but, rather, an advertising executive named Michael Patti who was at the game and went out and bought the helmet at a military surplus store on a whim. Patti was quoted in the papers a couple of days later as saying he was a huge Yankee fan who hated me when I was manager of the Red Sox, but now that I was with the Yankees he'd come to like me.

As much attention as all this got, I'd like to think I've been involved in a lot more significant events in my baseball career. For instance, if it wasn't for me departing the premises the Dodgers might never have won the 1955 World Series. Everybody remembers it was Sandy Amoros who made the saving catch off Yogi Berra in the seventh game that year. But Amoros was only in the game because our manager, Walter Alston, had the foresight to insert him in left field at the start of that inning as a defensive replacement. Jim Gilliam had been playing in left and moved to second base. The player who came out of the game for Amoros was me. I've always said the Dodgers would never have won their only World Series in Brooklyn if Alston hadn't had the good sense to take me out of the game.

Looking back, I can't believe how fortunate I've been to find myself a part of so much baseball history across seven decades—not to mention 46 years between two beanings. There was another bean-ing in between, too—which, looking back, was probably the worst of the three. I'll tell you about that after I tell you how I got my career re-started from the first one.

2

Dodger Blue

When I got out of the hospital at the end of that summer of '53, Buzzie Bavasi sent me a check for $1,500 and told me to go to Florida for the winter to recuperate. He didn't know my in-laws had moved there and that I had a free place to live. My sight seemed to have come back to almost 100 percent, and all my reflexes seemed fine. But I knew I couldn't be certain if I could still play until I got to spring training and started facing live pitching. What did concern me were these migraine headaches I kept getting. The doctors told me this was a natural aftereffect of the beaning, and that in time they'd go away. Nevertheless, they lasted for about a year, and if you've ever had a migraine, you know how awful they are. I was getting them two or three times a week.

It was nice being in Florida on Buzzie's money, but I was getting really antsy just sitting around, doing nothing. One day I was reading the sports pages and saw all these stories about the local softball leagues in St. Pete. "How do I get into this?" I said to myself. I'd played softball all my life back in Cincinnati when I wasn't playing baseball.

So I called the city recreation department and was put through to the head man, a guy named Don Donnelly, who later became a real close friend. I told him who I was and asked him if he could get me onto one of those softball teams. Right away I could tell he was thrilled at the idea.

"Give me 20 minutes and I'll be back to you," Donnelly said.

As promised, he called me back 20 minutes later with a proposition I could never have anticipated.

"There's a league that plays over in Largo that has a team from a prison camp in it," Donnelly said. "I've talked to the warden, who manages the team, and he said he'd love to have you if you're interested."

In my wildest dreams I never thought I'd ever be playing ball for a prison team, but this was an offer I couldn't refuse. I desperately wanted to get back onto a ballfield again, and I didn't care who it was with.

"When do I report?" I said.

"Tomorrow at 6:30 at Woodlawn Park," Donnelly replied. "You'll recognize your team. They'll be the ones arriving in a yellow truck with a wired fence on it. Their uniforms have stripes on them and the warden will be carrying a double-barreled shotgun."

Sure enough, as I was waiting with my wife and two baby kids at Woodlawn Park, this yellow truck pulled up with my new teammates aboard. The warden got off first, carrying his shotgun, and shook my hand.

"Great to have you," he said. "From here on out, you're the manager too."

The prisoners had been 0–4 up to that point, despite the fact the warden had promised to give them a pack of cigarettes for every game they won. So as soon as everyone got off the truck, we had a huddle.

Pointing to the fence that surrounded the outfield, I said to them, "All of you guys want to hit one over that fence, don't you?"

"Yeah," they said in unison.

"Well, that's why you're 0–4," I said.

I then picked three little guys out of the group.

"You three are gonna bat first, second, and third," I said, "and I want you to hit the ball on the ground and just run. I'm hitting fourth. You'll leave the homers to me."

Well, from that night on they started beating everybody. I was hitting the home runs and having a helluva time. Everyone knew who the manager was, too; I was the only one not wearing stripes. The warden was happy not to be managing anymore, but he was a little pissed about having to buy all those cigarettes. I wound up playing all that winter, as well as the next, with the prison team, and I got to be good friends with most of them. One of them, my second baseman, asked me after the second winter if he could take a picture of me to send to his kids.

"It'll really mean something to them," he said.

"No problem," I said. "Take the picture, and when you get it developed I'll sign it for you."

"You have no idea how much this means to me," he said.

Unfortunately, by the time he got the picture back, I'd gone home to Cincinnati to spend some time with my parents before the season started. The guy called me and told me he had the picture.

"I'm really sorry you can't sign it for me," he said, "but would it be okay if I signed it for you?"

"Sure," I said. "I don't have any problem with that if you don't."

We talked a little more—I really liked the guy—and then, before I hung up, I said, "By the way, what are you in there for anyway?"

"Oh," he said, "didn't I tell you? Sonovabitches got me for forgery!"

As it turned out, the following summer was the prison team's last in the Tampa–St. Pete–Largo recreation softball league. Apparently, they were playing a game at a different field that didn't have an outfield fence. When an opposing batter hit a ball to deep center, the prison center fielder ran for it—and kept right on running out to the street where a car was waiting for him. That was the one provision the warden had set down when he allowed the team to be formed. If anyone tried to escape, the team would immediately be disbanded.

I'm glad no one tried to escape when I was the manager. That first winter, especially, was a great confidence-builder for me. Even though it was softball, just getting out there, hitting the ball, and fielding got my juices flowing again and helped relieve a lot of my anxiety.

I reported with much anticipation to Vero Beach in the spring of 1954. The Dodgers had a new manager, Walter Alston, who had been promoted from their Triple-A farm in Montreal after Charlie Dressen resigned in a contract dispute. I was sorry to see Dressen go, if only because I knew how much he liked me from the brief time I had played for him in spring training. We also liked to play the horses together. I didn't know Alston and he didn't know me—a conflict that, in my opinion, had a lingering effect on my entire Dodger career.

Knowing I had no chance of making the team that spring and

that I was only going to get into games as Pee Wee's backup in the eighth or ninth innings, I asked Alston to send me out on the first round of cuts so I could play. He obliged me and sent me immediately to St. Paul where Clay Bryant was still the manager.

After my beaning, Buzzie had ordered protective inserts placed in all the Dodger caps throughout the organization, but as it turned out, even that couldn't prevent my head from being a magnet for errant baseballs. In our first spring training game against Minneapolis, the Giants' Triple-A farm, I was at bat with a runner, Walt Moryn, on first, and Bryant put a hit-and-run play on. Well, when the manager puts a hit and run on, you've got to swing the bat no matter where the pitch is. The pitcher, a big lefthander named Pete Burnside, threw a slider breaking in. I chopped at it to protect Moryn, who was running, and the ball hit me right square in the forehead where there was no insert in my cap!

I was momentarily dazed, and the next day Buzzie called and said, "I'm sending you home. You're gonna kill me!"

I assured him I was okay and managed to talk him out of it. Then once the regular season began, I started hitting homers again, just like the year before. This time, though, the opposing pitchers had begun to test me by knocking me down with regularity. It didn't bother me right then because I knew I had that part of it whipped. I wasn't afraid. I pretty much realized that the first time I faced Kirk again, early in the season in Columbus. I could tell he was scared to death, even though everyone knew his hitting me in the head the year before was an accident.

My dad was sitting in the stands right behind home plate this time, when some guy in the row in front of him started yelling, "Hey Kirk! This time hit him real good!"

The guy kept up his shouting at Kirk to hit me again when my dad finally tapped him on the shoulder and said: "Let me tell you something, buddy. If he does hit him, it'll be an accident, but just the same, if my kid gets hit I'm going to hit you!"

Even though I knew I had passed the point of any fear, when word of all these knockdowns got back to Brooklyn, Fresco Thompson, our farm director, was furious and ordered Bryant to start doing something to protect me.

In a game against Toledo, it got especially nasty when their pitchers knocked me down a couple of times, and afterward I heard two of their players, Bob Thorpe and Kermit Wahl, make some comments about how I could expect more of the same the next time we played them. We got back to St. Paul and our best pitcher that year, a lefthander named Wade Browning, called me aside before we were to play Toledo again. "I'm going to look your way at short before facing every batter," he said, "and if you tug at your belt I'm gonna knock the guy at the plate on his ass. You got it?"

I got it. When Thorpe came up in the first inning, I tugged at my belt and Browning threw a pitch right at his neck that just missed him. The next pitch didn't miss him. It was the same thing with Wahl. Browning had deliberately put the first two runners on base by hitting them. Now the third hitter in the inning, a big slugging first baseman named George Crowe, sees what's happening and he's halfway out of the batter's box as the first pitch from Browning comes in. That was the last time I had to give a tug. They had gotten the message.

A few days later, we were watching the Game of the Week on TV, which just happened to be the Dodgers. There was a ball hit to short, which Pee Wee backhanded. But when he came up to throw, his back buckled and he was forced to leave the game. That night, before our game in St. Paul, our general manager, Mel Jones, called me aside and said right after the game I'd be taking a red-eye flight to Philadelphia to join the Dodgers for their game tomorrow. I was hitting .291 with 17 homers and 53 RBIs in 73 games and I guess he wanted to get one more game out of me. I thought it was kind of selfish on their part, but I didn't complain. I was finally going to the Dodgers. My dad, who was sitting in the stands that night, started crying when I gave him the thumbs up. After the game, the media gathered around my locker said I'd be back in two weeks, as soon as Pee Wee was okay to play again.

"There's no way I'll be back," I said, defiantly. "I've got nothing more to prove here after hitting 40 homers in 150 games over two seasons."

They looked a little stunned to hear me say that, but I was right. My minor league apprenticeship was over.

When I arrived at Shibe Park in Philadelphia the next morning, the Dodgers greeted me warmly. I had gotten to know most of them from the previous two spring trainings, so even though I was now in the same clubhouse with Jackie Robinson, Duke Snider, Roy Campanella, Gil Hodges, Pee Wee Reese & Co., I wasn't at all overwhelmed.

Alston had me hitting eighth that day against Curt Simmons, a hard-throwing lefthander for the Phillies. In a lot of ways, my first at bat in the majors mirrored my entire career; it encompassed not only my determination to succeed and my ability to hit the longball, but also what might have been had fate not interceded.

Shibe Park, with its short left field porch and protruding upper deck, was a real good park for righthanded hitters. After the count reached 3–2, I fouled two or three balls back on Simmons. Finally, I hit a good one, although in my mind I didn't think I got all of it. As I was heading into second, I saw the ball coming back from left field. I kept on running and dove into third base. A triple in my first major league at bat! As I was standing on third, feeling about as good as anyone could ever feel, the third base umpire, Dusty Boggess, sauntered over to me.

"Be careful here, son," he mumbled. "You don't want to get yourself doubled off."

I thought that was a really great thing. In my first major league game the umpire was trying to help me. Years later, when I was managing, I didn't feel quite so kindly toward umpires.

It turned out, after the game there was a dispute about my hit. A couple of the Phillies told me the ball had actually hit off the upper deck overhang—which would have made it a home run. The umpires had ruled it hit off the lower railing, making the ball still in play. I wish I could say I hit a home run in my first major league at bat. Actually, I guess I did, but it went into the books as a triple and I'm probably the only person alive today who will testify the ball hit off the upper deck for a homer. Looking back, I should have seen that as an omen—that I was never going to get to the Hall of Fame unless it was on a tour bus.

As expected, Pee Wee came back to play about a week later and Buzzie called me up to his office.

"What do you want to do, son?" he asked. "We can send you back to St. Paul where you can play every day, or you can stay here and sit on the bench. It's your call."

"I've got nothing more to prove at St. Paul," I said. "I want to stay up here."

I got into only 24 games with the Dodgers that first season, but I felt confident I'd be getting a full shot the next year. As I said earlier, though, Alston didn't know me. He had managed at Montreal while I was at St. Paul, the Dodgers' other Triple-A farm. At Montreal, Alston had Jim Gilliam, Don Hoak, and Bobby Morgan, the Dodgers' other backup infielders at the time, and they were essentially his guys.

Even though I had another real good spring in 1955, I was prepared to spend most of the season as Pee Wee's backup. However, when we got home to Brooklyn for the start of the season, Pee Wee called me to his room at the St. George Hotel. I walked in and he was a mess. He was lying in bed and could hardly move. His back had gone out again. We called a doctor who gave him a shot, but it was clear he wasn't going to be able to play anytime soon.

So, lo and behold, when the 1955 season opened, I was the starting shortstop for the Dodgers. Since they won their only World Series in Brooklyn that year, this at least qualifies me as the answer to a good trivia question. The Dodgers staked their claim on first place early, reeling off a record 10 straight victories to start the season. As the streak reached eight, Pee Wee was ready to come back to play, but Alston didn't want to mess with a winning combination and he let me stay out there until we finally lost.

Not long after Pee Wee returned to short, Alston came to me and asked me if I could play second base. Now this wasn't like the minor leagues, where I had refused to move off short. You didn't say "no" to the man. I had never played second in my life, but I immediately told Alston, "Sure. I can play it." I knew nothing about the pivot or how to play the hitters from that side of the infield, but I wanted to play.

In my first game at second, there was a runner on first when the Giants' Willie Mays, who was one of the fastest runners in the league, hit a hard shot to Jackie Robinson at third. Robinson knocked it down, picked it up and fired over to me, covering second. I got the throw, turned and threw over to first a half-step ahead of Mays for the game-ending double play. From that point on, I was as much a semi-regular second baseman as I was the backup shortstop. I finished the season with 15 homers and 50 RBIs in 88 games. I also got into four of the seven World Series games against the Yankees, including the historic seventh when, as I said earlier, I made Sandy Amoros's saving catch off Yogi possible by getting taken out of the game.

Earlier during that '55 season there was a game in Brooklyn in which I hit two homers into the upper deck in left. Back then, there were no "high fives" or curtain calls after a home run. You came back to the dugout and everybody shook your hand. Anyway, it was an especially hot day and I had no jersey under my short-sleeved uniform top. The first home run was hit about three or four rows back in the Ebbets Field upper deck. The second one was hit even further. When I came into the dugout and everyone came up to shake my hand, Campy grabbed me by my biceps and, in that shrieking voice of his, yelled, "No wonder this little guy can hit balls like that! He's got arms like Popeye!" It was a nickname that stuck with me the rest of my life.

Even though I've always joked about being taken out of the seventh game of the '55 World Series, I can't gloss over the ruckus I caused when Alston benched me for Game 3. I had started the first two games of the Series at second and was hitting .400 with two RBIs. But when I got to the ballpark for Game 3, Milt Richman, the legendary baseball writer for UPI, approached me and asked me how I felt about not starting that day. I thought he was joking until somebody told me Alston wanted another lefthanded bat in the lineup against the Yankees' ace righthander, Bob Turley, and that Gilliam was playing second.

Well, I gave Richman an earful. I said it was pretty lousy the manager didn't even have the decency to tell me, and that I had to find out from a newspaperman. I went on to say even though I was no Ted Williams, I was doing okay. If I'd loused up in the field or something, I could understand.

The next morning, I picked up the paper at my hotel and saw this big black headline: ZIMMER BLASTS ALSTON. I knew I was in big trouble. Worse, I had to pick up Pee Wee and Rube Walker, our backup catcher, and drive them to the ballpark. I was nervous as all hell when I came by to pick them up. Here was Pee Wee, the captain of the team, and he's got to read this. I was sick and felt even sicker when the two of them gave me the silent treatment all the way to the ballpark. I had forgotten what team I was on, and the fact that the reason I was playing at all was because Jackie had been struggling and Alston had benched him! Once we arrived, it only got worse. Buzzie, as I fully expected, was waiting for me and he was steaming.

Pulling the paper out of his back pocket, he waved it in my face and screamed, "This is terrible! What the hell is the matter with you? We're trying to win a World Series here and you're popping off and thinking only about yourself!"

Before the Series, Buzzie had given me permission to play winter ball in Puerto Rico. I was to get paid $700 per month, which was going to go a long way toward paying my bills. But after dressing me down about my comments in the paper, Buzzie concluded by saying I could forget about playing winter ball. I tried to explain to him I was just upset about not playing and that I never mentioned Alston by name. He was having none of it. After hearing the commotion his story had caused, Richman came up to me at my locker and said, "I feel responsible for this. The headline on that story didn't reflect the content of what you said, but we don't write the headlines. If Buzzie insists on prohibiting you from playing winter ball, I'll give you the money you would have made."

That was the first time I learned the writers don't write the headlines on their stories. The editors in the office do. I really appreciated Richman's concern and generosity, but fortunately Buzzie got over it after we won the World Series for the first time. He relented and I went on to winter ball.

Looking ahead to 1956, it was pretty apparent Jackie Robinson's career was winding down and both the second base and third base jobs with the Dodgers looked to be wide open. I figured between the two and backing up Pee Wee I could probably get in 140-150 games. But then at the winter meetings in December of '55, the Dodgers swung a big trade with the Cubs in which they sent pitcher Russ Meyer, third baseman Don Hoak, and outfielder Walt Moryn to Chicago in exchange for a power-hitting third baseman, Ransom Jackson. That really hurt me. I had just hit 15 home runs in half a season and they give up three players for a guy who hit 20 over a full year.

I was also sorry to see Hoak go, even though we were often both competing for playing time in the infield. Because we were fellow scrubs, Hoak and I became good friends and we hung out together a lot off the field. He was an ex-marine and a real firebrand. They called him Tiger, and because our playing styles were similar, we were compared to each other a lot. The one difference was, after Hoak left the Dodgers, he had a couple of all-star seasons and became one of the better third basemen in the league. He stayed with the Cubs for only one year, then got traded to the Reds where he was involved in one of the biggest fights of the decade—against the Dodgers, naturally.

It was mid-July of 1957 and the Reds had a Cuban pitcher named Raul Sanchez who the Dodgers felt was a headhunter, especially after he had hit Charlie Neal with a pitch and knocked down Campanella in a game a month earlier. There was no question we were out for a little retribution against Sanchez. Early in the game, Junior Gilliam had bunted down the first base line and knocked Sanchez over as he fielded the ball. That was just a warning. The next time Gilliam came up, Sanchez fired a fastball past his head, dropping him in the dirt. That, in turn, called for another "set-up" bunt. This time Gilliam popped the ball up along the first base line. As Sanchez settled under the ball, Gilliam ran right at him and collided with him again. They began grappling on the ground as both dugouts cleared.

Hoak, who had been on the boxing team in the marines, was actually trying to be a peacemaker as he leaned over the pile of bodies all wrestling on the ground. It was then that Neal caught him square with a right hook under his left eye and sent him flying onto the grass. As baseball fights go, this one was a dandy, one of the better ones I've ever witnessed. Carl Furillo and George Crowe, a big first baseman for the Reds, were getting some pretty good shots in against each other with Furillo knocking Crowe's glasses off, and afterward Hoak was vowing vengeance against Neal.

Later Hoak moved on to the Pirates where he played a key role in their 1960 championship team. He was married to the singer Jill Corey when he died unexpectedly in 1969. The stories in the papers said he'd died of a heart attack in his car chasing some guy who had stolen his brother-in-law's car. That might be true, but I also know the Pirates broke his heart when they passed him over for their manager's job a week earlier. He had gone to the minors to apprentice for the job and he was bitterly disappointed when they lured Danny Murtaugh out of retirement to take it again.

When we broke camp in the spring of '56, Jackson was the third baseman and Jim Gilliam was the second baseman. I was both upset and frustrated, and I made some comments about not being one of Alston's guys. For the most part, Alston shrugged off my remarks as coming from a young player who was understandably upset about not playing. One day he said to me: "Stop going for homers and be more patient at bat. You'll get in a lot more games."

On May 14, the Dodgers sold Billy Loes on waivers to the Baltimore Orioles for $30,000. On the surface, it wasn't a transaction that got a whole lot of attention, if only because Loes had been bothered by a sore shoulder since the previous July and won only one game in the second half of '55. Just the same, Loes was an important pitcher on those great Dodger teams of the '50s—and quite a character, as well.

I didn't bum around with Loes the way I did with Podres—Billy was kind of a loner—but I enjoyed his company and was always amused by his comments and observations. He was an eccentric righthander who should have been a lefthander. A native Long Islander, he had signed with the Dodgers as a $22,500 "bonus baby" in 1949—a record amount to an amateur for the Dodgers at that time. In Loes' first four full seasons in the majors—1952–55—he won 13, 14, 13, and 10 games respectively. But never 20. Loes had a theory about that.

In 1954, shortly after the All-Star break, the Dodgers were in Cincinnati for a series against the Reds. Loes, who was something like 12–2 at the time, was walking along Fifth Street at Vine when he came across a pet store with a whole bunch of little puppies in the window. He saw this puppy that he decided he wanted to buy and bring home with him to New York. The problem was the puppy cost $100 and Loes didn't have the cash for it. So when he got to the ballpark, he asked Buzzie for a $100 loan. When Buzzie found out what it was for, however, he adamantly refused.

"No way you're bringing a dog back with you on the plane," Buzzie screamed.

"Okay," said Loes, "then I can't pitch anymore."

So it was that Loes sat out a couple of starts, supposedly because he had a sore arm. Then one day somebody pointed out to him that by missing those starts he was costing himself a chance to win 20 games.

"Oh hell," Loes said. "I don't want to win 20. Then people expect you to do it every year."

One time Loes stuffed his glove in his pocket and walked off the mound in the middle of a game. When he got to the dugout, he was asked what was wrong and he pointed to the home plate umpire, Hal Dixon. "I just don't like the way that guy is calling pitches today," he said. "He won't give me any strikes so I'm quitting for the day."

Loes could always be counted on to provide comic relief to clubhouse meetings, too. I had just joined the Dodgers in 1953 when, right before we were to play our first spring training game, Dressen called a meeting to go over the signs. It happened that Loes was pitching that first game and Charlie was going on and on about the bunt sign, making sure everybody got it. Finally, Loes pops up: "Geez, Charlie," he says, "I got to worry about all the signs from the catcher, the pickoff signs, all these other damn signs. I can't be bothered trying to remember all this. When I come up to bat, if you want me to bunt, just tell Billy Herman to square around in the third base coaching box."

Needless to say, Dressen went nuts. I've got to say, Loes was a helluva pitcher, a lot like Greg Maddux in the way he studied hitters; but he sure could drive managers to exasperation. Campy always said of Loes, "Billy's got a mind of his own. The problem is, you never know what he's going to do with it."

In spring training of '54, the Dodgers were in Miami and Loes had repeatedly broken curfew, prompting Dressen to fine him. But in a meeting with Dressen, the coaches, and Buzzie, Loes turned the tables on Charlie, saying: "Ah, c'mon, Charlie, you know I'm always ready to pitch when you want me. Forget about this fine business. What you should do is get me a $1,000 raise!"

That caught Dressen completely off guard and as he tried to continue stating his intentions to fine Loes, Billy persisted in demanding a raise, all the while gesturing at Buzzie and saying to Charlie, "C'mon, Charlie. Tell him to give me the $1,000!"

Word was he got the thousand, too. Only Billy Loes could turn a fine into a raise simply by befuddling people.

Another pitcher who played a significant role on those '50s Dodger teams was Clem Labine. Labine, also righthanded, never got the recognition he deserved as one of the most dependable and effective relief pitchers of that time. He had as good a curveball and sinker as any pitcher I knew. His curve was especially unique in that he threw it by holding his thumb parallel to his first two fingers, as opposed to the orthodox way of putting it on the opposite side of the ball. They called it a "cunny thumb" curve, which broke sharper and, as such, was much harder to follow.

Labine led the NL in appearances with 60 in 1955 while winning 13 and saving 11 in the Dodgers' world championship effort. In '56, he was 10–6 and led the league in saves with 19. He had this kind of strut when he walked, which gave off the impression of him being cocky. I guess maybe he was, but he backed it up.

A lot of folks in Brooklyn felt there was a case to be made for Labine being considered in the National League MVP voting because of his relief heroics in '56, but he got only one vote. That prompted the New York baseball writers to do a song parody—to "My Darling Clementine"—in tribute to Labine at their annual dinner that winter. The song went:

"Oh, my darlin', oh my darlin', oh my darlin', Clem Labine
We have won, but you're forgotten, dreadful sorry, Clem Labine."

I had a lot of fun with Labine, especially on the golf course. He and Duke had this rivalry on the golf course in which they'd bet each other $10 a round and then cheat like hell to win. You'd see one of 'em hit a ball into the rough, out of bounds, then suddenly discover the ball in play. I remember one time Labine hit a Titleist into the rough and as he went to look for it, he had a hole in his pocket where he could drop another ball down his pants leg without anyone noticing. On this day, though, Duke was noticing and when Labine announced he'd found his ball, Snider screamed at him, "Dammit, Clem, who the hell do you think you're kidding here! That's a Wilson ball! The one you hit off the tee was a Titleist!"

Oh, they were a couple of beauties, those two.

Despite Alston's admonition to be more patient and not to swing for homers so much, I wasn't getting to swing for much of anything the first couple of months of '56. I had only 20 at bats when Alston decided to give Pee Wee a day off and started me at short against the Reds on June 23, 1956—a date that is literally etched in my mind. The Reds' pitcher that day was a former outfielder, Hal Jeffcoat, who threw hard but was wild. A lot of the guys on our team also thought he tried to spike guys running to first base. Campanella and Gil Hodges (who was hitting ahead of me) had both homered off Jeffcoat in the second inning to give us an early lead. In my second at bat of the game, in the fourth, Jeffcoat threw me a fastball up high that I couldn't get out of the way of. The ball hit me right square in the cheekbone, and the next thing I knew I was lying in a hospital bed again. My teammates later told me they were convinced Jeffcoat was throwing at me, maybe in retaliation for Hodges' homer. I don't know. Only Jeffcoat does and he never called me or sent me a card when I was in the hospital. They tell me he lives in Tampa, right across the bridge from where I live in Treasure Island, Florida. But I've never seen him or talked to him since that day.

As they carried me off the field on a stretcher, I was still conscious, but numb. I didn't know where it had hit me. At the hospital, they put me on a slab for x-rays. My head had blown up like a watermelon and there was a huge black and blue mark under my eye, which they had to stick with needles to draw all the bad blood out. The doctors told me I had an almost-detached retina that was hanging by a thread, as well as a concussion. As a result, I wasn't allowed to bend over or do anything that would cause the blood to rush to my head.

They had to operate to repair the shattered cheekbone, which had caved in the left side of my face and compressed it much like a ping pong ball. For two weeks I had to wear a full blindfold so as not to move my eyes. When that time was up, they fitted me with pinhole glasses, so in order to see things to the side, you had to turn your whole head and not your eyeballs. It was another six weeks of wearing those. I was relieved they were able to save my retina and that my vision was okay after I gave up the pinhole glasses. It did affect my eyesight, though. I never told anyone when I was still playing, but to this day there's a black spot in my right eye. I'd especially notice it on day games when there'd be a ball hit in the air. I'd be looking up at the ball and this spot would appear and then disappear.

I never revealed this before, but I've always felt this beaning affected my career a lot more than the first one. The first one might have been life or death, but this one affected my eyesight and I don't think I was ever the same hitter again.

When I went down, the Dodgers recalled Chico Fernandez, another in the long line of shortstops who was never able to displace Pee Wee. I didn't play again that season, although the Dodgers did let me come back in September to work out with the team. I was also in uniform and sitting on the bench as an inactive player in the World Series, so I had a front row seat for Don Larsen's perfect game against us in Game 5. Who'd have ever thought, 42 years later I'd be sitting in the dugout on the opposite side of Yankee Stadium witnessing David Wells become the second Yankee pitcher to hurl a perfect game—and then a year later when David Cone pitched his perfect game?

This, I believe, makes me the answer to another trivia question. As far as I know, there are only two other people who were in Yankee Stadium for all three Yankee perfect games. Besides myself, there was Joe Torre, who was a fan sitting in the left field upper deck at Larsen's game, and Bob Sheppard, the longtime Yankees' public address announcer.

The 1957 season marked the end of an era in baseball in a lot of ways. For one thing, Jackie Robinson retired after the 1956 season—but not until the Dodgers traded him in one of the most shocking deals imaginable—to the Giants! We all knew Jackie was coming to the end of the line. He was 38, had slowed down and couldn't get around on the inside fastball anymore, and Alston was playing him less and less. But we never expected the Dodgers to trade him, especially to the hated Giants.

All I know is, Branch Rickey had to have been a very brilliant man to pick this guy as the first black player to play in the big leagues. Jackie had an inner fire about him like nobody else, but how he was able to contain it while being subjected to all that racial abuse when he first came up I'll never know. In later years, once he was established, he was able to retaliate—in the best way he knew how, with his God-given abilities.

One of the best examples of that was a game we played against the Giants. Sal Maglie, who hated us and showed it on many occasions when he'd knock us down with pitches, was pitching for the Giants. Maglie's favorite targets were Furillo, Campy, and Jackie. On this particular day, his first pitch to Jackie was a high inside fastball that just missed Jackie's head. What happened next was something I never saw before or after. Jackie stood there at the plate and started screaming at Maglie: "You dago bastard! You couldn't hurt me if you hit me! If you throw at me again I'm gonna bunt down the first base line and knock the shit out of you!" Sure enough, Jackie bunted Maglie's next pitch down the first base line and beat it out easily because Maglie never left the mound.

Just a word about Maglie. In one of baseball's great ironies, the pitcher we hated more than anyone else in the league wound up becoming one of us when the Dodgers got Maglie from the Indians for one dollar off the waiver list on May 15, 1956. Needless to say, there was a lot of tension in our clubhouse the day Maglie reported, especially with Furillo, who had been involved in a nasty bat-throwing incident with Maglie in 1952. The Giants' manager, Leo Durocher, had managed the Dodgers in the '40s and was there when Furillo first came up in 1946. Durocher and Furillo never liked each other, and after Leo left to manage the Giants in 1948 their rivalry intensified. Late in the 1953 season, they became involved in one of the most famous on-field fights in baseball history, with Leo breaking Furillo's left hand which, if nothing else, enabled Furillo to preserve his league-leading .344 average.

In a game the year before, Durocher ordered Maglie to throw at Furillo, and when he did, Furillo swung the bat and let it loose. The bat narrowly missed Maglie and the two of them remained enemies until the day Maglie joined the Dodgers.

We weren't sure what was going to happen that day, but Maglie and Furillo shook hands, and in a couple of weeks' time we considered "the Barber" one of us. Of course, it didn't hurt that he also became one of our most reliable pitchers, going 13–5 that year. He also pitched a hell of a game in the fifth game of the 1956 World Series against the Yankees, only to lose 2–0. The winning pitcher that day was Don Larsen, who happened to pitch his perfect game.

I actually had one of my greatest days in baseball in a game Maglie pitched against the Dodgers. It was July 8, 1955, at the Polo Grounds—and if you're wondering why I remember the date, it's because I didn't have a lot of big games in the majors, and the ones I did have I never forget. The Dodgers had a lot of guys banged up that day—Furillo and Robinson in particular had some nagging injuries. But Alston was tired of watching Maglie routinely beat us, so on that day he decided to start most of the humpties like myself. Gilliam moved from second base to right field in place of Furillo, Sandy Amoros played left, Don Hoak replaced Jackie at third, Rube Walker and Dixie Howell split the catching, and I was at second.

Alston's "humpties hunch" paid off as we knocked Maglie out of the game in the fifth inning. But it turned out to be one of the wildest and greatest Dodgers–Giants games ever played.

The Giants jumped out to a 6–0 lead, knocking out Don Newcombe (who was going for his 15th win) in just three innings. In the fourth, however, we got back into the game with five runs. My two-run homer capped the inning for us. By the time we got to the eighth inning, it had become a slugfest with the score tied 8–8. I was able to put us ahead, this time with the use of my speed. After singling, I took second on a long fly ball to Whitey Lockman in left and then stole third. When the throw by Giant catcher Ray Katt got past the third baseman into left field, I kept on running and scored what proved to be the winning run. The final score of the game was 12–8. I went 4-for-5 with three singles and the two-run homer. After Maglie and Newcombe left the game, there were nine more pitching changes made by the two clubs. One other thing: The time of the game was three hours and four minutes.

I mention this only to point out how different the game is played today. I realize they've added commercial time between innings to accommodate TV, but there's no way you could ever play a 12–8 game, featuring 11 pitchers, in three hours today. Besides the added commercial time, most people blame the pitchers for games dragging on the way they do. If you ask me, the biggest culprits are the hitters. How many times do you see a hitter get into the box, dig himself some footing, seemingly get set, and then put up his hand as if to say to the umpire, "Don't start yet, I'm not quite ready"? Guys today just aren't ready to hit. I know I couldn't wait to get into the box and take my swings.

There is no question Jackie Robinson was one of the best baserunners the game has ever known. He could stop and start as quick as any little man—and he was six feet, 200 pounds. I remember Maury Wills, one of the greatest basestealers ever, telling me you should never get out of a rundown if the fielders all execute properly. But Jackie got out of a lot of them.

Probably the most famous baserunning feat of Jackie's career was when he stole home against the Yankees in the eighth inning of the first game of the '55 World Series. To this day, Yogi Berra is adamant he had Jackie tagged out, and to be honest, I'd have to agree the film clips appear to bear him out. The batter for us when Jackie stole home was Frank Kellert, a reserve first baseman. Ordinarily in those situations, the batter is supposed to block out the catcher from getting a clear shot at tagging the runner coming home. But Kellert failed to do that and instead stepped out of the way as Jackie slid right into Yogi. Nevertheless, the umpire, Bill Summers, called Jackie safe, prompting a very vocal argument from Yogi that has been re-shown in pictures and film thousands of times since.

After the game, some writers asked Kellert if he thought Jackie was out and he said "yes." The next day, Jackie lit into him like I'd never seen before, screaming at Kellert: "What team are you playing for anyway?"

On December 13, 1956, the Dodgers announced they had traded Jackie to the Giants for a journeyman pitcher named Dick Littlefield and $30,000 cash. But a couple of days later, he pulled the plug on them by announcing he was retiring to accept an executive position with the Chock Full O' Nuts coffee company. The following winter, I got a call from him at my home in Treasure Island. He said he was coming to Tampa on business and asked me if I could get a golf game together. That was about as big a thrill as I ever had—Jackie Robinson thinking enough of me to want to play golf with me. He was a great friend and I miss him.

In the months leading up to the '57 season, there had been rumors the Dodgers were going to move because Ebbets Field had become antiquated. As it was, Walter O'Malley, the Dodgers' owner, had served notice on Brooklyn and the city when he switched seven of our home games in 1956 to Roosevelt Stadium in Jersey City and another eight in '57. I didn't get caught up too much in the Dodgers' move talks, mainly because I didn't live in Brooklyn like so many of the veteran players like Pee Wee, Gil Hodges, and Carl Erskine. Plus, I was more concerned with winning a regular job with the club.

It appeared this was finally going to happen, too, when Ransom Jackson wrenched his knee and Alston asked me to switch to third base. Late in '57 spring training, Dick Young of the *New York Daily News* called me "the guy they never take seriously, maybe because of last year's beaning." He went on to say that I was looked upon as an "all around fill-in and anybody's slob." That was Dick's way of complimenting you and I appreciated what he wrote. Dick was, in my mind, one of the greatest sportswriters ever. He was fearless and tireless. One time, after I made a couple of errors in a game, he wrote that I played like a Little Leaguer. The next day, the guys in the clubhouse told me I ought to pop Young for writing that. I said, "Why? He was only writing the truth. I did play like a Little Leaguer!" Typical of Dick, he came right up to me that day, probably waiting to see if I was going to confront him, and we talked like nothing happened.

I got off to a good start in '57 and was hitting .290 before we went on our first trip to the Midwest. Then I went into a terrible slump and I never could get it going again. I wound up doing mostly backup duty the second half of the season and hit only .219. All in all, it was a pretty depressing season, that last year in Brooklyn.

It wasn't until September 16 when the city fathers of Los Angeles actually made their formal presentation to O'Malley regarding the development of 307 acres of land in the Chavez Ravine section of the city for a new stadium. In the weeks that followed we read and heard about a lot of political bickering in both Los Angeles and Brooklyn, but there was no question now the Dodgers were leaving. Then, in the early morning hours of January 28, 1958, Roy Campanella was involved in a near-fatal automobile accident as he was driving home to Long Island from his Harlem liquor store. The roads were icy that night and Campy's car skidded on a slick spot and struck a telephone pole before flipping over, leaving him paralyzed from the waist down. Now, for sure, if there were any lingering questions in anyone's mind that an era was over, Campy's accident confirmed it.

It was often said Pee Wee was the heart of the Dodgers and Jackie was the soul. I would add that Campy was the conscience. He was such a good-hearted, sincere man, and nobody ever wanted him angry with them. The pitchers trusted him completely, and believe me— when Campy spoke his mind about something, everybody listened. I often heard writers describe him as a "manchild." I never knew exactly what that meant, but if you were to say he was a "man's man" with a boy's unlimited enthusiasm for the game, then you'd be pretty accurate.

To be honest, even if he hadn't had the accident, I still don't know if Campy could have made another season in Los Angeles. His last two seasons, '56 and '57, really took a toll on him physically and he'd become a shell of the Hall of Fame player he was. In particular, the muscles around the thumb in his right hand had completely deteriorated to the point where it was all hollow in there. He might have hit a few homers in LA because of that left field screen, but it had gotten to the point where he could hardly grip a bat.

On May 7, 1959, the Dodgers staged a special night in Campy's honor at the Coliseum. With the Yankees providing the opposition, they arranged an exhibition game in which all the proceeds went to help pay Campy's medical bills. An all-time record crowd for a major league baseball game—93,103—paid tribute to Campy. It was a night I'll never forget. They darkened the Coliseum in the fifth inning, then had the 100,000 fans all light up matches in unison. What an awesome sight! Afterward, all the players were given a silver tray with an inscribed commemoration of the event. I have that tray on the mantel in my house, and every day I look at it and think of Campy and that special night.

The tribute for Campy was typical of the things the O'Malleys did for the Dodger players and their families. I know the people of Brooklyn never forgave Walter O'Malley for taking their team away, but to me, he was a very special man in my life. When we left spring training for the West Coast in 1958, he had a separate plane for our wives and children. During spring trainings, he would fly the wives to Nassau for lunch! Everything with the Dodgers was always first class, and O'Malley treated everyone like family. Throughout my 10 years in the organization, I got to know Walter O'Malley and his wife, Kay, almost like second parents, and I watched his son, Peter, and his daughter, Terry, grow up. It was a sad day for baseball when Peter O'Malley sold the team to Rupert Murdoch's Fox News Corp. in 1997. You only wish there were more owners in baseball today like the O'Malleys.

A lot of the guys were excited about going to Los Angeles because they thought there would be a lot of extra money in it with all the endorsements and Hollywood movie deals out there. That turned out to be wishful thinking. They didn't realize we were leaving the biggest endorsement city in the world, and I don't think any of us got any real big movie or TV deals. Nevertheless, LA was a whole new experience.

It was going to take a couple of years for O'Malley to get his ballpark in Chavez Ravine built and in the meantime we were to play in the Los Angeles Coliseum, a huge 100,000-seat football stadium dressed up like a baseball field. The first time I stepped onto the field in the Coliseum, I couldn't believe it. This wasn't a place to play baseball. It was a place to stage chariot races. I couldn't imagine playing in this huge oval stadium with four times as many seats as what we had been accustomed to in Brooklyn.

I remember one day in that first spring of 1958, before one of our first games in the Coliseum, Duke Snider and I were out in center field shagging flies. Looking up at the seats, which were 77 rows high with another three-foot wall behind them, I shook my head in wonder. Then I had an idea.

"Do you think you can throw a ball out of this place?" I asked Duke.

After a few seconds of thought, he said, "I don't know, wanna try?"

So we decided to have a little contest to see which of us could throw a ball out of the Coliseum. Duke threw the first ball, which landed about 60 rows up. I threw mine almost as far. Duke's next throw was about 10 rows higher and mine was right there with his. On his third throw, Duke took a running start and unleashed a throw with all his strength. "Ooof!" he screamed, and right away I knew he'd hurt himself.

"Damn!" he said. "I hurt my arm, Zim."

All I could think was, *Oh shit, what do we do now?* So we did the only thing we could think of. We called Pee Wee out to ask his advice. In times of trouble, we always turned to the captain. As Duke explained to Pee Wee what had happened, I made a suggestion that he go in and take some batting practice and on his first swing, fall on his knees in pain.

The whole time this discussion was going on, Alston was standing behind the batting cage watching us. "I can't do that," Duke said. "I can't fake it. I've got to tell the man the truth."

And that's what he did. Alston's response was, "Yeah, you and Zimmer were trying to throw the ball out of the stadium." Then he sent us both to the clubhouse—Duke because he couldn't play and me because I was a party to getting him hurt. As our bad luck would further have it, every time something happened in the game that day it seemed to revolve around the No. 3 spot in the batting order where Duke would ordinarily have been. There were at least two or three times where the No. 3 hitter didn't drive in runs and we lost the game.

Now the coliseum clubhouse was divided into cubicles with separate doors to them, and Duke and I were hiding in ours when Buzzie came storming in after the game. He was livid. "Where are those two clowns?" he screamed.

Duke was the first to come out of his compartment and Buzzie started right in, yelling at him to pack his bags and go home to Fallbrook (his home) until he was able to play. Then I peeked out from behind my door and saw all these heads sticking out of their compartments. They were all trying to keep from laughing while wondering what Buzzie was going to do to me. I figured it didn't matter if he sent me home. I didn't play anyway.

"You're fined $500 too," Buzzie yelled, "because the other dummy can't play."

I'm glad Duke is in the Hall of Fame, but I always felt he never got his due in New York, mainly because he was always being compared to the two other great center fielders at that time, Willie Mays and Mickey Mantle. It always seemed Mickey and Willie were regarded as better fielders than Duke because they were faster and flashier. But part of the reason for that was the ballparks they played in. The Polo Grounds was 510 feet to center field and Willie is always remembered for that great catch he made off Vic Wertz in the '54 World Series.

At the same time, Yankee Stadium was 457 feet to left-center and Mickey had lots of room to make spectacular running catches. At Ebbets Field, Duke would go back 10 steps and he'd be at the wall. But he was as good a fielder as there was, and the catch he made off the Phillies' "Puddin' Head" Jones at Shibe Park in 1955—in which he climbed right up the center field wall to haul it in—was about the best I ever saw.

We played that entire first season in LA as if we had jetlag. It quickly became apparent the core of our team—Duke, Pee Wee, Gil, Furillo, Erskine—had left their best years behind in Brooklyn. Plus, that previous winter, Campy was paralyzed in an automobile accident, something else we never got over. We got off badly and it never got better. After finishing third in the last year in Brooklyn, we dropped to seventh place, 71–83 in 1958, the first time the Dodgers had finished under .500 since 1944.

I got in trouble again with Buzzie in spring training of 1958 when I was told I was going to be a utilityman. I had read in the papers where Birdie Tebbetts, the manager of the Cincinnati Reds, said he liked the way I played the game. So, in one of my frustrating days that spring, I was quoted as saying: "I'm in everybody's doghouse on this club. I figure they'll trade me for a lot less than I'm worth. Tell Birdie he can probably get me for a dozen bats."

You can imagine how much Buzzie loved reading that. The next day, he confronted me and told me to stop popping off. "Gilliam is a utilityman, too, and he's not complaining," he said.

Just the same, Pee Wee finally had come to the end of the line in 1958. In late April, after we lost two in a row to the Cubs, Alston decided to shake up the lineup. In addition to benching Furillo, he told me he wanted me to pick up Pee Wee at short. I got off to a good start and held the position the rest of the year. I hit .262 with 17 homers, and my .299 average at the Coliseum was second only to Furillo's. I also was successful in 14 of 16 stolen base attempts, and after the season Buzzie gave me a raise of $8,000 to $19,000.

Pee Wee retired that winter to become a coach and I thought I had at last fulfilled my destiny as the Dodger shortstop. But when I got to spring training in '59, there was yet another prospect being groomed as the successor to Pee Wee—Bob Lillis.

Still, Alston told me I was the shortstop when we started the season. Then I got into a slump right away, and before long, Lillis was starting to play. The only thing was, he was going just as badly as I had been. We both stunk. Meanwhile, word got back to us that down at the Dodgers' Triple-A farm at Spokane there was this shortstop they'd signed and loaned to the Detroit Tigers only to take him back. His name was Maury Wills and after a half-dozen undistinguished minor league seasons, he'd suddenly begun to blossom at Spokane after the manager there, Bobby Bragan, taught him how to switch-hit. Because both Lillis and I were going so bad, the Dodgers called up Wills at midseason.

They gave Wills the shortstop job; but in his initial stint there, he was no more productive than Lillis or I had been. I don't think Maury hit the ball out of the infield in his first 10 games, and finally the exasperated Alston said to me, "I'm tired of this. You're my shortstop."

I felt great. Finally, it seemed, I had beaten off all the competition and was ready to assume the Dodger shortstop job for good. In my first game as Alston's designated shortstop, we were facing the St. Louis Cardinals and their top righthander, Larry Jackson. After running the count to 3–2 on me in my first at bat, Jackson threw a changeup that, if I had not moved in, would have hit me on the foot. The umpire, Dusty Boggess, called "strike three."

I was furious. I couldn't believe he could ring me up on that pitch. I turned to him and screamed: "You fat bastard! How could you call that pitch a strike?"

"You're gone!" Boggess countered.

Remember, this was the day Alston said I was his shortstop. I left the game. Wills came in to replace me and immediately caught fire with his bat. He wound up hitting .260 the rest of the year and, as our leadoff hitter, was the most valuable player on the team. With Wills as a basestealing catalyst, we went on to win the National League pennant, beating the Chicago White Sox in the World Series. There was nothing I could say or do. This wasn't a matter of not being given the chance. I had the chance and didn't get the job done. Then, when I had the chance again, I got myself thrown out of the ballgame. I had no choice but to pull for Wills to get us into the World Series. I knew I had blown my last chance with the Dodgers. I'd like to think if Boggess hadn't thrown me out of the game, I'd have been the shortstop the rest of the year, but we'll never know.

There were a lot of reasons why the Dodgers were able to transform themselves from an aging seventh-place team in 1958 to world champions in 1959. But aside from Wills, the biggest factor was Wally Moon, a lefthanded-hitting outfielder we acquired from the Cardinals the previous December for another outfielder, Gino Cimoli. Moon had been an excellent player for the Cardinals, winning Rookie of the Year honors in 1954. But after hitting 24 homers in 1957, he slumped to just .238 in '58 and became expendable. Coming to the Dodgers, however, proved to be a re-birth for him because of the Coliseum's 251-foot left field line. In order to make such a "chip shot" home run distance more realistic, the Dodgers erected a 42-foot screen over the wall.

Moon was able to turn this wall into his own private shooting range. With his inside-out swing, he "golfed" nine of his 19 home runs that year over the Coliseum's left field screen. All the rest of the Dodgers' lefthanded hitters that year—Snider, Norm Larker, John Roseboro, Ron Fairly, Jim Gilliam, and Wills—hit seven homers combined over the screen. So adept was Moon at working that screen, his homers got dubbed "moon shots."

It was during that summer of '59 Moon arranged for a golf outing and a barbeque at his home in the San Fernando Valley for the whole team. Johnny Podres and I were living in a hotel in downtown LA and we drove out to the party. It was a great day in which we played golf all afternoon, drinking bloody marys and enjoying ourselves. Afterward, we had dinner at Moon's house and that led to all the guys sitting around in the backyard, telling stories and drinking some more. It eventually got to about one o'clock in the morning and only a few of us were left—Podres, myself, Ed Roebuck, and Don Drysdale—the usual roustabouts.

By this time, Mrs. Moon clearly wanted us out of there, so we all got up to leave. Drysdale, who lived a few houses away, offered to let Podres and myself stay at his house for the night, but Podres insisted on driving home.

"Okay," Drysdale said, "but at least let me lead you out to the freeway back to LA."

So we followed Drysdale out to the freeway and were on our way. I fell asleep almost immediately, only to be awakened by sirens and a whole lot of commotion. We had been pulled over by a cop and Podres was in a heated argument with him. He's yelling: "What the hell are you pulling us over for? We weren't speeding. If we weren't ballplayers, you wouldn't be stopping us!"

The cop didn't say anything at first and I tried to calm Podres down, but he kept on.

"We weren't speeding, dammit!" he hollered. "Why the hell are you bothering us?"

Finally, the cop seemed to have had enough of Podres' protesting.

"Who said anything about speeding?" he replied. "You're going the wrong way on the freeway!"

I shook my head to figure out if I was hearing right. It seemed Drysdale had led us to a freeway exit, not an entrance. Who knows how far we had driven the wrong way? It was a miracle we were alive. Although as it turned out, we wound up in jail. The cop put us into his car and drove us off to this tiny little jail in the middle of nowhere. Now I was really scared. I'd never been in jail in my life and I couldn't believe this was happening. They put us in this three-foot square cell and told us to wait there. I figured if I could just get Pod to behave, I could talk our way out of there. Awhile later, a couple of more cops came by and Pod started in on them too. Finally, I was able to shut him up and call a friend of ours who came out to get us. That was the first and only time I've ever been in jail and about the only thing more unbelievable than the incident itself was that no one ever found out about it. I know one thing: If it had happened today, Pod and I would be all over ESPN before we even got out of the slammer, our mug shots playing over and over all morning long.

I was most thankful Buzzie never found out about it. My relationship with Buzzie Bavasi was unique, to say the least. I know I drove him crazy with my frequent outbursts about not playing, but from the time I was first beaned in St. Paul, Buzzie was always there for me. Somehow, he always found it hard to stay mad at me, and he was especially always there for me when I needed a little extra cash for the racetrack. Of course, Buzzie loved being there for me for that.

When we were training in Vero Beach, every chance we got we'd go down to Gulfstream Park. Problem was, we never had any money. So I'd be sitting in the lobby of the hotel and Buzzie would walk by and say, "What's this? You're not going to Gulfstream with the rest of the guys?" I'd say I had no money and Buzzie would reach into his pocket and ask, "How much do you need?"

Well, there was a reason Buzzie was so generous with his racetrack loans to us. He loved it when you owed him money because he would take it out on you when it came to negotiating your contract at the end of the year. It was his way out of having to give us a raise. He'd simply deduct all the racetrack loans. That's why I never asked for a round number in cash from Buzzie. He'd ask me how much I needed and I'd always give him an uneven number because it was too hard for him to remember.

About the only time I can think anyone ever got the best of Buzzie in a contract negotiation was when Sandy Koufax and Drysdale got together and staged a mutual salary holdout in spring training of 1966. The previous year, they'd combined to win 49 games while pitching the Dodgers to the world championship, which obviously gave them considerable leverage—especially as a tandem. Though they were forever linked, both because of the holdout and the fact they were the heart of those pitching-driven Dodger teams of the '60s, Koufax and Drysdale were very different personalities. Drysdale was a hell-raiser, which is why he, Podres, and I all seemed to naturally gravitate toward each other. Sandy was much more of a loner.

Even though Sandy didn't really run with us that much as players, I remained friends with him over the years. A couple of years ago, I was sitting around in the coaches' room at the Yankees' spring training headquarters in Tampa when the security guard came in and said there was a guy at the clubhouse door who wanted to come in to see me. The guard said he didn't recognize him, so he wanted to check with me. I went out there, and who is it but Sandy. I couldn't help but laugh. Only Sandy Koufax, for all his greatness, could walk into a spring training camp unrecognized. He came in and sat with the coaches for an hour just talking about pitching. After he left, Billy

Connors said it was the greatest hour he'd ever spent in baseball. Every time I'm around Sandy it's a thrill for me. I've told him I wish he'd come around more often!

Koufax came to the Dodgers in 1955 out of the University of Cincinnati where he'd had a basketball scholarship. Back then, baseball had a bonus rule, which required players given a bonus in excess of $6,000 to be kept on the major league roster for two years. Koufax's bonus was $14,000, so there he was, mostly sitting around in the bullpen on this veteran team that was always fighting for a pennant, while Don Newcombe, Carl Erskine, Billy Loes, Podres, and the others did all the pitching.

Because they didn't want Koufax to rust away from lack of use, the Dodgers arranged a lot of simulated games for him to pitch during the season. Naturally, they had all the humpties like me hit against him. Sandy is always telling people that the stories about him being wild back then are exaggerated. Let me tell you something: He was wild. And, boy, did he throw hard! When you think of Sandy Koufax, you immediately think of this overpowering fastball—but he had an unbelievable curveball too.

One time, in spring training at Vero Beach, Sandy was pitching an intra-squad game. My first time up against him, I hit a home run over the orange trees in left field. Now I was always a wild swinger who would swing at anything even remotely close to the strike zone. My next time up against him, Sandy threw me three straight curveballs. All three of them paralyzed me! They came in looking like they were over my head and I stood there and watched them drop into John Roseboro's glove, belt high. When I came up again, it was the same thing—three straight curveballs and I can't pull the trigger. At that point, Fresco Thompson was sitting in the seats behind home plate and yelled out, "Take a damn cut!"

There was no doubt—in my mind at least—that Sandy Koufax was going to be a great pitcher. He didn't put it all together until after I got traded, but when he did, he put it together like nobody else before or after him. People have asked me who was the greatest pitcher I ever saw and I answer without hesitation: For five years, Sandy Koufax was the greatest pitcher there ever was. I have to believe that. From 1962 until 1966 when he retired because of arthritis in his arm, he was 111–34 with 1,444 strikeouts, 33 shutouts, five straight ERA titles, three no-hitters, a perfect game, three Cy Young Awards and one MVP! It was no wonder Buzzie had no chance in that great holdout.

I know Sandy, too, and he has a long memory. In 1959, he pitched in two of the World Series games against the White Sox and gave up just one run in nine innings. But when he slumped off to an 8–13 season in 1960, Buzzie cut his salary. He was only 36–40 overall at that time, and he grumbled to Buzzie, "What does a guy have to do to get to pitch around here?"

"Get somebody out," Buzzie snapped.

"How can I get anybody out when I don't get to pitch?" Koufax persisted.

"Get the ball over the damn plate when you do pitch!" Buzzie countered. "You've got one pitch—high!"

By the time Drysdale and Koufax announced they were holding out after the '65 season, Buzzie was singing a decidedly different tune. He was prepared to offer them both modest raises, $80,000 to $90,000 for Drysdale and $85,000 to $100,000 for Sandy. After bickering all spring with Buzzie, the two pitchers managed to get two of the biggest contracts ever for that time—$125,000 for Koufax and $110,000 for Drysdale. Buzzie later conceded neither of them would have gotten close to that amount negotiating individually.

"I stood there with a bloodstained cash box," he said.

That was Buzzie's life back then: talking to the players about their family, their salary, and all the other things we were involved in. When the agents came in to baseball, it all changed for Buzzie. The personal relationships he had with players ended. I saw that when I worked for him years later as manager of the Padres. The fun had gone out of the game for him.

As I said, the Dodgers went from a seemingly aging, faded-out, seventh-place team in our first year in LA in 1958 to world champions again in 1959. The '59 team was not nearly as good as the '55 Brooklyn world champions, mostly because it was a team in transition. Hodges, Snider, and Furillo, were all nearing the end of their careers, while Wills, Roseboro (who had taken over the catching after Campy was paralyzed), and rookie reliever Larry Sherry were all coming into their own. Sherry had replaced Clem Labine as our top reliever. He was 7–2 with a 2.19 ERA and three saves for us in '59 and was the hero of the World Series against the Chicago White Sox, winning two games, saving two others, and allowing just one earned run in 12 ⅔ innings of brilliant relief work. Sherry had a routine that became a very familiar and reassuring sight for us that year. He'd be summoned in from the bullpen, and would take the car past the Dodger dugout where he'd flip his jacket in to us and say: "Have no fear guys, the super Jew is here."

To get to the World Series in 1959, we had to first dethrone the two-time defending National League champion Milwaukee Braves. In a reverse of their "miracle" comeback-to-the-pennant over the Dodgers in 1951, the Giants lost seven of their last eight games in 1959 to tumble out of the league lead and allow both the Braves and us to tie for first place, setting up a best two-out-of-three playoff. Our first-game starter, Danny McDevitt, failed to get out of the first inning, prompting Alston to bring in Sherry, who served notice on his World Series heroics to come by shutting the Braves out over the last 7 ⅔ innings for a 3–2 win.

We had to again come from behind in Game 2 at the Coliseum, overcoming a 5–2 Braves lead with three runs in the ninth. After Braves starter Lew Burdette faltered in the ninth, giving up singles to Moon, Snider, and Hodges, Milwaukee manager Fred Haney brought in Don McMahon and even Warren Spahn in relief to get out of the inning. The game wound up going 12 innings with us winning when Felix Mantilla, who had been moved from second base to short, made a wild throw to first on Furillo's grounder, allowing Hodges to score.

In a way, that win was typical of that '59 Dodgers team. We were no longer a powerhouse, but we were good enough, and had enough savvy veterans and hungry, talented new players who knew how to win. The White Sox team we were to play in the World Series was billed as the "Go-Go Sox" because of their slap-hitting, speed-oriented style of play. They didn't have any power hitters to scare you, other than Ted Kluszewski, the slugging first baseman with the huge biceps who they had acquired from the Pittsburgh Pirates to help out in the stretch drive. Kluszewski was 35 and past his prime, but he still had some big pop left in his bat as he proved in Game 1 of the Series. Otherwise, the White Sox were a team that relied heavily on their top-of-the-order hitters—Luis Aparicio, Nellie Fox, and Jim Landis—getting on base and using their speed to create runs. They also played solid defense and had a solid veteran pitching staff led by future Hall of Famer Early Wynn, Billy Pierce, Dick Donovan, Bob Shaw, and relievers Gerry Staley and Turk Lown.

In Game 1 of the Series in Chicago, the White Sox stepped out of their "Punch and Judy" mold and clobbered us 11–0 behind two homers by Kluszewski and four other extra-base hits. As I sat in the silence of the bus ride back to our hotel after the game, I was seething. Finally, I couldn't hold it in any longer.

"Go-Go Sox my ass!" I shouted, touching off a roar of laughter throughout the bus.

I can't say I contributed a whole lot to the '59 world championship effort—I got only one pinch-hit at bat in the Series—but Pee Wee always credited me for providing the tension-lifter with that remark. Our pitchers held the White Sox to only 12 runs over the next five games, and Roseboro did a great job in shutting down their running game as we wrapped the Series up in six games. Years later, whenever we'd play golf together, Pee Wee would bring up that "Go-Go Sox, my ass" remark and loved re-telling the story.

"I still can't believe you said that!" he'd exclaim.

"Why?" I'd say. "It's what I felt. They weren't that good! We were a better team and I believed that."

One of the real unsung heroes of that '59 Dodgers team was Chuck Essegian, who made baseball history with two pinch-hit home runs in the World Series. We picked up Essegian in a minor league trade from the Cardinals on June 15 for Dick Gray, another in that long line of shortstops who was unable to take Pee Wee's job. Essegian was a big, strapping former football player from Stanford. Besides his two pinch home runs in the Series, he's the answer to another trivia question: He and Jackie Jensen are the only two players to have played in both a Rose Bowl and a World Series.

As a fellow permanent tenant of Alston's bench, Essegian and I became quick friends, and to this day, whenever I'm on the West Coast, he always looks me up. He became a lawyer after his playing days.

Essegian was always calling me aside to complain about Alston in '59.

"The man never uses me," he'd say. "I'd like to walk up and punch his lights out. At least in football there's always someone you can take your frustrations out on by cracking their head on the field."

Essegian hit his first pinch-hit homer to tie up the second game in the seventh inning. It was an upper-deck shot to left in Comiskey Park, and to give you an idea of how strong this guy was he broke his bat! He hit his second homer pinch hitting for Duke Snider in the ninth inning of Game 6 when we were already ahead 8–3.

After the World Series I remember somebody asking Roseboro how this aging Dodger team that had finished seventh the year before could have come all the way back to win another World Series.

"Very simple," Roseboro said. "What made this team was black power, white power, and a super Jew reliever."

He could've probably added Maury Wills' speed.

With Wills having established himself as the Dodger shortstop in 1959, I knew my days were numbered with the ballclub. At the winter meetings in St. Petersburg that December, there were all sorts of trade rumors involving me. One had me going to the Washington Senators for Roy Sievers, their slugging first baseman; another had me going to the Milwaukee Braves, who were now managed by Charlie Dressen. That one got started when I came over to the meetings from my home and people saw me leaving the hotel with Dressen. What they didn't know was we were just going to the dog track.

I really did expect to get traded at those meetings, but it didn't happen. So I reported once again to Vero Beach for spring training in 1960 and assumed my familiar role as a backup infielder. Late that spring, we went out to Arizona to play our last exhibition games on our way to opening the season in Los Angeles. A writer told me: "It looks like you're still going to be a Dodger. If they were going to trade you, they'd have done it in Florida. They wouldn't have brought you all the way out here."

The next morning at the Adams Hotel in Phoenix, I ran into Del Rice, an old friend who was now a backup catcher with the Cubs.

"I think you're gonna be with us," he said to me.

I said: "No way, they would have traded me by now."

In the fifth inning of the game that day, Buzzie summoned me to the clubhouse.

"Son," he said, "by six o'clock tonight I'm gonna trade you, but I'll tell you what I'm going to do. I'm talking to both the Cubs and the Cardinals and it doesn't matter which team I trade you to. So I figure I owe this to you. Take the next four innings to decide where you want to go."

I didn't know what to say. I went back to the dugout and started to think about my options. I knew if I went to the Cardinals, it would mean six weeks of spring training at home in St. Petersburg. But they wanted me to play second base, and by this time my preference was to play third. The Cubs wanted me to play third, but they trained in Arizona. Plus, they played all day games at home and I hit better at night.

Buzzie had given me this piece of paper to write the team of my choice on, but after thinking about it all that time, I folded the paper up, threw it away and told Buzzie: "I don't care where you send me. You make the deal."

A short time later, Buzzie announced he had traded me to the Cubs for infielder Johnny Goryl, two minor leaguers, pitcher Ron Perranoski, and outfielder Lee Handley, plus $25,000 in cash. It turned out to be one of the best trades Buzzie ever made, if only because Perranoski became one of the best relief pitchers in Dodger history. In '63, he played a major role in the Dodgers' world championship season, going 16–3 in relief, and leading the National League with 69 appearances. Buzzie rightfully took credit for that deal, but I'd like to state here that I at least deserve an assist.

After Buzzie announced the trade, I had to go to the team bus to get my luggage off it. Podres and Drysdale were both crying.

Podres hugged me and said: "Zim, I promise you one thing. If there's ever a time I'm out there pitching and the game is settled, you'll get a fat one. Be ready. I hope you hit it a mile."

Later that year, the Dodgers came into Chicago and were beating us 9–1 in the ninth inning of a game Podres was pitching. I came to bat and I suddenly remembered that promise he had made me. I'm thinking, *I hadn't lived with John for five years for nothing.* I was looking for anything, but I wondered if he had remembered.

His first pitch to me was a curve above the knees that dived into the dirt. It was John's best curve. Strike one.

Next comes a searing fastball on the outside corner. Strike two.

After wasting his third pitch outside, he throws a ball that starts out like it's going to hit me. Then it suddenly starts breaking away and finally dives down just below the strike zone. I swung at it almost in self-defense and missed.

As I turned to walk back to the dugout, I said to John Roseboro, the Dodgers' catcher: "What the hell was that?"

"Don," he replied, "all I can say is that's probably the only spitball John's ever thrown in his life."

And all I can say is, this just shows the fairness, honesty, and integrity of baseball. No matter how close the friendships guys might have, the name of the game is to win.

3

Cubs
to Casey
to Home

I didn't have to go far after the trade was announced that made me a Cub. The Cubs were finishing up spring training right there in Phoenix, and as the Dodgers left town I simply took my bags to the Cubs' hotel where they were packing up to go to Las Vegas. We had one more exhibition game scheduled in Vegas Sunday and then we were to fly to Los Angeles to open the season—ironically—against my "newly former" Dodger teammates.

I have to admit, it felt a little strange walking into the Coliseum that Tuesday afternoon, wearing a Chicago Cubs uniform and standing for the national anthem in front of the visiting team dugout. There were about 68,000 fans at the Coliseum and Don Drysdale, who obviously had gotten on the freeway the right way this day, was the Dodgers' pitcher. It was scoreless going into the third inning when I hit a homer off him. I figured I owed him that for nearly getting me killed the year before.

The next inning, Drysdale hit a ball to right-center that got through the gap for extra bases. I'm playing third base and watching the 6-foot-5 Drysdale chugging around the bases, heading toward me. It was a close play but Drysdale slid in safely, just ahead of the throw. Now this guy was one of the fiercest competitors I ever knew in the game. He was also one of my best friends on the Dodgers. I didn't know quite what to do or say so, instead, I just glanced away. After a few seconds, Drysdale broke the tension: "You hit that sonovabitch pretty good, didn't you?" he said.

"Oh hell," I said. "I just got lucky."

The Dodgers wound up winning the game, 3–2, and Drysdale was the winning pitcher. Afterward, I was walking up the ramp to the Coliseum exit and all the Dodger wives were waiting there for their husbands. When they saw me, they all came over to me and hugged me, wishing me good luck. In the middle of them, was Drysdale's first wife, Ginger, who gave me a big hug and a kiss. I looked at her and said, "Do you think I'd be getting kissed by you if that homer had beat your husband 1–0?"

The Cubs got off to a bad start in 1960, which was not unusual for them, and they quickly fell into last place. We were 5–11 on May 4 when the front office took Lou Boudreau out of the broadcast booth to replace Charlie Grimm as manager. Grimm was a terrific guy who only got fired because he didn't have enough good players. The Cubs had already fired him twice previously as their manager, so this was nothing new to him. I don't think he particularly minded going up in the booth and trading jobs with Boudreau.

One of the few good young players the Cubs had that year was Ron Santo, a third baseman who I kind of took under my wing in spring training. I worked with Santo on playing third, and away from the field he followed me around like a puppy. I knew he was going to be an outstanding ballplayer, even though they sent him back to the minors at the start of the season to get a little more experience.

In the middle of the 1960 season, we were in Pittsburgh when Boudreau summoned me to tell me they were bringing Santo up. I had been playing third, but I assumed I'd be moving over to second where Jerry Kindall wasn't hitting a lick. There was no manager's office in the visiting clubhouse in Pittsburgh and Boudreau was sitting on a stool in a corner of the room.

"Santo's coming up," he said to me. "He'll be playing third."

"I figured that," I said. "So I'll be moving over to second?"

"Well, not now anyway," Boudreau said. "We're going to leave Kindall there."

"You mean to tell me I'm not at second either?"

"We just feel right now we want to go with the younger guys," Boudreau replied.

Younger guys? I said to myself. Kindall was like two or three years younger than I was and I was out-hitting him by nearly 100 points.

"What's wrong?" Boudreau said. "Don't you want to be a Chicago Cub?"

"Screw the Chicago Cubs if I can't play here hitting .270 when the other guy's hitting .180!" I said.

It just so happened about a week later, Boudreau benched Kindall and put me at second base and I wound up playing there for most of the rest of the season. The Cubs made few waves that season, nestling in at the bottom of the standings. On August 4, however, we created some unwanted fireworks when Jim Brewer, a rookie left-hander for us, got involved in a nasty fight with Billy Martin that made some baseball history.

Martin, a World Series hero with the Yankees in the '50s and a notorious scrapper, was winding down his career by then, playing second base for the Reds. In the second inning, Martin was at bat when Brewer's first pitch to him came in high and tight. The ball wound up hitting Martin's bat as he backed away from it. Martin swung at the next pitch, and the bat flew out of his hands toward the mound. As Martin slowly walked out to retrieve his bat, Brewer stepped off the mound. Then, suddenly, Martin charged Brewer and let loose with a right hook that fractured the bone underneath Brewer's left eye.

Billy later insisted he hadn't thrown the bat intentionally at Brewer—that it slipped. He said the only reason he swung at Brewer was because Brewer had said some things to him when he came out to get the bat. The next day, I was standing by the batting cage when Martin came up to me.

"You're a baseball man," he said. "Tell me the truth. Was Brewer throwing at me?"

I had seen the whole incident from the bench and I couldn't lie to him.

"In my opinion, he was," I said.

Martin thanked me and I figured that was the end of it. But a couple of weeks later, Brewer announced he was suing Martin for $1,040,000 in damages. It was the first time anyone could remember a player suing another player in baseball. I've got to say, Martin's response to the suit was classic.

"How does he want it," Martin said, "cash or check?"

I didn't think any more of the incident until a year later when I was playing for the Washington Senators and I got a phone call from Martin.

"Do you remember when you told me that day you believed Brewer was deliberately throwing at me?" he asked.

I couldn't say I didn't remember because I did. The next thing Martin said was that he wanted me to come to court in Chicago and testify for him, as the case was being decided. I really didn't want to get involved, but the man had asked me to give my opinion and I had. I even called Buzzie to ask for his advice. He told me to do what I thought was right.

So I went to Chicago and walked into the courtroom and immediately I see a half-dozen of my former Cub teammates sitting there. They obviously thought I was there to testify for Brewer, so when I got up and spoke in Martin's defense I think they were a little surprised.

The case wound up getting settled with Brewer being awarded $10,000 for his medical expenses. Martin later thanked me for my testimony and said I probably saved him a lot of money. I couldn't help remembering that after I went to work for him as a coach with the Yankees in 1983 and he made a statement about some of his coaches being disloyal to him.

My second—and last—season with the Cubs in 1961 proved to be one of my best, but as usual I got myself embroiled in a hotbed of trouble with the front office by speaking my mind. Since winning the pennant in 1945, the Cubs had had 13 losing seasons, including the last eight in a row. The owner, chewing-gum heir Phil Wrigley, wasn't one to spend wads of money or make sweeping changes to improve the club. He just fired the manager every two or three years, as he did in 1961 when he had Grimm and Boudreau change places in the broadcast booth.

But after Boudreau brought the club home seventh in '60 with 94 losses, Wrigley decided he was going to do something totally unconventional in order to rid the Cubbies of their losing ways. Instead of a manager, Wrigley announced he was creating a college of coaches who would take turns running the team. The theory was that while one of them was serving as head coach, the others would devote their time to teaching the finer points of the game to the players. The original college of coaches consisted of Bobby Adams, "Rip"

Collins, Vedie Himsl, Goldie Holt, Elvin Tappe, Fred Martin, Verlon Walker, Lou Klein, and Harry Craft. Of them, only Craft had ever managed in the majors. That didn't matter to Mr. Wrigley. The idea was to educate us.

And just to be sure the college of coaches had everything covered, Wrigley and general manager John Holland named me the team captain! Himsl, who became the first head coach, made the announcement on Opening Day that the organization felt they needed a captain. That's when I knew captains were a joke. To me, there was only one captain in baseball and that was Pee Wee Reese. So what if you had a reputation for working hard? Wasn't that what everyone was supposed to do? It was primarily because of my work with Santo that Wrigley felt the college of coaches needed a veteran "assistant" on the field.

I suppose I should have been honored—after all, Ernie Banks was on this team—but when you're a lifetime .235 hitter, being a captain doesn't mean a whole helluva lot.

Nevertheless, I quickly found out the captaincy had its advantages. Not long after Himsl informed me of the front office's decision, I called Pee Wee and asked him if being the captain was worth any extra money. Much to my surprise, he told me the Dodgers gave him an extra $500 every year he was the captain.

Well, when the first paychecks arrived that season, I discovered an extra check with mine for $500. Suddenly, I started having a different outlook about being the captain. It might be a crock, but at least it was a worthwhile crock. Fifteen days later, the next check came and, much to my surprise, there was another extra check for $500. I figured this had to be a mistake, but I didn't say anything.

Then, two weeks later, I got another $500 check with my regular check and now I was worried. I didn't want to have them come to me at the end of the season and say they'd made a mistake and that I owed them all this money—or that I had to pay extra taxes on all these captain's checks. So I went to Holland and told him I thought there was a mistake here. He said: "Mr. Wrigley wants it this way as long as you're doing your job with the young players."

I didn't know what to think. I could sneak $500 from the wife once, but not every week!

I don't think the captaincy had anything to do with it, but I had a pretty good year in 1961, hitting .252 with 13 homers, and Pirates manager Danny Murtaugh picked me for the All-Star team. That was one of the years they played two All-Star Games and I was in both of them. Today, I can tell my grandkids I was good enough to have played in two All-Star Games. Why does anyone have to know they were both in the same year?

I suppose this has happened before in baseball, but almost as soon as the season was over—in which I was named team captain and an All-Star—the Cubs got rid of me. Of course, I did my best to make sure of that.

To the surprise of probably no one except Mr. Wrigley, the college of coaches was unable to "educate" the Cubs into winners. We finished seventh again, losing 90 games, and about the only thing we learned was that seven heads are definitely no better than one. It was nothing more than a popularity contest.

That first year of the experiment, four of the coaches, Himsl, Tappe, Craft, and Klein alternated as the head coach, each serving two-week stints at a time. Now you can't tell me, if you're not the head coach, you're rooting for the guy who is to succeed! Every guy had a different philosophy and different opinions of the players. Himsl, Tappe, and Craft all left me alone to play second base and fulfill my "duties" as the captain. Then, Lou Klein took over and the first thing he said to me was, "You're my holler guy out there. I'm looking to you to take charge of the infield."

That was fine with me, except when I went to check the lineup card the next day, I wasn't in it. Klein had apparently meant I was to do my hollering and taking charge from the bench. Even though I had a decent year, it was one of the most disheartening seasons of my career, and in the last week I let my feelings be known.

Boudreau had gone back up to the broadcast booth after being replaced by the college of coaches and he asked me one day if I would do the pre-game interview show with him.

"Sure," I said. "What will we talk about?"

"Oh, I don't know," Boudreau replied. "Just the way the season has gone and your assessment of the college of coaches."

I knew I had an assessment for him that the front office wasn't going to want to hear, but I didn't care. I let it all out, while being careful not to mention any of the players. I wanted to make it clear this was me speaking for myself. I said the college of coaches was a joke that was doomed to failure the moment it was created. The Cubs were even worse under it, I pointed out, but what can you expect when you have nine guys giving nine different pieces of advice?

It was nothing but a popularity contest, I said, and to them we were nothing but chessmen, not thinking, breathing players. I went on to say it didn't take me long to discover Tappe thought I could play and Klein thought I couldn't. Meanwhile, Santo was going goofy with all these different coaches giving him all these different instructions on how to play third base.

They had the radio on in the clubhouse and everybody heard the interview. When I walked back to the dugout, Rip Collins was waiting for me. I wasn't sure how he had reacted to my blasting of the coaches, and I was relieved when he put his arm around me and said: "I respect you for what you said. You said what you feel."

Now I saw Grimm walking toward me.

"I just heard your interview with Boudreau," he said. "You spoke what you felt and that's okay. You're entitled to your opinion. But I can assure you, you won't be here next year."

That winter, the National League was to conduct its expansion draft to stock the two new clubs coming into the league for 1962, the Mets and the Houston Colt .45s. The established clubs had to have their lists of eligible players filed before the end of the season. I later found out that before my interview I was on the Cubs' protected list. But the day after I said what I did about the college of coaches, they removed relief pitcher Barney Schultz as one of their two $125,000 "premium" players available for drafting and replaced him with me.

In a way, that was an honor since the $125,000 premium players were considered the most valuable to the clubs. According to the rules of the draft, they only had to designate two players as $125,000 premium players and they could only lose one of them. Fortunately for me, the Mets took me with one of their first picks. I was moving on again.

Going to the Mets was a sort of "double homecoming." They trained in St. Petersburg, about 15 minutes from my home, and of course, New York was where I began my major league career. There were plenty of old familiar Dodger faces there too. Besides me, the Mets had Gil Hodges, Roger Craig, Clem Labine, and Charlie Neal as former favorites from Brooklyn for the New York fans. Because I was the only player on the new team who lived in St. Pete, I was asked to come over to Miller Huggins Field one winter afternoon to model the new Mets uniform. I brought my son Tommy with me and, with him sitting on my shoulders posing for all the photographers, I became the first player ever to wear a Mets uniform.

It never crossed my mind I might soon become one of the first players traded by the Mets.

I've got to say, one of the greatest strokes of genius in baseball history has to be George Weiss picking Casey Stengel as the first manager of the Mets. Weiss had served as Casey's boss for over 10 years with the Yankees. After the 1960 season, they were both let go—Weiss as general manager, Casey as manager—because they were supposedly too old. When the Mets were formed a year later, Weiss was named president, and the first person he hired was Casey as manager.

The wisdom of that decision was evident the very first day of spring training in St. Pete in 1962. As I drove up to Miller Huggins Field that first morning I couldn't believe what I saw. There must have been fifty camera crews, from all three networks, all the local New York stations, and stations all over the country. There were also well over 100 newspapermen there. You'd have thought the Mets had won four straight world championships, not starting out their first year. It was like that every morning. All these TV crews and sportswriters, waiting to talk to Casey. We'd watch in amazement as Casey would do one interview after another, all the while selling the ballclub, not just to New York but to the whole country.

As I said before, we had a lot of big name players on that first Mets team; players who had all had a lot of success in the big leagues— Hodges, Neal, Frank Thomas, Gus Bell, and Hobie Landrith. Unfortunately, they were mostly all past their primes, their best seasons left with other teams. Landrith was a catcher whom the Mets had made their first pick in the expansion draft. Typical of Casey, when he was asked why the Mets took Landrith first, he said, "Because he's a catcher. In baseball I've learned you've gotta have a catcher because if you don't, you're gonna have a lot of passed balls."

Richie Ashburn had been a roommate of mine with the Cubs. He was still a terrific leadoff hitter, and in 1995 got elected to the Hall of Fame. He hit .306 that year and quit to go into broadcasting for the Phillies. When I saw him in spring training the next year, I asked him, "How could you quit on a .300 season? Unlike a lot of the other guys, you were still a good ballplayer!"

Ashburn's answer was: "I'm a competitor. I don't like to lose and I was just afraid they were going to have another 100-loss season and I just didn't want to be involved in that."

It was understandable. Years afterward, Ashburn loved telling the story about winning the Mets' most valuable player award in 1962. It was a hollow honor, to say the least. Just the same, his prize for winning it was, of all things, a boat. There was only one problem: Ashburn lived in Nebraska. "What was I gonna do with a boat in Nebraska?" he asked. So he docked the boat at a yacht basin in Ocean City, New Jersey where about a year later it sank. It took him five days to raise it up and he sold the remains to a scrap dealer. The fitting end to the story was when Ashburn went to cash the check, it bounced. That pretty much typified what the 1962 Mets were all about.

The Mets lost a record 120 games in 1962 although, thankfully, they can only blame about 10 of 'em on me.

It was hard to tell that first spring we were going to be so bad. So much of the spring focused on Casey that nobody paid much attention to the quality of play on the field. Casey didn't know any of our names. You have to remember, he was used to the Yankees where the same players—Mantle, Berra, Ford, Bauer, McDougald, Collins, Coleman, and the others—were there year after year. This was an entire team of new faces for Casey and he'd simply call us by different names every day and, usually, we knew who he meant.

When we started playing the exhibition games at Al Lang Field in St. Pete, we'd watch Casey as he came in. If his shoulders were slumped, we knew he'd been out drinking and telling stories to the writers until 4 A.M. Usually when that was the case, Casey would sit on the grass at the far end of the dugout, leaning up against a wire fence.

I got off to a great start that spring, hitting home runs all over the place, and Casey would give me a wink as if to say "nice going, kid."

During the course of those games, as he'd sit on the grass, his head would start to nod and, as I watched him, I got to know that when he nodded for the third time, he was off to sleep.

Well, I couldn't resist needling him, and when it happened, I'd run down to the end of the dugout and shout out something like, "Let's go, now! Shake 'em up out there!" Casey would jolt up from his nap and give me that wink.

Spring training was always the best time of year for ballplayers. It was a time for getting in shape. The games didn't matter, unless you were trying to make the club. There was one game none of us wanted to play in, however, and that was Fort Myers. Back then, it was about a five-hour bus ride from St. Pete to Fort Myers, and as soon as the Fort Myers game got close on the schedule, guys started coming up with hamstring pulls and sore arms. I was always a humpty when I played with the Dodgers, so I always had to make the trip to Fort Myers, but with the Mets in '62, I quickly became one of Casey's favorites. I was hitting well and he also knew me from the World Series when the Dodgers played his Yankees. The day before the Fort Myers trip, Casey came up to me and gave me another wink, which I knew was his way of saying I could stay back the next day. He thought he had a helluva player in me. I only wish I could have justified that confidence.

Unfortunately, my great spring quickly dissolved into a horrible slump as soon as the season began. I couldn't hit anything. I'd like to say I was just hitting in bad luck, but that wasn't the case. I was just plain awful and didn't hit even one ball hard. After 14 games, I was hitting .077, 4-for-52 with no homers and one RBI. We were in Philadelphia and had just lost another game and I was in the shower when Casey called me out. I had no idea what he wanted with me and even less idea when he began talking.

"I got something for you," he began. "You'll love it. That left field fence is just right and your dad is gonna be delighted. They got that little hill out there in center field and the beer tastes good and the people are just great, especially in the summer."

He was going on and on in his famous "Stengelese," not making any sense except to himself. Finally, I stopped him and said: "Casey, what in the hell are you talking about?"

"Oh," he said, "Didn't I tell you? We traded you to Cincinnati."

I didn't know what to say. I felt bad that I hadn't been able to produce for Casey, and unlike with the Dodgers and Cubs, I didn't ask for this trade. But if I had to be traded, Cincinnati was the one place I would have chosen. It was home. My dad's health was starting to decline, and it was an opportunity to bring my wife and two kids back home. The Mets got a young third baseman, Cliff Cook, and a left-handed pitcher named Bob G. Miller for me. If nothing else, I had the distinction of being the Mets' first third baseman, and they ran through 39 more in their first seven years.

Fifteen years after they had recruited me in high school, I was finally a Cincinnati Red. And as baseball often works, my hitting stroke suddenly came back when I changed teams. On the second day I was with the Reds, I got a pinch hit. Then I got a couple of more pinch hits right away. Part of the reason, I think, was the extra practice I took with Reds coach Reggie Otero. They were aware how badly I'd been going with the Mets and they set up extra sessions for me.

It was not long until I started platooning at second base with Don Blasingame, and then I started playing a little everywhere, even in the outfield. I remembered what Buzzie Bavasi had once said to me when I was a young player with the Dodgers: "There's nothing wrong with being a utility player. Sometimes, those are the most valuable players on the team for a manager."

I got off to an 18-for-51 (.354) start with the Reds, and at one point George Weiss was quoted as saying: "We possibly made a mistake in trading Zimmer, but he wasn't doing anything for us."

Our manager with the Reds was Fred Hutchinson, a big bear of a man who despised losing. Hutch was a guy you loved to play for because he was honest, fair, and smart. But he had a temper that would make players and writers cower in fear. After a bad loss, you didn't dare try to talk to him, much less approach the postgame "spread" table. More times than not, Hutch had already tossed it over in a rage anyway.

I'd like to think, when I became a manager I took something from every manager I played for. Charlie Dressen was accused of being an "I" guy who gave himself all the credit. "Just keep it close," he was quoted as saying, "and I'll think of something." That's a mistaken portrait of Charlie, though. He had a big heart and it hurts when I hear people say that about him. Walt Alston taught me patience and to never get too high or too low. Casey taught me how to motivate players, and Gil Hodges showed me how a manager gets the players' respect. Under Hutch I learned how to treat people the way you'd like to be treated. He was a man's man, tough on the outside, but understanding and fair beneath that leathery skin of his.

A month or so after I joined the Reds, we had a four-game series against the Mets. Now you have to remember, the Reds were the defending National League champions in 1962, and to lose to the Mets was unacceptable—especially to Hutch. We won the first two games of the series on Friday and Saturday, only to screw up the first game of the Sunday doubleheader. So Hutch was already hot when we started the second game.

In the third inning, "Hot Rod" Kanehl, one of Casey's favorites because he was always hustling, was leading off. I knew Kanehl was a good bunter and I was playing up at third for just that reason. Well, he couldn't have laid a more perfect bunt down, and while I fielded it cleanly, Kanehl just beat my throw over to first. From the dugout I heard this crash, and when I looked over, I saw that Hutch had kicked an ammonia bucket clear into the back wall. Guys were scattering all over the place and I knew I didn't want to get anywhere close to Hutch when I came in after the inning was over.

Fortunately, the Mets didn't score that inning, but that didn't stop Hutch from confronting me in the dugout in front of all the rest of the players.

"How long have you been playing this game?" he screamed.

I tried to explain to him that I knew Kanehl was probably going to bunt and that I was playing him properly.

"He was safe, wasn't he?" Hutch railed.

It so happened we lost the second game too, and when we got into the clubhouse, Hutch was still outside in the dugout, all by himself. Reggie Otero went around to everyone, instructing us to "get showered and dress quickly and get on the bus. He doesn't want to see anyone when he gets in here."

The next day, we were in Philadelphia and I was sitting in the dugout when Hutch came up to me and put his arm around me.

"Let me tell you something," he said. "I was really hot yesterday, but not at you. I had to take it out on somebody. Just disregard it. That's the reason I didn't come into the clubhouse. If I had, I might have killed somebody."

I thanked him, while at the same time promising myself never to get Hutch really mad at me. If only I was able to keep that promise.

When I got to the Reds, Otero told me the only time Hutch ever had curfews was in Pittsburgh, which back then was a dry town. Hutch didn't believe in bedchecks, but to appease management he had them in the one city where guys couldn't get in trouble anyway. We were flying from Cincinnati to Pittsburgh after a Sunday game and Jerry Lynch, one of the best pinch hitters in baseball history, was sitting with me. Lynch and Gene Freese, the third baseman who had been sidelined most of '62 with a broken ankle, were my running mates. (Ironically, it was because of Freese breaking his ankle in spring training that the Reds acquired me.)

"I know a private place you can go to in Pittsburgh to get a belt, if you're interested," Lynch said.

"Sure," I said.

As soon as we landed, Freese and I grabbed a cab and went to this place that had a door with a little window in it. The guy inside opened the window, recognized us, and let us in. There were just a few stools and a bar, and we sat down and ordered some drinks. We were into our second drink when the proprietor of the place announced from behind the bar that in 15 minutes the bingo game was going to start. I looked at Freese and said, "What's this all about?"

"Oh, this'll be fun," said Freese. "Maybe we'll even come out ahead here."

So we started ante-ing up five dollars a game, and before we knew it, it was nearly 2 A.M. When I got back to my room, Blasingame woke up and said, "They had a bedcheck at 12:30 and marked you missing."

"Oh shit," I thought. "What am I gonna tell Hutch?"

Needless to say, Hutch was waiting for us when we got to the clubhouse the next day and he was steaming. He shut the clubhouse door and began dressing us down, the veins in his neck bulging as he got more and more worked up.

"I try to treat you guys like men and you pull something like this," he bellowed. "The only place I have a bedcheck is in a dry town, and still you guys go and break it. Now I ask you Zimmer, what in the hell were you doing till 2 A.M.?"

I didn't know what to say. I didn't want to lie to him, but I also knew if I told him the truth, he'd think I was making fun of him.

"We were playing bingo, Skip," I gulped.

I braced myself as I said it, and as I expected, Hutch exploded. I don't remember what he said next because I kind of blotted it out of my mind. I just wanted to get out of there and onto the safety of the field. I had never seen a manager so teed off.

I waited a day for him to cool off before attempting to explain to him that we really were playing bingo and had just lost track of the time. He listened to what I had to say and said that it was forgotten. I think I even saw him crack a little smile.

I'm only sorry I got to play for Hutch just that one season. The next year, he developed lung cancer and I had been traded again. Thank goodness I never saw him after he got sick and his body withered down to nothing. I want to always remember him for the bear of a man he was.

The last time I saw him was at a party he had at his home in Anna Marie Island in Florida. He had just been diagnosed with cancer, and there was a reporter there waiting to interview him but hesitant to approach him. Finally, Hutch got right in the guy's face.

"What is it you want to ask me?" he said. "You want to know if I've got cancer, right? Well, I've got cancer and I'm gonna die. What am I gonna do about it?"

That was Hutch, straightforward, no nonsense, speaking his mind. I respected him like I respected Gil Hodges.

4 | From Washington Senator to Foreign Correspondent

I wish I could have done more for the Reds to make up for the broken ankle that knocked Freese out for most of the '62 season. Hutch used me a lot as a pinch hitter and as an occasional starter at third. Although we won 98 games and had a few players with career seasons—Bob Purkey, Joey Jay, Leo Cardenas, Frank Robinson—we could never quite catch either the Dodgers or Giants. At season's end, they wound up in a tie, with the Giants winning the NL pennant in a three-game playoff.

In March of 1962, Bill DeWitt purchased the Reds from the estate of Powell Crosley, who had owned the team since 1934. DeWitt had previously owned the old St. Louis Browns in the American League—a sad sack team that always seemed on the verge of bankruptcy until they were finally sold to a Baltimore group and became the Orioles in 1954. In any case, DeWitt came from a long line of old-fashioned, tight-fisted baseball executives, which I was soon to discover.

I was making $19,000 when I went to Cincinnati, and I thought I did a decent job for the Reds in the limited role Hutch used me. But after the season, DeWitt sent me a contract calling for a 20 percent pay cut with a note in it saying he can't pay utility infielders that kind of money. I wrote back a letter to him that said I'd busted my rear end all my life to make a halfway decent salary in baseball. I went on to say I didn't think it was right to cut me after what I'd done for the ballclub. I told DeWitt I'd rather quit than accept this cut. His response came a couple of weeks later when he traded me back to the Dodgers for a young pitcher named Scott Breeden.

I'd like to say that was the worst trade DeWitt ever made, but in baseball's big picture it was just another in more than 10,000 that did nothing for either club. Two years later, however, DeWitt did make a trade both he and the Reds would come to forever regret when he dealt Frank Robinson to the Orioles for pitcher Milt Pappas. While Frank was unquestionably one of the best players in all of baseball and the Reds' leading run producer ever since breaking in as Rookie of the Year in 1956, DeWitt thought he was a troublemaker. After making the trade, DeWitt actually said Frank didn't hustle. That would have been incentive enough for anyone, but Frank really embarrassed DeWitt by leading the Orioles to the world championship in 1966, winning both the Triple Crown and the MVP award. He remains today the only man to win the MVP in both leagues.

I wonder, if he were alive today, what DeWitt would say about Frank being named baseball's vice president of on-field discipline. Frank Robinson is one of the most respected people in the game and, in my opinion, one of the five greatest competitors I ever played with or against. And believe me, it was a lot easier playing with him. I don't think he ever meant to hurt anybody, but nobody ever went into second base harder than Frank.

I remember one time during that '62 season he was in a slump and, like a lot of us when that happens, he said he was going to quit. I went over to his locker and grabbed his big glove, which I felt would be perfect for my Sunday softball league in the winter. "What are you doing?" Frank yelled, "That's my glove!" I said, "What do you need it for? You quit didn't you?"

He laughed and realized I was giving him the business. He later gave me the glove anyway, which, like that Babe Ruth baseball, I wore out using it playing softball.

Even though I was going back to the Dodgers, I was a little annoyed at getting traded again. After all, this was the second time now my hometown team had rejected me. I felt shortchanged. There was even more irony to it this time. The following year, one of the players who replaced me on the Reds' roster was Pete Rose. That's another trivia question about me, which I didn't realize until years later: Who wore No. 14 on the Reds before Pete Rose?

The irony of Rose joining the Reds the year after I left was that we both went to Western Hills High in Cincinnati and my father and his father were great friends who played softball together. When I was growing up, my father would take me to watch the local Sunday football game in town. This was real, hard-nosed sandlot football, and Pete's dad was one of the best football players in Ohio. I'd see Pete in diapers on the sidelines as his dad played one great, inspired game after another. When Pete grew up, he was one of the best baseball players in the area, but because he wasn't a power hitter and was pretty much a self-made player, he didn't get any offers from the major league teams. Finally his uncle, Buddy Bloebaum, who was a bird dog scout for the Reds, talked them into signing him for a bonus of $7,000.

I followed Pete's career all through the minors. Every week I'd get *The Sporting News*, which published all the minor league averages and box scores. I got a real kick when he made it with the Reds in '63 and went on to win Rookie of the Year honors that year. Another victory for Western Hills.

I know Pete had a problem and it's the reason he's not in the Hall of Fame. But my feeling about that is, if they want to put something next to his name or on his plaque, so be it. He should still be in the Hall of Fame. This man did something no one in the history of the game ever did. He got 4,256 hits! I know one thing, if he did bet on baseball—and I'm not saying he did—there's no way he'd ever bet against Pete Rose.

My second stay with the Dodgers proved to be a whole lot shorter than my first one. They really didn't have a specific job for me, except as a pinch hitter. On June 24, 1963, after I'd gotten just five hits in 23 at bats, they sold me to the Washington Senators in the American League. Alston had some kind words in parting ways with me again: "He knows how to play the game the way it's supposed to be played. He tried to do the job we got him for. He just wasn't the pinch hitter we had to have."

I appreciated those words, just as I looked forward to trying to resurrect my career in a new league. The manager of the Senators— and the primary reason why I had been sold there—was my old Dodger teammate and pal, Gil Hodges. He had begun that season as a backup first baseman with the Mets, but willingly retired when the Senators inquired about him becoming their manager.

It didn't take Gil long to realize he needed a lot of help before the Senators—who had joined the league as an expansion team only two years earlier—could be respectable. So he turned to our old friend, Buzzie Bavasi, who was still running the Dodgers. I was just the first of many Dodgers Buzzie sent over to Washington. The next year Sandy Koufax was diagnosed with an arthritic condition in his elbow late in the season, leaving his future uncertain. Buzzie immediately set out to acquire a starting pitcher who could give the Dodgers the 250 innings they were accustomed to getting from Koufax. The object of his affection was the Senators' ace, Claude Osteen, a lefty who fit the bill, having won 15 games for a ninth-place team that won only 62 in 1964.

I'll say this, Gil and Senators GM George Selkirk made Buzzie pay the price for Osteen. The two of them got together and swung a monster deal at the December '64 winter meetings in which Osteen and infielder John Kennedy went to the Dodgers for outfielder Frank Howard, third baseman Ken McMullen, first baseman Dick Nen, and pitchers Pete Richert and Phil Ortega. I use the word "monster" literally because Howard was a 6-foot-7, 260-pound giant of a man who hit home runs befitting his physique. He and the four other players the Senators got represented the cream of the Dodgers' abundant farm system at the time and immediately became the core of the rebuilding Senators.

Later on, a few more ex-Dodgers joined the Senators—catchers Mike Brumley and Doug Camilli and my old buddy, reliever Ed Roebuck. One time, I was playing third base and some fan in the box seats yelled out to me: "Hey Zimmer, you and the rest of that bunch are nothing but a lot of Dodger rejects!" I just shook my head. What could I say? The guy was right.

I flew into Kansas City to join the Senators that June of '63. Gil had assumed I'd been out most of the previous night, saying my goodbyes to all my friends with the Dodgers, and he was right. "I'm not gonna play you tonight," he said.

The next night, in my first game as a Senator, I hit a homer off A's righthander Dave Wickersham. It was on a high slider and I hit the ball real good into the left field seats. The next 10 times I faced Wickersham, he threw me nothing but screwballs in the dirt and I just kept swinging at them and missing. I finally told Gil that I might get another home run off Wickersham but if I do, it'll be on the first bounce.

That season and the next, Gil was never satisfied with his three catchers: Brumley, Camilli, and Joe McCabe. On the last day of the '63 season, we were playing in Boston. Brumley, who was a lefthanded hitter, was catching, and in the middle of the game the Red Sox brought in a lefthanded reliever. I was sitting on the bench and Gil called me over.

"Can you catch?" he asked.

Well, I had caught in our fast-pitch softball games in Cincinnati when I was a kid, but that was the extent of it.

"Sure," I said.

"Okay," Gil replied. "I want you to pinch hit for Brumley and then take over the catching."

I have to say I was really excited. I was actually going to get to catch the last four innings of the game!

After the side was retired, I rushed out to behind the plate and began warming up our pitcher. All of a sudden the third base coach, Eddie Yost, started yelling something at me that I couldn't understand. Then just before the first batter came up to bat, the home plate umpire, John Flaherty, said to me, "Don, didn't you forget something?"

I looked around and couldn't figure out what he was talking about.

"Your chest protector," Flaherty said. "I think you may need that."

After the game was over, Gil called me aside and suggested that if I was really serious about catching, I should go to the Senators' instructional league that fall under the direction of George Case. Case was a wonderful man who played 11 years in the big leagues with the old Washington Senators in the '30s and '40s and led the AL in stolen bases six times. Gil also told me I should talk to Jim Hegan, a Yankee coach who was working in the instructional league for them. Hegan had been one of the great defensive catchers of all time with the Cleveland Indians in the '40s and '50s.

So I went to Tampa for the Senators' instructional league and I immediately hooked up with Hegan, who gave me two of the best pieces of advice a would-be catcher would ever want to know.

"How do you catch a ground ball?" Hegan asked me. "Out in front, right? Well, that's the same way you catch a pitcher. Catch the ball in front of you with full arm extension."

Hegan's other piece of advice was just as valuable. "Sometimes," he said, "the tendency of catchers is to play lazy when there's no one on base. Because of that you should approach catching the first pitch of the game as if there's a runner on third base and keep that mental thought in your mind all the time."

Case asked me, "How much do you want to catch?"

I said, "Every day, if I can."

Well, that happened to be a fall in which there was almost no rain in Florida and the ground was rock hard. By about the fourth day of catching, I was really hurting from all the squatting and running on that hard ground. I was massaging my legs every night to ease the pain. Then a guy took a half-swing and caught my middle finger with a foul tip. The finger was sticking straight up in the air and I knew it was hurt pretty bad. All I could do was scream, "Hodges! You SOB! Why am I doing this?"

It turned out I had a little chip in my finger that kept me on the sidelines for about a week. But I was quickly learning why they called catching "the tools of ignorance."

When I reported to the Senators' spring training in 1965, Gil told me to take both my fielder's glove and catcher's glove and work out with both. It was hard enough what catchers went through, running back and forth to the bullpen, working out pitchers, and trying to squeeze in their at bats. Around all that, I was working out at third base and second base. I was quickly becoming worn out. All the while, Gil was switching his three other catchers, trying to settle on one of them. Finally he did, with Brumley.

I was really ticked off. All the while I thought Gil had asked me to go to the instructional league in order to prepare myself for being his catcher. I told him: "Hey, I busted my ass all winter and again this spring. Why not me now? What was all that about?"

He said: "How are these guys gonna feel about me bringing an infielder in to catch?"

I was really steamed. I felt I had been misled and had wasted all that time trying to learn how to catch. Then early in the season, I was staying with a few of the other players at the Windsor Park Hotel in Washington when Rube Walker, a former Dodger teammate and now a coach for Gil, called me one morning in my room and invited me to have breakfast with him.

As I sat down at the table, Walker said, "Did you hear about Gil? He had some kind of an indigestion attack and he's in the hospital. I've got to take over."

After breakfast, Rube and I drove out to the ballpark together. I knew as soon as he got to the park he was going to call Gil to ask him about the starting lineup. I told him I wanted to catch. When he asked Gil who he wanted to catch, Gil said it was his call. "Okay," Rube said. "you're in there."

Our pitcher that day was a bespectacled righthander named Howie Koplitz who looked as much like an English professor as he did a ballplayer. He's a guy I'll always have in my memory bank as the first pitcher I caught an entire game for. We beat the Kansas City A's 7–4, and the highlight for me was throwing out a guy named Nelson Matthews, who was one of their best basestealers. After Matthews singled, I knew he was going to try and steal. I got myself ready to throw, and as he took off I tossed the mask over the side of my head. The problem was the mask was too big for me and it stayed all askew on the side of my head. I never saw the throw, but it somehow was in time to get Matthews. Meanwhile, everyone in our dugout was laughing since I looked like a complete rube, standing there off-balance with the mask hanging off the side of my head. I didn't care. He was out and I had my first baserunning victim as a catcher.

I really got to like catching. One day we were playing the Yankees at Yankee Stadium in the Game of the Week on NBC. Pee Wee, Dizzy Dean, and Gene Kirby were the announcers. Mike McCormick, who would later win a Cy Young Award with the Giants, was pitching for us and I was catching. In the fourth inning, it started raining and the game had to be stopped. Kirby came down to the dugout and asked if I'd be willing to do a rain delay interview. I said okay. But when I walked across this little gangplank into the TV booth, Pee Wee and Dizzy got up and left. It was their way of immediately making me uncomfortable.

A few minutes later, Pee Wee, laughing, came back into the booth and started kidding me about calling signs. When the game went into the rain delay there was a righthanded hitter at the plate for the Yankees with a 2–2 count on him.

"If you're so smart," Pee Wee asked, "tell me what pitch do you call next? Fastball, curveball, or screwball?"

I told him: "I'm gonna call a screwball."

Sure enough, when the game resumed I called a screwball and we struck him out. Then later in the game, someone hit a high pop behind the plate. I started circling under it, getting dizzier and dizzier as I waited for the ball to come down. As I staggered around, the ball finally glanced off my mitt onto the ground. From up in the booth I heard this shrieking whistle. It was Pee Wee, getting the attention of Hodges. Gil looked up and Pee Wee was holding his head as if to say: "Get your catcher a helmet!" Some pal. Pee Wee. He was a dandy.

As I said, that Senator team wasn't very good. We improved from 62–100 in '64 to 70–92 in '65 after making the big Osteen trade with the Dodgers. There were some good young players on the team, outfielder Don Lock, shortstop Eddie Brinkman (who was also a graduate of Western Hills High), and of course big Frank Howard. But we struck out a hell of a lot—1,125 times to be precise. by far the most of any team in the American League. Howard had 112 of them. I had played a little bit with Howard with the Dodgers. Besides being a fearsome slugging outfielder with enormous power, he was also an All-America basketball player at Ohio State when the Dodgers signed him to a $108,000 bonus. "Hondo," as we called him, was just a big old friendly giant. Everybody loved him, especially Gil.

I reported early to spring training in '65 with the catchers and pitchers, and one of the first things I did was to go over to Hondo's locker and tie all his socks and pants in knots. One of the other players saw me and said, "You better be careful. When that big guy gets here he'll bite your head off!" I knew different. I knew Hondo would be pissed, but he'd see the humor in it too.

Anyway, he reported a week later weighing nearly 280 pounds. Hodges came over to his locker and said: "Big boy, it looks like you've got some work to do."

We started playing Grapefruit League games and it quickly became apparent Howard was having trouble getting around in the outfield. Balls were dropping in front of him with regularity and it looked like he was running in quicksand. One day, one of our young pitchers who was trying to make the club complained to me after Howard couldn't get to a ball that dropped in for an RBI single. "Is that guy that bad an outfielder?" he said.

"I don't know," I replied. "He wasn't that bad when I played with him with the Dodgers. I can't believe he could fall off so quickly."

So I went up to Howard after the game and said, "Is something wrong with you?"

"Why do you say that, Popeye?" he asked.

"Well, you're not catching a lot of balls out there and it looks like you can't run too well anymore."

"Oh hell, Popeye," he said. "I'll catch 'em when the bell rings. I'm playing with five-pound weights in my inner soles!"

I couldn't believe it. "Are you nuts?" I said. "We got pitchers here who are trying to make this club and they're losing games and getting their ERAs swollen because of hits dropping in that you should be catching!"

"Geez," Howard said. "I never realized that. I guess I better start playing without weights, huh?"

What a beauty. That was Hondo's way of losing the extra pounds. And he could sure put 'em on. One of the great experiences for anyone in baseball is to be a witness to Frank Howard eating breakfast. Or, more precisely, watch the look on the waitress's face when he orders it. A typical Frank Howard breakfast was a half-dozen eggs, a half-pound of bacon, six or seven pieces of toast, two large orange juices, and a pot of coffee. That was the first course. When he was finished with that, he'd order a couple of stacks of flapjacks with sausage.

Howard was still a raw talent when he came to the Senators and hit 21 homers with 84 RBIs that first year. By 1968, however, he had developed into one of the premier sluggers in the game. He led the league in homers with 44 in both '68 and '70, and also led the league in RBIs with 126 in '70. By then, Hodges had moved on to the Mets as their manager and I was starting my own managing career in the minors, employing a lot of things I learned from Gil.

It didn't take long for people in baseball to recognize Gil's ability to manage. He was one of the few people in the game ever to go right from playing into managing without any prior experience. He was a student of the game and a master at handling ballplayers. He was great at motivating players, making them want to play for him, but he also was a strict disciplinarian. I saw that right away in that first season, 1963, I played for him.

Chuck Hinton, our best player, and Minnie Minoso, our oldest player and a bit of a legend by then, were late for a game one day. In front of everyone in the clubhouse, Gil really lit into them. I thought that was a hell of a thing. They weren't two rookies. I took that lesson with me for the rest of my life in baseball. The one thing I wouldn't stand as a manager was guys being late to the ballpark. You don't have to be there until 4 P.M. I've always said if you're there early, you can't be late. That sounds like something Yogi would say, but he adhered to it too.

In late July of '63, Ed Roebuck joined us from the Dodgers in a trade for second baseman Marv Breeding. Eddie was one of my long-time comrades, going all the way back to Elmira, New York, where we both got married on the same day. It was supposed to be a dual ceremony at home plate, but because he was a Catholic, he had to get married in the church. That night, after I got married at home plate and Roebuck got married in the church, he pitched the game for us. Because of that, he got the next three days off to go on a honeymoon to Niagara Falls. Me? The next night I got to hit against 6-foot-10 Gene Conley, who was on a fast track to the big leagues with both the Braves and the NBA Celtics. Some honeymoon. Roebuck and I came up together through the Dodger minor league chain and were both there for the '55 world championship team. My favorite memory with him was a game we played against the Phillies with the Dodgers in '55.

I was playing shortstop and Roebuck had come in to relieve. It was a close game. We were winning 5–2, but the bases were loaded. The batter for the Phillies was "Puddin' Head" Jones and the catcher, Stan Lopata, was on deck. Roebuck was a sinkerball pitcher, and the first pitch he throws to Jones is low for ball one. The next pitch is low again and so is the third pitch. With that, I hollered "time out" and went to the mound to talk to him.

"Eddie," I said, "we ain't got any room on the bases for this guy!"

"Oh yeah," he said. "Well he's gonna get another one just like those first three!"

I thought he had gone crazy on me. Sure enough, he walked Jones on four pitches to force a run home—only to get Lopata to hit an inning-ending ground out. When we got back to the dugout Roebuck explained his strategy to me.

"You may not know this," he said, "but Puddin' Head Jones never hits singles against me. He hits only doubles and homers. I wouldn't have minded giving up a single to him, but a double or homer would have cleared the bases. So I walked him, figuring that one run wouldn't hurt and was far better than three or four."

That was Roebuck. He got the job done more often than not—he was 10–2 with nine saves for the Dodgers in his best season, 1962—but he sometimes had some goofy reasoning. By the time he got to the Senators, his arm had started to wear out and Gil used him mostly in a middle relief role. Our closer was another righthander, Ron Kline, who had begun his career as a pretty good starting pitcher with the Pirates in the '50s. He switched to relieving after coming over to the American League, and in 1965 he led the league in saves with 29 for us.

Kline was one of the toughest guys I ever knew in baseball. One day he came to the ballpark and said to me, "You wouldn't believe what I got." He then lifts up his arm and shows me these two huge boils.

"You can't pitch with those," I said.

"Yes, I can," he said.

"I'm telling the manager you need the day off," I replied.

"You do that," Kline said, "and I'll never talk to you again."

He wouldn't have, either.

As I said before, those Senator teams did strike out a lot, and it would drive Hodges crazy when guys would take third strikes with men on base. He never chose to remember all the years he struck out 100 or more times as a player, and one day after he was particularly upset with our free swingers, I said to him, "Do you think I never saw you take a called third strike?"

"Yeah," he said, "but that don't count."

One of the few contact hitters we had on the Senators was Joe

Cunningham, a lefthanded-hitting first baseman who had hit .345 in 1959 with the St. Louis Cardinals. Cunningham always played in the shadow of Stan Musial in St. Louis and probably never got the credit he deserved as a hitter. He had a great eye, though, and was a real tough out. He just didn't hit for much power.

In the middle of the '65 season, the Senators called Dick Nen up from the minors. Nen, who was also a lefthanded-hitting first baseman, had been acquired from the Dodgers in the Osteen deal. He had some power, and it was clear the front office intended him to play. But when he reported to the team and was greeted by Hodges, he informed Gil he couldn't hit lefthanders. It was a strange thing for a kid to tell the manager right off. Anyway, Cunningham wound up playing only against lefthanded pitching, even though he was left-handed. I have to think that experience hastened the end of his career.

By 1965, the Senators and I were going in different directions. The team was getting better under Gil's leadership, but I was getting worse. I hit only .199 that year, and as I got less and less playing time I began hearing rumors that I'd be released over the winter. I finally went to Hodges and asked him about it, and he said the matter had not even been discussed.

"I don't care," I said. "I understand if you feel you have to do it. I just don't want to get released in the middle of winter because I've got a chance to play in winter ball and get better with my catching." The general manager, George Selkirk, gave me the same reassurance, but then, sure enough, Gil called me in the middle of the winter to tell me they had to take me off the roster to make room for a younger player.

"It's not like we're releasing you," he said. "We want you to come to camp next spring, and you'll still be on the team. We just need a roster space right now."

Well, I had my pride. Plus, I had passed on winter ball because of their assurances I wasn't going to be released. I told Gil I wanted no part of that and said I was just going to quit. He tried talking me out of it, but my mind was made up. Then a couple of weeks later, Al Campanis, who had been the Dodgers' farm director when I came up through the system, called me and asked me if I'd be interested in going to Japan.

The Tokyo Toei Flyers made me a very generous offer—$30,000—which was $9,000 more than I ever made in the big leagues. They also offered to pay for my family to make two trips over to Japan. Needless to say, I had some difficulties adjusting to a whole new culture. For one thing, the yen was valued something like 360-to-one with the dollar, and on payday you needed a shoebox to collect your money. Then there was the racetrack.

We had an outfielder on our team named Hocku, who was Korean and spoke English. He was kind of our interpreter. One time on an off day he asked me, "Jimma? [that's the way he pronounced my name] You like horses? I take you to the track!"

I was really excited. I was almost feeling like I was back home—that is until we arrived at the track and I bought a racing form which was all in Japanese. I couldn't figure out a word of it. Then I'm watching the races and the horses are running in the opposite direction as they do in the U.S. That was the first and last time I went to the track in Japan. I told Hocku I might have gone back if I could read the damn racing form and if the horses didn't run backwards.

As for the food in Japan, I don't eat all that raw fish. I couldn't stand the smell. I lived on a diet of Campbell's tomato soup and flounder. I would have killed for a hamburger. Nowadays, Tokyo has been pretty much Americanized with McDonalds all over the place. It wasn't like that in the '60s.

Each Japanese team was allowed to have two Americans on it. My American mate on the Flyers was Norm Larker, who had been my teammate with the Dodgers. Larker had been there the year before, and he was a real hothead who kept running off our interpreters. He kept insisting they wouldn't say the things he wanted to say. I didn't care what they said for me.

There's no doubt, however, if they had a chance to belittle you they would. Our manager, Shigeru Misuhara, was a legend over there, like Casey Stengel, and I don't think he liked having American players. I never had a problem with him, although there was one time when we kind of tested each other. He coached third base as well as managed, and he liked to wait until a player got all the way to the plate before he would pinch hit for him. This one day, I had a feeling he wanted to pinch hit for me, but I walked up to the plate and paid no attention to him down in the third base coaching box. I heard him yelling, "Bat! Bat!" as if to say "pinch hitter." I've got to admit, it was fun watching him frantically trying to get me out of there.

The caliber of play in Japan in the '60s wasn't nearly as good as it is now. I'd have to say there were only two Japanese players then who could have played in the big leagues—Sadaharu Oh, their all-time home run hitter, and Shigeo Nagashima, a third baseman who won a bunch of RBI and batting titles from the '50s into the '70s.

One of the all-time best American players in Japan was Joe Stanka, a righthanded pitcher who had briefly played for the Chicago White Sox in 1959 before becoming one of the first U.S. pitchers to forge a new career in the Far East. Stanka pitched in Japan for five or six years and was very popular over there. He was a big guy, who towered over most of the Japanese players. He and I became good friends while I was there, and I know Joe really loved it in Japan. While he was there he suffered a terrible tragedy when his son was taking a shower in the two-story house where he lived. There was apparently some sort of gas fumes coming out of the shower, which overcame his son, and he died. Joe had him buried in Japan.

I never brought my family to Japan, mainly because I just didn't think they would like living in a foreign country for a summer. My daughter, Donna, was only 12 and my son, Tommy, was 14, and I'm sure they would have gotten pretty tired of the Campbell's soup and flounder. Today, it would have been different for them with all the short-order American food over there. It wasn't easy being so far away from my family, but baseball was my profession and I was making more that season in Japan than I ever had before.

I hit seven homers in the first two weeks over there and thought I'd really discovered a second career. Then I broke my toe on a foul tip. I tried to keep playing on it and was still going pretty good until I tore something in my shoulder trying to make a long throw from deep in the hole at short.

That was, for all intents and purposes, the end of my playing career. I wound up hitting just .182 with nine homers in 97 games. Still, they wanted to give me another contract to come back in 1967. Much as I hated the thought of not playing anymore, I couldn't in good conscience take their money. I told them, "I'd be cheating you and cheating myself."

I headed home to my wife and kids, uncertain of my future, knowing only that if it still involved baseball, it was no longer going to be as a player.

I didn't think I'd ever go back to Japan, but as events turned out, I wound up managing an all-star team that toured there for some exhibition games in the fall of 1990. Unfortunately, my managing experience wasn't much more fruitful than the one I had as a player. I was impressed at how the Japanese players had improved. At the start of every game, I'd bring the lineup card to home plate and this nice little Japanese girl would bring a bouquet of flowers out to me. She'd bow and I'd bow. We'd wave goodbye. Then I'd take the flowers back to the dugout, lay them down real nice, and turn around and watch us get the crap beat out of us. Oh, it was a lot of fun, all right, if you liked flowers.

If I didn't like an umpire's call—and there were a few I didn't like, believe me—I wasn't about to kick and scream and throw dirt for fear of creating an international incident. Besides, the umpires wouldn't have understood me anyway.

I'd also forgotten how expensive Japan is. One night, Soot and I were with a group of 12 people having dinner in one of those Japanese steak houses where they cut the meat up with these fancy knives and cook it right in front of you. I got the bill and it was 182,000 yen. I peeled off 182,000 yen and went to bed. What's a few yen when you're having a good time? We got upstairs to the room and I asked Soot, "How much is 182,000 yen?"

"About $1,500," she said.

"That's a lot of yen," I said.

5

Back to
the Bushes

I knew I couldn't play any more. My arm was shot and I couldn't run. I was 35 years old and I felt all of it. So when I got home to Treasure Island, I called Buzzie just to let him know I was finished as a player and that if he had any kind of a baseball job for me I'd be interested.

"This is what I can do for you," he said. "All my minor league managing jobs are filled, but come to Vero Beach next spring and we'll get you some coaching work and take it from there."

There was no signed deal, just an agreement, but that was fine with me because it was Buzzie. A couple of weeks later, however, I got a call from Jim McLaughlin, the farm director of the Reds. McLaughlin was a tough little Irish guy who'd been around baseball for years and had been especially instrumental in developing those championship Baltimore teams in the '60s. I had gotten to know and like him during my one season as a player with the Reds in 1962.

"I heard you were back from Japan and decided to hang 'em up," McLaughlin said. "Would you be interested in managing in our organization?"

I told him Buzzie had offered kind of an open job, but not in managing, which is what I really wanted to do. McLaughlin said he definitely had a managing job if I wanted to come to Cincinnati and talk about it. I told him I did, but I wanted to call Buzzie first. Buzzie, as I knew he would be, was great.

"That's terrific, Zim," he said. "Take the job. You can always come back to me."

In my meeting with McLaughlin, he said, "You're a Cincinnati boy coming home, and that's the way we want to present this at the press conference. It'll be a lot of good publicity for you and us. The only thing is I can't pay you a lot of money."

"What's not a lot of money?" I asked.

"Eight thousand," McLaughlin replied.

Eight thousand? I thought. *I got two kids and a wife to support.* If nothing else, I knew I was back in the minor leagues!

"I don't know, Jim," I said. "I'm really appreciative of you offering me this job, but I've got to think about it."

The problem was, what did I have to think about? I didn't have another job, and I knew Buzzie's job wouldn't have paid any more and probably would have been less. The next day, McLaughlin called me with another proposal.

"How does this sound?" he asked. "You manage Double-A Knoxville for us, and then when the season's over you go to our instructional league in Tampa, and we'll make your salary $12,000."

"Perfect," I said. I get the extra money and I can work right at home after the season.

The night before the press conference in Cincinnati to announce my signing, I went to dinner with McLaughlin. At one point, he suddenly asked me: "I'm just wondering. If I should call you during the season and say, 'Do this and that with your team,' how would you feel?"

"I'd tell you to go shit in your hat."

"That's what I like," McLaughlin exclaimed.

Unfortunately, I never got to manage a game for him. Shortly after I got hired, Bill DeWitt sold the ballclub for $7 million to an Ohio syndicate, headed up by the publisher of the *Cincinnati Enquirer*, Francis Dale. Bob Howsam, who had been the general manager of the St. Louis Cardinals, was brought in by the new group to head up the front office, and the first thing he did was replace most of DeWitt's people, including McLaughlin. The new farm director was Sheldon "Chief" Bender, a longtime scout and a good baseball man.

Late that winter, Chief called me and said they'd like me to come to spring training early to work as an extra instructor and coach for Reds manager Dave Bristol. That was easy for me, just driving over to Tampa every day from Treasure Island. Bender told me there were a lot of veteran players assigned to the Reds' Triple-A farm in Buffalo, managed by Lou Fitzgerald, a longtime minor league manager who had worked for McLaughlin in the Orioles system.

"We've got high hopes for the Buffalo team," Bender said. "That's why I don't want you to get discouraged this season. We're not going to be able to send you too many good players at Knoxville. Don't worry if you don't win a lot of games there. We understand that."

I thought it was real nice of him to say that, especially since he hadn't been the guy who hired me.

Once spring training got underway, I was assigned to my Knoxville club and we started playing our own Grapefruit League games. I suppose it was only fitting, given my stubborn nature, that I almost got fired before I ever got out of spring training.

We were playing a game against the Detroit Tigers' Double-A team over in Lakeland. For nearly a week before, it had rained almost every day. Because of that, the pitchers didn't get their work in and every team in spring training was in chaos. I had just enough players to play this game. Other than extra pitchers, I hadn't been sent any reserve players yet. Sure enough, the first player up to bat for me, my center fielder, Clyde Mashore, gets called out on strikes on a pitch that damn near hit him in the foot. Mashore immediately goes nuts and gets right in the home plate umpire's face, calling him every name in the book. Before I knew it, he's tossed out of the game and now I'm suddenly left with only eight position players and a couple of extra pitchers.

I went up to the home plate umpire to explain my problem but he would have none of it. Mashore was out of the game, he said, and that's final.

"Okay," I said, "if that's the case, I'm not gonna put a pitcher in the outfield and risk him getting hurt and ruining his career. We're out of here."

I knew it was wrong and might very well cost me my job, but I couldn't go through with this. As we were packing up our bats and equipment, Frank Carswell, the Tigers' Double-A manager whom I had played with in winter ball in Cuba years earlier, was talking to the home plate umpire.

"C'mon!" I heard Carswell saying, "let the guy play! We've got pitchers here who need to pitch. These are only exhibition games designed to get guys their work!"

Finally, the umpire called me and Mashore back over.

"Okay," he said, "I'll let Mashore stay in the game." Then, looking at Mashore, he added: "I'm letting you back, but when the game is over I want you to take five laps in the outfield."

This was about the silliest thing I had ever heard in all my years in baseball. After the game, Mashore came up to me and asked if he should start running the laps.

"Get back on the bus," I said.

Bender wasn't lying when he told me I wasn't going to have much of a team at Knoxville. I had only two players who went on to have major league careers, Mashore and Hal McRae, and as I expected, we got off badly and never got any better. I was still having the newspapers sent home to my dad, and I knew he had to be getting pretty tired of reading about us losing six in a row, winning one, and losing another four. One day he called me.

"I know you're having a tough time," he said. "I've just got one piece of advice for you. Don't expect all your players to play the game the way you played it."

It was something I never forgot. I played the game hard all the time, but not every player is like that. Some guys are just soft, and some are laid-back. You have to adjust and deal with players' different approaches and different makeups.

In the middle of the season, we were in last place, 26–46, when I got another call from Chief Bender. It seemed the Buffalo club, in which they had invested all their top prospects and veterans, wasn't doing well either.

"I'm coming to town tomorrow," Chief said. "There's some things I want to discuss with you."

The next night we had dinner and Chief asked me if there was anyone on the Knoxville club who could help Buffalo. I told him McRae and Mashore.

"Okay," he said. "We'll send them to Buffalo only on the condition that you go with 'em."

They were obviously unhappy with Fitzgerald's handling of the team, and they wanted to make a change. The next day, McRae, Mashore, and I were on a plane to Buffalo.

The Buffalo team I inherited did have a lot of players who had had major league experience—pitchers Ernie Broglio, Jack Baldschun, and Jim Duffalo; outfielders Duke Carmel and Bob Perry; third baseman Steve Boros; first baseman Cal Emery; and shortstop Frank Obregon. Unfortunately, they were all on the way down, not up. We also had a 19-year-old catcher named Johnny Bench.

When I got there Bench was only hitting about .250, but you didn't need to be a real great baseball mind to see that this kid was going to be one helluva major league player. He was struggling because he was in the army reserve, going back and forth from the team to training exercises. We just never really got going, and then Obregon broke his hand and that pretty much finished us. We wound up in seventh place.

All in all, it was a pretty depressing experience in Buffalo. The ballpark the team played in—War Memorial Coliseum—was located in a real bad part of town, and because of the racial unrest the city had been experiencing, we only played there on Sunday afternoons. All the rest of our "home" games were played in a rickety old ballpark in Niagara Falls with a picket fence in the outfield.

We had another pitcher on that team who had pitched in the majors, a chunky righthander named Dom Zanni. The players who had been there all season told me that whenever Zanni got into the sixth inning with a lead, he'd immediately start looking to the manager to get him out of there.

It so happened the first time I started Zanni was on a hot Sunday afternoon in Buffalo. As I said, the Coliseum was a terrible baseball park and among its many faults were the dugouts that sank way down, almost to the point where you had to stand all the time to see the field.

Sure enough, after the fifth inning we were winning and Zanni goes out to the mound, and after his first pitch he looks in to me and starts rubbing his arm. He throws another pitch and does the same thing and repeats it after his third pitch. At that point, I said to my players: "On his next pitch I want everyone to go belly down on the dugout floor!"

You can imagine the look on Zanni's face when he looked into the dugout and no one was there.

I had an offer to manage the San Juan team in the Puerto Rican League that winter, and I took Bench with me. San Juan had not made the playoffs in eight or nine years, and while we didn't get off to a good start, I knew we had a good team, capable of winning the championship. Besides Bench, I had Tony Taylor, the Cuban second baseman who had a long and successful career in the majors with the Cubs and Phillies. I also had two good major league pitchers, Pat Dobson and Rick Wise, and about once a week Roberto Clemente, the hometown hero, played for us.

I lived in a hotel right on the ocean. The general manager of the team gave me a car to use, but what was I gonna do driving around Puerto Rico? We were well on our way to winning the championship when the general manager announced he had acquired Ramon Hernandez, a lefthanded sidearm pitcher who had pitched in the majors for the Atlanta Braves that year and would later go on to spend a half-dozen seasons with the Pittsburgh Pirates. Immediately, the talk around our clubhouse was about what a bad character Hernandez was. It didn't take me long to find out they weren't wrong.

We were playing a doubleheader in Mayaquez, and I was coaching third base as well as managing. Our starting pitcher had tired, and I yelled into the dugout for someone to get Hernandez up.

"He's not here," they said.

"What do you mean, not here?" I said.

After the inning was over, I ran off the field into the clubhouse where I found Hernandez sitting in front of his locker in his undershorts, drinking a beer.

Hernandez was said to carry an army knife and a gun with him, but at that moment I didn't care. I lit into him.

"What do you think this is, a damn picnic," I shouted.

A week later, we were playing a game in Ponce, and Hernandez didn't show up. I decided at that point I had had enough of Ramon Hernandez. We had a team meeting when we got back to San Juan and with Hernandez in attendance I said, "Fellas, you've done a great job for me and we will win the championship, but not with Hernandez. He will not pitch for us."

Later that night, the GM confronted me.

"What's going on here?" he said. "Hernandez says you've gone goofy."

"I've gone goofy?" I replied. "Call the coaches and ask them who's the goofy one here."

Four days later we clinched a berth in the playoffs. I was sitting by the pool at my hotel, half asleep, when the team's traveling secretary tapped me on the shoulder. It was the 15th of the month and I figured he had come with my paycheck. He handed me an envelope, and I said thanks.

"You better open it up before you thank me," he said.

I opened the envelope and there was a letter from the GM informing me that, "as of today your services as manager have been terminated."

The first guy to greet me when I went to the ballpark to clean out my office was Tony Taylor, who was in tears. Then Bench came over and told me he was going home. I said to him, "No way, John. Baseball doesn't work that way. I appreciate your support, but you have a contract here and you must fulfill it. Even though the man fired me over Hernandez, you must stay here and finish what we started." I did think it was interesting, though, that the GM waited until we clinched a playoff berth before he fired me.

Bench was just 19 and he didn't need to get a reputation. He stayed, and the next year he was voted Rookie of the Year in the National League. He went on to become one of the greatest catchers in baseball history, and I was proud to have managed him that one season. I might also add he never went out there without his chest protector.

The Reds got out of Buffalo after the 1967 season. The next year their Triple-A affiliate was in Indianapolis, and I was asked back to manage it. This time I had a much better club. Ironically, my shortstop, Jimy Williams, my catcher, Pat Corrales, and one of my outfielders, Jim Beauchamp, all wound up coaching together for Bobby Cox with the Braves in the early '90s. Williams and Corrales also went on to become big league managers. I still had McRae and Mashore with me, too. My best starting pitcher was a righthander named Jay Ritchie, who had pitched briefly in the majors with the

Red Sox and Braves, and I had a reliever, Steve Mingori, who went on to have some good years with the Kansas City Royals in the late '70s and '80s.

After another slow start, we got it going and were in contention for first place when we were about to embark on our first big road trip, to San Diego and Tulsa, the two teams that were in front of us. I felt really confident we could come back from the trip in first place when the night before we left, the general manager, Max Schumacher, called me at home.

"Can you stand a right to the chin?" he asked.

"Yeah," I said.

"Well, how about a left to the other chin?"

Schumacher explained the Reds had undergone a shakeup and they were calling up Corrales, McRae, Ritchie, and Beauchamp. Suddenly, I was left without my 3-4-5 hitters and my best pitcher. And there were no adequate replacements coming for them.

Still, I was thrilled my guys were going up to the big leagues. That's what it's all about, isn't it? Not surprisingly, though, we lost every game on the trip, and when I got back Schumacher called me to his office. Sitting there with him was Donie Bush, the owner of the ballclub who was in his 80s. Bush, who was the Detroit Tigers' starting shortstop from 1909 to 1921, was a legend in Indianapolis. He was born and raised there, and owned the ballclub for years. I sat down and listened politely as Bush said, "I don't think you handled your pitching staff too well on the trip."

I respected the fact that he was an old man, and I managed to control my emotions while I was laughing inside. There was no point in telling him I had no ballclub left.

We wound up in fifth place, 66–78, and at the end of the season I decided to call Buzzie again. By this time, Buzzie had left the Dodgers after nearly 30 years with the organization and was running the new expansion team in San Diego, which was scheduled to join the National League in 1969.

"Go ahead," said Schumacher, "call your man."

Buzzie informed me he had two minor league teams, being that the Padres were just starting up operations and only had about 60–70 players under contract. One was a Class-A team in Elmira, where I got married, and the other was a Rookie League team in Key West.

"I've already hired Harry Bright (a former first baseman for the Pirates and Yankees) to manage one of the teams," Buzzie said, "but you can have first choice."

I thought about the two places, and I figured Key West would be great since it was in Florida and had to be fairly near where I lived. How did I know it was on the other side of the state? I'd never been to Key West in my life. I thought it was a bicycle ride from Miami. I was and always will be a baseball man. I don't know anything about geography—which is why it came as a rude shock to me to discover Key West was three and a half hours south of Miami and in the middle of nowhere. By the time I discovered that, it was too late. To top it off, Buzzie gave me the usual line: "I can't pay you too much."

"How much is not too much?" I asked once again.

"The best I can do is $7,500," he said.

"Terrific," I said to myself. "I just quit a $15,000-a-year job in a Triple-A city to work for half as much in Key West. Some businessman I am!" Nevertheless, this was the choice I had made.

I took over the Key West club at our spring training camp in Leesburg in March 1969. It was a ramshackle facility with no air conditioning in the clubhouse—remember, this was the most southern tip of Florida where the games were going to be played in the dead of summer—and the field conditions were even worse. On the first day, I'm in my office and I hear this terrible screeching and grinding sound coming from the parking lot.

"What in the hell is that?" I asked one of my coaches.

"Oh," he said, "that's the bus driver. He's learning how to drive the bus."

As I later found out, this was the least of my transportation problems. The bus driver also had a drinking problem—which Buzzie had neglected to tell me when he gave me this job. He also led me to believe we'd be transported from place to place in a nice air-conditioned Greyhound bus. What is it the Hertz people say in their commercials? Not exactly? The bus, which my impaired driver was trying to learn how to operate, was an old rattletrap with holes in the floorboard, which allowed all the fumes from the engine to seep through. Needless to say, there was also no air conditioning, no toilet, and the tires were almost bald.

This is just great, I thought. *We're going to have to go on five- and six-hour bus trips everywhere on this thing?* Welcome to the Beverly Hillbillies.

I needed only about 15 minutes on our first trip to realize this was going to be just about the worst experience of my life. My players were gagging from the fumes and sweating profusely from the heat as we chugged along into the night. Finally, most of them just fell asleep—I only hoped they hadn't died—as we were driving through the swamps of no-man's land in the middle of the state. I was about the only one on the bus who was still half-awake when I noticed the bus driver's head was starting to bob.

"Hey," I yelled at him, "are you all right?"

That startled him and he straightened up, but only for a few minutes.

Suddenly, as I'm now watching everything out the windshield, I see this stop sign up ahead, only the driver isn't slowing down. At the last second, I yelled, "Are you gonna stop?" The next thing I know we're careening to the right, and by no more than a couple of inches we miss crashing head-on into a blueberry pie truck.

That was enough for me. The sweat pouring off me was no longer from the heat. I told the bus driver to pull over and I called back to my players, asking if any of them knew how to drive a bus. One of my pitchers, Vic Albury, who turned out to be the only one on that team to make the major leagues, said he'd been a truck driver in the offseason, and he drove us the rest of the way.

The next day, in a rage I called Buzzie's son, Peter, who was the farm director: "I'm done unless you get rid of this bus driver and this bus! How could you guys do this to me? Between the two of them, they almost got us killed before we played our first game!"

I had all kids on that Key West team, and while none of them other than Albury, a lefthander, ever made it to the majors, it was rewarding for me to see how they all improved as the season wore on. We won our share of games—we finished third in the Class-A Florida State League, 67–63—but I don't think I've ever spent a summer so hot as that one.

Speaking of hot, in my career I've probably been thrown out of more than 100 baseball games, but only once did my ejection from the premises prompt the fans to stage a riot. That, too, happened during that long, hot summer of 1969 in Key West. The Key West ball-park, as you might have suspected by now, was very unusual. The clubhouse was in center field, and out beyond the center field fence there was this huge telephone pole that looked like a sequoia.

This one day, we were playing the Reds' Tampa Rookie League club and there was a play at second base in which my player was called safe and then out. The umpire on the bases, a big bald guy, made the call, and I came running out to ask why he had reversed himself. As I complained and asked for his explanation, he just stood there, arms folded, looking toward center field. After this stalemate lasted a few minutes, the home plate umpire came out and said: "Let's go, Don." To which, I said: I'm not leaving until I get an answer from this guy."

Well, it was obvious by this point the bald guy wasn't going to give me an answer, and the home plate umpire insisted I had to go. I refused, and told him he was going to have to get the police to take me off the field. A couple of the ballpark cops were my friends, so I felt safe telling the umps that. Finally, the cops arrived and escorted me off the field as the fans—there were about 1,700 of them in the park—started getting really worked up.

When I walked around the center field fence, I saw this ladder that was used to pick oranges lying against the back of the clubhouse. I leaned it up against that big telephone pole and proceeded to climb up on it. From the infield, it looked like I was on top of the fence but I was really behind it. So I told our center fielder to go tell the ump on the bases that I'm sitting on top of the fence. Moments later, the big bald guy comes running out to center field yelling at me to get off the fence, and as he does, the fans begin to riot. They were pelt-ing him with garbage and oranges, and the game had to be stopped.

The next day, Peter Bavasi called me, asking as calmly as he could what in the hell was going on down there. First, we nearly got wiped out in a bus wreck and now I had started a riot. I'm sure Peter must've thought it was the same old story with me that he'd heard from his dad, always causing headaches.

The league suspended me three days for the pole-sitting incident, and now we needed someone to step in and manage in the interim. The honor went to my old running mate, Johnny Podres, who had also been hired by Buzzie to serve as a roving minor league pitching coach. Podres had been up at Elmira when the riot occurred in Key West, and when he got his orders to replace me for the three days, I called him right away.

"You'll do fine, Pods," I said. "Just call me after every game and fill me in."

The first night we got beaten real bad and Podres calls and says to me, "You can have this managing." The next night we lost badly again, and he calls and says, "I'm telling you, this managing really stinks." On the third night, we were winning the game and this big righthanded hitter for the other team ties it up with a home run into the left field seats. Two innings later, we got another lead and this same guy hits another homer into the left field seats to tie it up again. Now it's the ninth inning and we've taken the lead again, 7–6.

"This time," Podres related to me, "I was ready for the big ox. I had a lefthanded relief pitcher on the mound, there are two guys on base, and as I see this guy coming again, I immediately signal for my best righthanded reliever. *Gotcha!* I said to myself."

"So what happened?" I asked.

"Well," said Podres, "wouldn't you know the sonovabitch turned around lefthanded and hit a game-winning homer over the right field fence! How the hell did I know he was a switch hitter? This managing is a bunch of bullshit! You can have your damn team back."

I know now why Peter Bavasi went on to become a real good baseball man as president of the Toronto Blue Jays and Cleveland Indians. He'd call me almost every day, and he came to Key West on a number of occasions to learn about both the operation of the club and the game itself. We'd stay up until 3 A.M. just talking situations in managing. He really wanted to learn. I used to take matchsticks and put 'em in positions where players would be, then move them all around to show him where the players were supposed to go in certain situations.

That winter, Peter called me and told me they wanted me to take over their Triple-A club at Salt Lake City for 1970. Once again, there wasn't a whole lot of major league prospect talent there, since the Padres were still pretty much in the starting-up stage. My best player was catcher Fred Kendall, who went on to play a number of years for the Padres and also raised a darn good catching son, Jason, who's become an all-star with the Pirates. My utility player was Walt Hriniak, who later became one of the best hitting coaches in the majors with the Red Sox and White Sox. And I had Albury, my emergency bus driver, with me again. There was also one other player to whom I was to give special attention.

"We're giving you a pitcher named Eli Borunda," said Peter. "Take very good care of him. We gave him our biggest bonus of any player we signed."

I understood. However, there was an added complication with the care I was supposed to give Borunda. Peter informed me that Borunda was a Jehovah's Witness who could only pitch certain days of the week. The other days he had to go to church between six o'clock and nine at night to pray.

Okay, I said to myself. *We'll just have to figure this thing out.*

So when I gathered the team in Salt Lake City to start the season, I called Borunda in and told him he had to let me know when we went into every town which days he was available to pitch. "I've got to work my starting rotation around you," I explained.

I started pitching him regularly and in his first few starts, the harder he threw, the harder they hit him. He had a good fastball, but they were hitting the hell out of him. Meanwhile, I've got this piece of paper from Peter Bavasi that says he can't pitch on these days, and I'm starting to go cuckoo trying to make this rotation work. It doesn't seem to matter what day Borunda pitches, he's getting bombarded.

I had heard, the year before he'd been at Salt Lake City and had gotten into some trouble, which made me a little skeptical about his religious convictions. They told me he had taken a leak out on Main Street and came back to the Ramada Hotel where the players were staying and starting shooting the lights out with a bee-bee gun. I just had bad vibes about this guy, and not just because he couldn't get anybody out.

One day, we were in Phoenix to play the Giants' Triple-A farm— this was a day Borunda wasn't supposed to pitch. In his last start he had gotten really pounded again, and this night he's supposed to be in church from six to nine. I called our trainer, Doc Cole, into my office and said to him, "You know the situation with Borunda?"

"Yeah?" he said.

"Well, I've got funny feelings about this guy. Something just doesn't seem right to me. He's supposed to be in church from six to nine tonight. I want you to go over to the hotel at seven to see if he's there."

So at 7 P.M. Doc left the ballpark and went over to the Ramada. He went to Borunda's room, knocked on the door and found him drinking a beer and watching an exhibition football game on TV. Needless to say, when Doc reported back to me I was fit to be tied. The next day I had a meeting with Borunda and read him the riot act. I left nothing unsaid. I told him he was supposed to be a franchise player and I'd done everything I could to accommodate his religious convictions only to have him take advantage of me.

When I got done, Borunda looked at me and said he wanted out, that he was going to quit. Now I had to call Peter and tell him his franchise player, who I was supposed to be handling with special care, just quit. Peter wasn't real happy when I told him the news, but after explaining the whole story to him, he was more disappointed than angry. The next day I heard Borunda's wife was so upset with him she had him put in the army. I don't know what army he went into. I never heard from him again.

The Pacific Coast League, which Salt Lake City played in, was a real fun circuit that season, even if our team was by far the worst one in it. Before the season, at the press conference in Salt Lake announcing my hiring, I told the local media and fans, "I know I will do a few things out on the field you people won't agree with." I guess I pretty well backed that up, too, being that we finished 44–99, 52 ½ games behind Hawaii in the Southern Division.

The Northern Division was won by Spokane, the Dodgers' top club which was managed by my old teammate, Tommy Lasorda. Tommy had a real powerhouse, the best team in the league, with all those guys who would go on to Los Angeles with him—Steve Garvey, Bill Buckner, Bobby Valentine, Davey Lopes. I think they beat us something like 16 out of 17. We didn't belong on the same field with them. After every game we'd play in Spokane, I always would meet Tommy in the general manager's office. We'd spend an hour or so telling stories over sandwiches and beer, and there was always this priest friend of Tommy's named Tom Mulcahy there.

Well, this one night we got lucky and actually beat Spokane. After the game, I went up to the general manager's office, only Tommy wasn't there. I sat there by myself for nearly 45 minutes, all the while wondering what had happened to Tommy. Finally, he showed up with Tom Mulcahy but said nothing to me other than a curt "hello."

We went out to the car to go to dinner, and Mulcahy was driving with Tommy sitting next to him in the front seat, still not saying a word.

"What the hell's wrong with you?" I said to him.

"What's wrong with me?" Tommy repeated. "I'll tell you what the hell's wrong with me! I'm so goddam mad about losing to that sorry, sack-of-shit team of yours! After all, what's one more loss to you?"

I couldn't believe this. As if Tommy didn't have enough with all those good players he had, making him look good. I told him: "You've got to be kidding!" Tommy's one of the funniest guys I've ever been around in the game, and I admit I had to laugh—him getting so worked up about my team not losing to his again.

Fortunately, Buzzie and Peter knew what they had at Salt Lake City—or, more accurately, what they didn't have—and they weren't judging me on wins and losses. I figured I would either manage again at Salt Lake City in 1971 or maybe go up to the big club in San Diego as a coach. But then I got a surprise phone call from Gene Mauch, who was managing the Montreal Expos.

Mauch had come up as a player in the Dodgers system in the '40s—before I got there—and I really didn't have any kind of relationship with him. Nevertheless, he called Buzzie for permission to hire me as his third base coach and Buzzie, as he had done before when I went to the Reds, gave me his blessings and assured me I could always come back to him at a later time.

After my fourth year of managing in the minors with Salt Lake City, I thought I had a chance to manage in the big leagues some day. I had learned a lot about handling players and running a ballgame. But after being with Mauch for one year, I knew I was ready! To me, he was as sound a baseball man as I had ever been around. To this day, when people ask me who was the best manager you ever saw, I tell them Mauch.

"Oh yeah?" comes the usual response, "What's he ever won?"

"Well," I say, "if he's never won anything, then how did he manage 26 years in the big leagues?"

Gene's always gotten a bum rap for never having managed a team to the World Series. That shouldn't diminish his record or his ability. The man won 1,900 games with mostly second-division teams and he always made his teams better. He had a quick mind and he knew talent.

In that 1971 season I worked for Gene we had only one major disagreement. We were playing the Cubs, who were managed by Leo Durocher. I was coaching third base, and before the game, Mauch told me that Durocher's third base coach, Peanuts Lowrey, was probably the greatest sign-stealer in baseball.

"I'm pretty sure," Mauch told me, "that Peanuts has my signs to you."

So Mauch decided for this series he was going to change the signs from him to me. We went over and over them, and I knew the one thing I never wanted to do was to miss a sign from Mauch.

In the first inning, Boots Day led off for us with a single. As Ron Hunt, our No. 2 hitter, got into the box, Mauch flashes me the old hit-and-run sign. I do nothing and Day stays at first base.

Now the home team dugout in tiny Jarry Park, where the Expos played in those days, was almost right behind the third base coaching box, well within earshot, and all I can hear is Mauch screaming: "What's going on, you rockhead?"

I don't say a thing. I knew he'd forgotten to give me the new hit-and-run sign. The next pitch to Hunt is the same thing. He gives me the old hit-and-run and I just look at him and give him a wave.

When I came into the dugout after the inning, Bobby Wine, our shortstop, says to me: "You can't act that way to the 'general.'" I glared at him and said: "Screw you and the 'general.'"

Meanwhile, I could see Durocher and Lowrey having a real good time over in the Cub dugout, watching Mauch screaming at me. I was really hot and when the game was over I dressed quickly in the clubhouse and began heading out the door without talking to anyone. On the way out, I had to go past the manager's office, and as I did, Mauch called out, "Where are you going?"

"Okay," I muttered, "let's go get it on."

"Look," Mauch said, "I get really wrapped up managing a game..."

"Don't go no further!" I shouted. "I'm your third base coach. I get just as wrapped up during a game as you do. I'm trying to do a good job for you."

That's the way we left it. Mauch never acknowledged that he had given me the wrong sign, and I never told him he did. To this day, we remain great friends. I love the man.

6

No Day at
the Beach

I had been home only a couple of weeks after the 1971 season when
I got a call from Buzzie, who was experiencing the growing pains
that come with running an expansion franchise. In three seasons the
Padres had lost 110, 99, and 100 games.

"I've got an opening for a third base coach," he said. "Would you
be interested?"

The prospect of going back to work for Buzzie certainly appealed
to me, but I wanted to make sure it was okay with his manager,
Preston Gomez.

"I am," I said, "as long as Gomez is comfortable with it."

"No problem," Buzzie said. "We all want you to come aboard."

So I called Mauch and told him about Buzzie's offer.

"I appreciate the call," he said, "but don't worry about leaving me.
Buzzie's your man. You've got to take the job."

While I was happy to be back working for Buzzie, I was uncomfortable with all the speculation in the newspapers that I was hired as
the heir apparent to Gomez. I had absolutely no thoughts about managing in the big leagues. I figured I'd have to be a coach for a few
years before I got any consideration for managing. I've got to say,
though, I didn't look forward to doing my coaching apprenticeship
in those hideous brown and yellow uniforms the Padres wore in those
early years of their existence. In all my years in baseball, I never
thought I'd ever see yellow sannies on top of brown socks. The first
time I stood in the third base coaching box in that uniform, some fan

in the box seats yelled, "Hey Zimmer, you look like a pregnant canary." Unfortunately the Padres played like their uniforms looked. They had lost 100 games the year before, and 11 games into the '72 season, on April 27, Gomez was fired with the club 4–7. I was playing golf when I got a call from Buzzie, asking me to come over to the stadium. Remember, Buzzie had been general manager of the Dodgers all those years when Alston managed from year to year on one-year contracts. As a result, he had never fired a manager before and when I arrived at his office I could see he was very upset.

"Thirty-two years in baseball," he said, "and I'm forced to do something like this."

Even though I was being given the job, I felt just as bad. Finally, Buzzie made us both feel better by making a joke.

"You'll probably mess this job up like everything else," he said to me, "but what the hell. Let's give it a try."

I was suddenly and unexpectedly a big league manager, but I didn't know nearly what I had gotten into.

Not long after I had taken over, Buzzie already had a suggestion for me. I had put our hitting coach, Bob Skinner, at third base, replacing me; and Buzzie thought it would be better if I stayed as third base coach and managed from there. I did it for awhile, remembering that's what Charlie Dressen had done with the Dodgers.

My pitching coach was Roger Craig, my old Dodger teammate, and that, too, posed a problem for me. Years earlier when I left the Dodgers the second time as a player, I had told Johnny Podres that if I ever got a big league managing job, he'd be my pitching coach. Now, Podres was coaching the Padres' minor league pitchers, right there in the organization. I didn't know how to explain this to Craig. Finally, toward the end of the year, I called him into my office. He came in laughing.

"Why are you laughing?" I asked him.

"I know you're bringing in Pods," he said. "Don't you remember? I was standing right there that day when you promised him he'd be your pitching coach when the time ever came." That was Roger, a terrific, understanding guy and a friend for life. I ended up coaching third base for him in 1987 when he was managing the Giants and then, in another bit of irony, managed against him in the 1989

National League Championship Series when I was with the Cubs.

San Diego was a great place to live and manage. The weather was always sunny and warm. Jack Murphy Stadium was one of the best facilities in the league and I lived in an apartment not more than 200 yards from the ballpark. I got to walk to and from work every day.

Too often, though, that walk home was a lot longer.

Even though the Padres were barely two years removed from being an expansion team, Buzzie was convinced the talent was there to start playing respectably. In particular, he was high on the second base-shortstop combo of Derrel Thomas and Enzo Hernandez. "The best middle infield in baseball!" he exclaimed to me. Well, Enzo was a helluva fielder, and he could steal a base. The problem was he never got any opportunities because he never got on base. He hit .195 for me that season, and I didn't know what Buzzie was looking at.

Thomas was something else. Derrel had a lot of ability. It was just overrated. He hit .230 that year, but really aggravated me by being late to the ballpark all the time—that and the fact that he wouldn't accept advice. He later became one of the best utilitymen in the game, but in the beginning of his career I had my problems with him.

After 59 games, Thomas was struggling both at the bat and in the field. He had stolen only four bases, after bragging in spring training that he'd steal 104. And he'd already committed 13 errors at second. In one of the many conversations Buzzie and I had after I took over as manager, I told him that Joe Torre, who had won the MVP Award with the Cardinals in 1971, was the one guy I would never let beat me. So we were in St. Louis for a series in June, and Torre wasn't having nearly as good a year as he'd had in '71. A situation arose in the ninth inning where we were winning by a run, but the Cardinals had runners at second and third with two outs. Torre was the batter, with Ted Simmons, a real good switch hitter, on deck.

I could have walked Torre to the open base, but instead I chose to pitch to him rather than give Simmons an opportunity with the bases loaded. Torre then hit a ground ball right to Thomas, which should have been the game-ending out. Instead, Thomas kicked the ball into the right field corner and we lost the game. Afterward, Buzzie called and said: "I thought you said you'd never let Torre beat you?"

Well you can imagine how hot I was. I had a meeting after the game, and I lit into Thomas in front of the whole team. I said: "We're going home tonight, but there's one thing for sure. There's not enough room in our ballpark for both of us. One of us will be gone."

Naturally, somebody told the media what I had said, and Buzzie was on the phone to me first thing next morning.

"What the hell is this 'Thomas or me' stuff all about?" he demanded.

I told him I wasn't going to put up with Thomas any more and I was just being honest about it with him.

"Well," Buzzie replied, "you could have at least given me two or three days to do something."

"No way," I said.

"Go home and think about it," he said.

"There's nothing to think about," I said. "Are you going to back me up on this?"

The next day Thomas was sent to our Triple-A farm in Hawaii.

Thomas spent 10 days at Hawaii and it did him good. When he came back, he did everything I asked of him and I never had a problem with him again. He didn't quite become the player he'd been touted to be, but he went on to a pretty decent career, lasting 15 years in the big leagues as an all-purpose, Jack-of-all-trades utilityman.

The first thing I did when I took over as Padres manager was to loosen up on some of the team rules in an effort to make the players feel better about coming to the park. I told them they didn't have to wear ties on the road, and I allowed beer back on the team flights. It seemed to boost spirits and they played hard for me. By late May, we were 15–18 and in fourth place, and there was a lot of optimism about the club, even after we settled back down to last place before the All-Star break and finished 54–88.

My best pitcher, Steve Arlin, had good stuff and deserved much better than his 10–21 record that year, in which he led the league in losses. I've always said for a guy to lose 20 games in a season he must be a pretty good pitcher if the manager keeps running him out there every five days. On July 18, 1972, Arlin came within one out of pitching a no-hitter against the Phillies. With two outs in the ninth, Phillies second baseman Denny Doyle bounced a slider off the plate and over the head of our third baseman, Dave Roberts, who was playing in. After the game, I took the blame for Arlin not getting his no-hitter.

When the media came into my office, I said, "Arlin will have to make the Hall of Fame some other way. I fouled it up. I told Roberts to play in for a possible bunt."

I had been told that my best pitcher was Clay Kirby, another righthander who was 15–13 for the last-place Padres in 1971. Kirby had also gained a lot of acclaim when my predecessor, Preston Gomez, pinch hit for him in the eighth inning of a game in July 1970 in which he was pitching a no-hitter, but losing 1–0. I always admired Preston's guts at making that move. The irony of it was that he did it again when he was managing the Astros and pinch hit for Don Wilson who was losing a 2–1 no-hitter. Kirby was 12–14 for me in 1972, but never quite lived up to expectations. He wound up being traded to the Reds in 1973 and was out of baseball by 1976. We had one minor confrontation during a game in San Francisco when I came out to the mound to take him out and he didn't want to leave. I had also heard he was one of the players who had been grumbling about my handling of the club.

"What do you want?" he said to me.

"I don't want much," I said. "I just want the ball."

With that, he mumbled something and I shot back: "If you don't like the way I'm running the club, then just go home."

Before I had come out, he had thrown five pitches in the dirt, walked the pitcher and the next batter too. It wasn't like he was pitching another no-hitter.

We had some other good players. Fred Kendall, our catcher, didn't hit much but did a good job handling the pitchers. Leron Lee, a lefty-hitting left fielder, hit .300, and then there was Nate Colbert, who was pretty much our whole offense. Colbert was a big, imposing, righthanded-hitting first baseman who hit 163 homers in six seasons with the Padres from the club's inception in 1969 to 1974. In '72, he hit 38 homers and knocked in 111 runs, and on August 1 in a doubleheader in Atlanta had one of the greatest days in baseball I've ever witnessed. He hit five homers in the two games, tying a record set by Stan Musial, and his 13 RBIs were the most ever by a player in a doubleheader. To top it off, after the game Colbert, who grew up in St. Louis, told me he was in the stands the day Musial hit his five homers in a doubleheader in 1954.

Like I said, San Diego was a great place to manage, and I had a lot of good, hard-working players. We just didn't have enough of them, and our lack of depth, especially in the bullpen, made it a tough place to win. Probably my biggest thrill managing in San Diego was in September 1973 when I tried to help my old pal Sparky Anderson win his second straight National League pennant with the Big Red Machine in Cincinnati. The Reds were involved in a real tight race with the Dodgers when they came to San Diego for a three-game series, August 31–September 2. They pounded us 10–4 in the first game behind Don Gullett, beat us 3–2 in the second game, and then completed the sweep with an easy 6–1 win in the third game. Three days later, we were scheduled to go up to Los Angeles for a four-game series against the Dodgers. After sweeping us, Sparky came over to me and said: "I hope you got enough to go up there to LA and help us out by getting at least one game from the Dodgers."

Well, the first night in LA, we beat the Dodgers 3–2 with Randy Jones—a rookie lefty, who four years later would lead the NL in wins and win the Cy Young Award—outdueling Don Sutton. After the game, "Snacks" Shore, the Reds' chief scout, came into my office and congratulated me on the win.

"What do you say we call Sparky?" I said.

When I got Sparky on the phone, he was thrilled we had won, but then he said: "Do you think you can do it again?"

"You told me all you wanted was for me to win one!" I protested.

The next night was another nip-and-tuck game and I wound up squeeze bunting the winning run home, 4–3. Naturally, I had to call Sparky again.

By the third night, I was getting real cocky and I squeezed a couple of more times and put on all kinds of hit-and-run plays and we won 9–6. At one point, Tommy Lasorda, who was coaching third base for the Dodgers, shouted over at me: "Who the hell do you think you are, managing like that? Mugsy McGraw?"

I could only laugh. But again I called Sparky after the game and, wouldn't you know, he says to me: "Do you think you can sweep them?"

As it turned out, we didn't have a sweep in us. The Dodgers salvaged the fourth game of the series behind Andy Messersmith, but the Reds went on to win the NL West division, thanks in small part, I guess, to us. I'd have to say that Big Red Machine team of Johnny

Bench, Pete Rose, Joe Morgan, Tony Perez, Ken Griffey, Davey Concepcion, Gullett, and their kid relievers Rawly Eastwick and Will McEnaney was as good a team as I've ever seen. I don't like comparing teams because you really can't do it. But I'd put them right up there with the Dodger teams of the '50s and Joe Torre's Yankees.

One of the biggest reasons for the infusion of enthusiasm with that first Padres team in '72 was Dave Roberts, our No. 1 draft pick out of the University of Oregon. Roberts, a big righthanded hitter, was signed as a third baseman but he really had the ability to play anywhere—as he would later prove when he left the Padres after the '78 season and signed a huge free-agent deal with Houston, specifically to be a utilityman. The plan was to take Roberts on one road trip and then send him out to our Alexandria, Louisiana, farm club that was managed by Duke Snider. The first day, however, he was hitting ball after ball out of the park in batting practice, and then in the game he kept on hitting the ball all over the place. I said to Buzzie, "We've got to keep this guy up here at third base."

"No way!" he screamed.

"Why not?" I countered. "We don't have anybody here who can fill the position better than he can. Why not let him get his experience right here?"

I finally was able to talk Buzzie into letting me keep Roberts, and, the kid did okay for going straight from the college campus to the big leagues. He hit .244 in 100 games, but was worried about looking bad and striking out against the good pitchers. That caused him to lose a lot of the aggressiveness he showed in his swing and his approach. The next spring I had a talk with him.

"I know what you're doing," I said. "You're worried about looking bad against the good pitchers and you're satisfied with hitting weak grounders instead of striking out. I want you to go out there and swing aggressively and be the old Dave Roberts we gave all the money to."

"I know I can swing hard," he said—and he did, hitting .286 with 21 homers in '73.

I had a similar battle with Buzzie over our No. 1 draft pick in 1973, and fortunately was able to win that one, too. Like with Roberts, we used our No. 1 pick on a college player who, our scouts felt, wasn't that far away from the majors. He was Dave Winfield, and he was about the most awesome physical specimen I had ever seen: 6-foot-6, with great mobility and a rifle arm. He had just incredible God-given skills. Besides us, he had also been drafted by the NFL Minnesota Vikings and both the NBA Atlanta Hawks and ABA Utah Stars.

Winfield joined us shortly after the June draft, and again the plan was to send him to Alexandria with Duke after he took one road trip with us, primarily as a spectator. But as soon as I saw him, I decided to put him into left field. I called Buzzie and told him of my intentions.

"Oh geez, no!" he shrieked. "He just got out of college!"

"Buzzie, he's better than anyone I got here," I pleaded, sounding like a replay tape of my argument for Roberts the year before.

Once again, I was able to win my point and Winfield more than justified my faith in his ability. He got into 56 games that year and hit a respectable .277. More to the point, he played a terrific left field for us and showed absolutely no trepidation about being in the big leagues. And needless to say, he went on to a Hall of Fame career, with 3,110 hits, 465 homers, eight 100-RBI seasons, and seven Gold Gloves. He was also about the most exciting player you ever saw going from first to third with those huge strides of his.

Besides being his first manager, I was fortunate enough to be with him again when I was a coach for the Yankees under Billy Martin in 1983. That was the year he got involved in that goofy seagull incident in Toronto in which he attempted to scare a gull off the field of Toronto's old Exhibition Stadium by throwing a ball at it. The ball wound up hitting the bird and killing it, and the Canadian authorities turned it into an international incident. They arrested Winfield after the game, charging him with cruelty to animals, and detaining him for an hour and a half in jail while the rest of the team was waiting in our chartered plane at the airport. The whole thing was nuts, about the craziest thing I've ever encountered in baseball. I guess it showed just how great a natural athlete Winfield was. I mean, what are the odds of hitting a bird with a baseball from 75 feet? Maybe I should have tried him as a pitcher too.

I want to say this about Dave Winfield: He left the game hustling, and he remains to this day one of my all-time favorite baseball people.

A quick postscript here on Roberts and Winfield. I heard years later when Duke was asked by a reporter why he gave up managing after just those couple of years in Alexandria, he joked: "I never had a chance to succeed. Zim grabbed all my best players before I ever got them!"

In my tenure in San Diego we had one other No. 1 draft pick with whom I didn't have so much success. In 1970 the Padres made Mike Ivie, a strapping high school catcher from Atlanta, the No. 1 overall pick in the June draft and gave him an $80,000 bonus to forego college. Ivie never got to play for me, but I had him in two spring trainings.

Not long after he signed with the Padres and went to the minors, he developed a mental thing about throwing. He couldn't throw the ball back to the pitcher. As a result, he told the Padres he couldn't catch anymore and asked to be switched to first base. My job, Buzzie informed me, was to change his mind.

We had a real good relationship—I really liked Ivie. It was during the spring of 1973 when he asked the Padres to move him out of catching. I called him aside and had a long talk with him, trying to convince him what he could do for us if he could catch. We trained in Yuma at the other end of Arizona and were going on a four-game trip to Phoenix, and finally I got him to agree to catch. So I called Buzzie and said: "I think we got the problem solved."

I told Ivie, "Don't worry about botching a throw." I was like a father to him, trying to protect him, and at the same time boost his confidence. He caught the first game in Phoenix and did well, and afterward I'm pumping him up sky-high. I thought he'd gotten over the hump, but the next day he came to my hotel room and started crying.

"I just can't do it," he said. "That's it. I can't do it."

Fortunately for Ivie, he was a pretty good hitter and was able to play 10 years in the majors, mostly as a first baseman. But the Padres had made him a No. 1 pick because he was a catcher, and in 1978 they traded him to the Giants, getting Derrel Thomas back in return.

The 1973 season was the Padres' fifth in the National League, and as such, Buzzie regarded it as a pivotal, turn-the-corner year. For me, it turned out to be about the toughest season I ever endured in the majors. Despite supposedly being ready to come of age, we started the season with seven rookies and four second-year men on the roster. Then in late May the team owner, C. Arnholt Smith—who I never met in my entire time as Padres manager—announced he intended to sell the team for $12 million to a group that planned to move it to Washington, D.C.

Because Smith was experiencing such severe financial problems, the club was forced to make a couple of "salary dump" trades that only further depleted a roster that was close to threadbare anyway in terms of experienced players. We sent Fred Norman, a useful little lefthanded pitcher, to the Reds for Gene Locklear, a full-blooded Cherokee Indian who was a pretty good lefthanded hitter but really just a reserve outfielder. Not long after that, we dealt Dave Campbell, who had been our regular second baseman in 1971, to the Cardinals for a young second baseman, Dwain Anderson, who had trouble picking up the ball. Our infield was pretty much a shambles, Kirby and Arlin went backward, and we still weren't able to bolster our bullpen. We scored the second fewest runs of any team in the league and were also next to last in pitching.

Needless to say, we finished last again for the fifth straight year, 60–102. Throughout the season, I was trying to please three bosses, Buzzie, his son Peter, and the general manager, Bob Fontaine. They all had different ideas about how we could improve things, and I just got sick of it. I didn't want to end up in the nuthouse. With about 30 days left in the season, I told Buzzie I'd had it, that I was going home as soon as the season was over and that was it.

"Don't you want to manage anymore?" he asked.

"Not under these circumstances," I said.

"Well, why don't you just give yourself some time to think about it for awhile," he replied.

"I already have," I said. "At the end of the season, I'm going home and that's it."

And that's exactly what I did, but not before telling a friend in San Diego there would probably be some stories coming out in the newspapers and to please send them to me.

I hadn't been home more than a few days when a letter arrived from the Padres informing me I was officially no longer under the employ of the ballclub. Not long after that, my friend in San Diego sent me a tiny little newspaper clipping that said: "Zimmer fired as manager of the Padres; [John] McNamara hired." There were no quotes from Buzzie in the article—just a straightforward story that McNamara was replacing me.

"Well ain't that nice," I said to myself.

Later that winter I went to Giants owner Horace Stoneham's annual golf outing in Arizona. I was invited because as far as anyone knew I was still manager of the Padres, since nobody had formally announced I wasn't. As I was walking through the locker room, somebody came up to me and said, "Congratulations, you just got Willie McCovey."

"No," I said, "they just got McCovey. I don't manage San Diego anymore."

Later, I was sitting in the hotel lobby with Gene Mauch when Dick O'Connell, the general manager of the Red Sox, walked by. Mauch immediately introduced me and said, "This man doesn't have a job."

"What are you talking about?" O'Connell asked. "He's the manager of the Padres, isn't he?"

"Not anymore," Mauch said, "and you could use him."

O'Connell acknowledged that his manager, Darrell Johnson, was looking for a third base coach, but said he was leaving the choice up to him.

"Here's Darrell's number," O'Connell said. "Go call him up and tell him you're interested in the job."

I called Johnson and he said he'd be glad to consider me, but that he was probably two or three weeks away from making a decision. That was fine with me and I told him so. Three days later, O'Connell called me and asked: "Are you interested in that third base job?"

I told him I was and he replied: "Good. You got it."

Meanwhile, I was still carrying around that "Zimmer out, McNamara in" newspaper clip in my wallet, and I showed it to Phil Collier, the longtime, Hall of Fame baseball writer in San Diego.

"I never thought in my wildest dreams Buzzie would ever fire you," Collier said.

"He wouldn't," I replied.

But as Casey Stengel said when he was let go by the Yankees in 1960, it didn't matter whether I was fired or quit. There was no question I had to leave.

7

Banned
in Boston

Little did I know when I accepted the Red Sox third base coaching job I'd wind up staying in Boston longer than any other major league town I've worked in. My only experience in the American League to that point had been the three years I'd played for Gil Hodges in Washington. I looked forward to Boston and Fenway Park because of the deep-rooted baseball tradition there. I would soon find out on an up-close and personal level that the passion Boston fans have for their baseball and their team is second to none anywhere, even in Brooklyn for the Dodgers.

Darrell Johnson had taken over as Red Sox manager from Eddie Kasko after the 1973 season. It was a veteran team he inherited, led by Carl Yastrzemski, Luis Tiant, Bill Lee, and Rico Petrocelli. Unfortunately for Darrell, maybe it was too much of a veteran team because it pretty much collapsed over the final month of the '74 season. At one point in late August, the Red Sox had a seven-game lead in the AL East, but over the final 28 games, they won only eight as the Orioles and Yankees went storming past them. The entire Red Sox team hit only eight homers in the month of August and if you know Fenway Park, you know that isn't going to get it done.

Tiant won 20 games, Lee 17, and Yastrzemski hit .301, but for the most part, the highlight of the '74 Red Sox season was the emergence of two young players, shortstop Rick Burleson and right fielder Dwight Evans. Burleson, who got the nickname "Rooster" because of his fiery and aggressive style of play, became an immediate favorite with the Boston fans. He hit .284 in 114 games after taking over as shortstop from Mario Guerrero, a weak hitter who was really more of a backup player. For seven years in Boston, from 1974–80, Burleson played as good a shortstop as it can be played, and he developed into a real good hitter too. His strong arm enabled him to make the play from deep in the hole as well as anyone I've ever seen, and he was exceptional at coming across the bag on double plays. Evans hit .281 with 10 homers and 70 RBIs, and quickly showed himself to be a brilliant defensive right fielder.

I don't believe in using injuries as an excuse, because like it or not, they are part of the game. That said, the '74 Red Sox were beset with a siege of injuries, the worst of which occurred June 28 in Cleveland when Carlton Fisk, our mainstay catcher and team leader, tore up his knee in a home plate collision with Leron Lee, one of my former Padres. That finished Fisk for the season. In addition, Rick Wise, a 16-game winner for the Cardinals in 1973 who O'Connell had acquired for outfielder Reggie Smith in his biggest deal of the offseason, hurt his arm pitching in cold and damp weather in his first start and won only three games.

The bad taste of the '74 season was removed almost as soon as the Red Sox broke camp in spring training the following year. After just two weeks of the 1975 season, I knew it was going to be a much different story. What gave me that optimism was the arrival of two of the best looking rookies I ever saw: outfielders Fred Lynn and Jim Rice. I can't remember two rookies with so much ability breaking in with a club in the same season. After watching them both for about a month, I got a baseball and had Yaz sign it for me. Then I had Lynn and Rice sign it. I felt I might have the first baseball with three Red Sox Hall of Fame outfielders on it. That's how much I thought of Rice's and Lynn's talents.

I don't think I ever saw a player contribute as much to a championship team as Lynn did for the Red Sox in 1975. Defensively, he made plays in center field that were not to be believed. It just seemed he got to everything, and he demonstrated one of the best arms of any center fielder in the majors. He batted .331 with 21 homers and 105 RBIs, and led the league in runs (103), doubles (47) and slugging (.566). Whenever the Red Sox needed a hit, he just seemed to get it. Every opportunity that came up, he took care of it. It was no surprise to me that he became the first player in history to be named Most Valuable Player and Rookie of the Year in the same season.

Then you had Jimmy Rice, who hit .309 with 102 RBIs and led the team in homers with 22. It wasn't long before he began playing more and more in left, with Yaz taking on the designated hitter duties. Rice worked hard at becoming a good outfielder, especially learning the tricks of playing left field in Fenway, and he didn't make an error that season. That was just a small preview of what was to come.

Besides the pleasant arrivals of Lynn and Rice, Darrell got more good news in spring training when Fisk reported with his knee completely healed. In mid-May, Cecil Cooper, another really impressive hitting prospect, forced his way into the lineup at first base; and on June 13 O'Connell solidified the infield defense by purchasing second baseman Denny Doyle from the California Angels. Doyle proved to be a perfect complement to Burleson, and hit .310 for us out of the No. 2 slot in the order.

Another big contributor to the '75 pennant-winning season was Roger Moret, a lanky lefthander who was 14–3 that year as a long reliever and spot starter. Moret, because of his delivery, could be really nasty on hitters, but he tended to be erratic. He was also a strange character off the field. One time in Boston, Moret was scheduled to be our Sunday starting pitcher and the night before, after batting practice, Darrell told me he was planning on letting him go home and get a good night's sleep. From some things I'd heard about Moret, I didn't think that was a good idea. My suspicions turned out to be well founded when Moret got in his car and drove all the way to New York to pick up a girlfriend. Then, driving back to Boston, he crashed his car into the back of a trailer truck at 3 A.M.

I got to the park early that Sunday morning and Jack Rogers, our traveling secretary, was in the clubhouse with a frowning look on his face.

"Moret's been in an accident," he said. "Crashed his car up on the highway. He's got cuts all over his face and he's probably lucky to be alive. He sure as hell can't pitch today."

Moret recovered and really served as a good luck charm for us all year. It seemed every time we brought him into a game, we'd end up winning. If it was 6–1 when he came in, we'd wind up rallying to win 7–6. He had three good pitches—a curve, overhand fastball, and a changeup. The best comparison I could make to him is Ramiro Mendoza with the Yankees, in that he could start or relieve with equal effectiveness. Unfortunately, he went goofy after the Red Sox traded him following the '75 season. In Texas two years later, he'd go into these trances in which he didn't know who or where he was. I heard that even after getting released from baseball he never did recover from whatever it was that had afflicted him.

Anyway, with that cast—plus Tiant, Lee, and Wise anchoring the pitching with a combined 54 wins—the '75 Red Sox took control of first place in the AL East in June and went on to win the division by four and a half games over the Baltimore Orioles. Unfortunately, Rice broke his arm in Detroit on September 21 and missed the rest of the season. In the American League Championship Series, the Red Sox ended Oakland's three-year reign as world champions with a three-game sweep, and for the first time since 1959 I was going back to the World Series. And what a World Series it was! Only about the greatest ever played.

Our National League opponent was Sparky Anderson's "Big Red Machine" Cincinnati Reds, and although the Series was to open and close in Boston, we were regarded as the underdogs. Game 1 was all Luis Tiant, who pitched a five-hit, 6–0 gem in front of his parents, who had been given a special diplomatic dispensation to fly in from Cuba for the game. It rained periodically throughout the game, but the ageless El Tiante was simply superb, and we were able to break up his scoreless duel with Don Gullett by scoring all six runs in the seventh. What I'll always remember about that game was that Tiant, who had batted only once all season because of the designated hitter rule, started the six-run rally himself with a single. Tiant was a true showman. He'd smoke those big Cuban cigars and he had that distinctive herky-jerky motion when he pitched. They loved him in Boston. He was also a helluva pitcher. Once he got to the ninth inning, you could sit your bullpen down. He knew how to finish a game. He was his own closer. His teammates all loved him too. El Tiante was always the life of the party in the clubhouse, and on the plane flights—which he dreaded—you'd hear him screaming (while everyone else was laughing), "Get up! Get up!" every time we took off.

At the Monday workout before the Series got underway, I was standing in the outfield at Fenway while our guys were taking batting practice. I had something on my mind and Darrell must have sensed that as he strolled over to me.

"What are you thinking?" he asked.

"Well," I said, "I know Bill Lee hasn't pitched well the second half of the season (he hadn't started in three weeks and hadn't won since August 24), but I've just got a hunch about him. I saw a lot of this Cincinnati team when I was in the National League, and they're pretty much a free-swinging team. I think a lefty like Lee who throws all that off-speed stuff and keeps the ball down might give them trouble, especially in this ballpark with the grass. I'd recommend pitching him in the second game."

Darrell looked at me as if I was crazy. For a moment, I thought he was going to tell me to go to the clubhouse and take a cold shower.

"I just have a feeling Lee might pitch well here," I insisted.

He said he'd think about it before he had our meeting with the coaches. After the meeting, Darrell told the media he'd decided to pitch Tiant in Game 1 and Lee in Game 2. The Lee part of the announcement drew howls of disbelief from the media who thought Darrell was showing desperation before the Series even began.

When I heard and read all the criticism of giving Lee the Game 2 start, I said to myself: "I hope to hell this works or I'm gonna feel pretty bad, not just for me, but for the manager." I have to say, I never rooted so hard for Bill Lee to pitch well than I did that day. He doesn't know it, but that was one day when the biggest fan Bill Lee had in the ballpark was me. And I've got to say he rewarded my faith by holding the Reds to just two runs over eight-plus innings and carrying a 2–1 lead into the ninth. He definitely pitched well enough to win.

Unfortunately, the Reds bullpen of Pedro Borbon, Rawley Eastwick, and Will McEnaney completely shut our hitters down over the last three innings, and the Reds scored a pair of two-out, ninth-inning runs off Lee's reliever, Dick Drago, to win 3–2. It was a tough loss, but at least nobody could blame it on Darrell's decision to start Bill Lee.

Our Game 3 loss in Cincinnati was even tougher, if only because of a controversial call that prompted death threats from Boston against umpire Larry Barnett. We had been down by as much as 5–1 in the game before coming back to tie the score 5–5 in the ninth and send it into extras on a two-run homer by Dwight Evans. In the bottom of the 10th, Reds center fielder Cesar Geronimo led off with a single. The next batter, Ed Armbrister, pinch hitting for Eastwick, attempted to sacrifice Geronimo to second, but after successfully laying down the bunt in front of the plate, he got in front of Fisk, attempting to field it. There was a collision, and Fisk wound up throwing the ball wildly into center field trying to nail Geronimo at second. Fisk argued vehemently that Armbrister had interfered with him, but Barnett stood firm in contending it was a clean play. When Joe Morgan later singled Geronimo home for the winning run, all of New England was in a fury. To this day, I don't know if it was interference. It all happened so fast and you couldn't see from our dugout. I just know it was a call made against the Red Sox and you have to live with it. The way I look at it, if nothing else Barnett assured himself of being one person who consistently got booed louder in Boston than I did over the next 20 years.

The Red Sox evened the Series in Game 4 when Tiant again went all the way—this time using 163 pitches to close out his own game—a 5–4 win. But when the Reds, behind Gullett, won Game 5 to go up 3–2 in the Series, a lot of people pretty much figured we were done. And it surely looked that way when the Reds wiped out the 3–0 first-inning lead we took in Game 6.

I don't think you'll get too many arguments about Game 6 of the 1975 World Series being one of the greatest baseball games ever played. I know I probably was never part of a better one (although for sheer wacky drama, Game 4 of the '96 World Series comes close). After Lynn had gotten us out front quickly with his three-run homer in the first inning, the Reds came back to tie the score off Tiant in the fifth and went ahead 5–3 in the seventh on a two-run double by George Foster. They added another run in the eighth, and at that point, Fenway Park was about as quiet as I can ever remember it when the place was filled. It was in the bottom of the eighth when we tied it in the most surprising and unlikely manner. I say unlikely because it was Bernie Carbo, pinch hitting, who tied it up with a three-run homer off Eastwick into the center field bleachers—after taking two of the weakest swings I've ever seen. If Carbo had made contact on either of those two previous swings—even on the fat of the bat—he wouldn't have gotten the ball past the pitcher. He had no chance and looked totally fooled. I don't know if he ever explained why he had such weak swings prior to hitting the home run, but then he was always a little goofy.

Coaching at third base, I'll never forget Pete Rose, playing third for the Reds and shouting over to me after Carbo's homer: "Win or lose, Popeye, we're in the greatest game ever played." He was like a little kid in the candy store.

We had a chance to win the game in the ninth when Denny Doyle led off with a walk and made it around to third on a single by Yastrzemski. After Fisk was walked intentionally to load the bases, I told Doyle: "Bases loaded, nobody out. Anything that looks like a line drive, you can't go nowhere. We can't have you getting doubled up here. Anything in the air, I'll watch it while you just tag up."

Lynn then proceeded to hit a fly ball to shallow left about 180 feet from home plate. As Foster came in to make the catch, I started down the line and yelled to Doyle to tag up. But as soon as I realized it was too shallow to score him, I knew he was going to have to hold. I was stunned when I turned and saw Doyle already breaking for home.

"No!" I screamed. "No! No! No!"

Instead of heeding my cry, he kept running for home and was thrown out easily. Again, Rose hollered over to me: "How many times do you have to tell a guy not to go?"

Doyle later explained he thought I was yelling "Go!" to which I said to myself, "What about when I was next to him and said 'You can't go nowhere'?"

If we had lost that game, I already decided I was going to get dressed and out of the clubhouse before the media got there. The last thing I wanted to do was to criticize a player for losing a World Series.

After that botched opportunity, the game continued on, tension mounting, into the 12th inning. In the bottom of the 12th, Fisk led off for us and hit a high drive down the left field line right at the foul pole. It happened so suddenly, at first I just thought it would go foul. Coaching third base, you can't see around a part of the Fenway wall that juts out beyond third base. I had to get out, probably into fair territory where I wasn't supposed to be, to see the flight of the ball. I've never seen any film clips of me, but I'm sure I was doing the same thing as Fisk—trying to wave the ball fair. I see that home run over and over in my dreams. It was—and still is—one beautiful sight.

In the papers the next day, Rose was quoted everywhere saying the Red Sox probably should have won the game in the ninth inning had Doyle not tried to score against my instructions.

I am not one of those who believed the Red Sox' dramatic win in Game 6 destined them to win the World Series. I've been around baseball long enough to know you can never predict what's going to happen from game to game. As pumped-up as Fisk's homer got all of New England, Game 7 was another night.

Once again, Darrell turned to Lee, only this time with no input from me. Lee was really all we had left and, in truth, the most logical choice after the way he'd handled the Reds in Game 2. His opponent, Gullett, had control problems and helped us to three runs in the third inning with a couple of bases-loaded walks. The Reds got two runs back in the sixth when Rose slid hard into second to break up a likely inning-ending double play and Tony Perez homered. They tied it in the seventh, but missed an opportunity to break it open when reliever Jim Willoughby got Bench to foul out to Fisk behind the plate, leaving the bases loaded.

Willoughby went on to pitch a scoreless eighth, but when Darrell replaced him with rookie Jim Burton to start the ninth, the second-guessers began to form a line. As it turned out, Burton gave them something to debate all winter long—and for many winters to come—when he gave up the Series-winning run on a soft, looping RBI single to center by Joe Morgan. "He never should have taken out Willoughby" was the tortured chorus heard all over New England. But you know what? Don Drysdale could have given up a hit like that. If Darrell didn't think Burton could do the job, he wouldn't have put him in there. If Burton had popped Morgan up—as he damn near did—would Darrell have ever been given the credit? It was just one of those things that happens in baseball. Somebody always has to lose, but as our owner Tom Yawkey said afterward, there were no losers in this World Series.

He backed up that statement by giving us all World Series rings.

The only thing that separated our rings from the ones the Reds got for winning the Series was the diamond in the middle.

Mr. Yawkey was a truly wonderful man. Before day games, he'd come into the clubhouse and sit right down at my locker, which was just outside the manager's office. He knew I always got to the park early, around 8:30, and he'd come in with a cup of coffee and we'd talk baseball. One time, after we lost a 9–8 game the night before—in which I got a baserunner thrown out at the plate—I got to the park early, and instead of sitting in the clubhouse I went out to left field and sat down at the base of the Green Monster. I was just sitting there, thinking, and taking in the ballpark, when I saw Mr. Yawkey coming down through the stands behind first base. He came out onto the field and started heading out to left field, right at me.

"Oh boy," I said to myself. "He's probably still upset about last night's game."

Mr. Yawkey had a favorite phrase that he used all the time, especially after the '75 World Series. "It wasn't meant to be." That's all he had to say to me when he got out to left field that morning.

There appeared to be a hangover from our hard-fought, tough loss in the '75 World Series. For one thing, Fisk, Lynn, and Burleson got embroiled in a nasty contract squabble with the front office that lasted nearly half the 1976 season. The media maintained the contract disputes of the three players had an overall negative effect on the team's play. I can't say that it did or it didn't. I just know we didn't play very well the first half of the season. About the only highlights early on that year—if you want to call them that—were a couple of big fights we got involved in that got a lot of attention.

It became clear early in 1976 the Yankees were once again a team to be reckoned with. After years of decay under the ownership of CBS, the Yankees had begun their revival when George Steinbrenner bought the ballclub in 1973. They made a series of successful trades, bringing Graig Nettles and Chris Chambliss over from Cleveland; Ed Figueroa and Mickey Rivers from California; and with the dawning of the free-agent era, Steinbrenner was ahead of the pack in signing Catfish Hunter from three-time world champion Oakland.

Hand-in-hand with the Yankees' resurgence was the renewal of the Yankees–Red Sox rivalry, and at Yankee Stadium in May 1976, hostilities boiled over between these two historic rivals like never before. It all began in a typically tense game when the Yankees' Lou Piniella barreled hard into Fisk at home plate, bringing both players to their feet, fists flying. What evolved from there was one of the wildest brawls you ever saw, with Bill Lee winding up the principal victim. First, Lee got rabbit-punched by Rivers, and later he got punched and thrown to the ground by Nettles. When order was finally restored, he left the field crying in pain, his left shoulder broken. In my opinion, he was never the same pitcher after that. I remember, the next day he held a press conference and called Billy Martin, the Yankees' manager, a "Fascist."

The next month, we got involved in another melee in Cleveland, and this time I was almost the prime victim. I was coaching at third base when Carbo hit a ball to deep right-center into the gap. As he was tearing around the bases, I hollered "down!" expecting him to slide into third. Instead, he doesn't slide and tries to run Indians third baseman Buddy Bell over. Naturally, the two of them came up swinging and both benches cleared with me ending up at the bottom of a heap of players. I kept thinking of the left side of my head where there was a soft spot from my beanings, and I just didn't want to get stepped on.

Finally, I heard Dave Garcia, one of the Indians coaches, scream: "Don't hurt Zim! Don't hurt Zim! He's got a plate in his head!" If only it was a plate. Finally, order was restored and I escaped with only a small spike mark in my cheek.

In between the fights and the players' contract squabbles, we were playing badly and the speculation naturally started up about Darrell Johnson's job security. Then on July 9 Mr. Yawkey died, which cast a further pall over the club. Darrell was supposed to manage the All-Star Game, which he did. But right after the break, the club lost five out of six games to Kansas City. When we arrived in Texas, July 19, the club was 41–45 and I got a call in my room from Dick O'Connell. I knew O'Connell and Darrell were pals, so I was little bit surprised to hear what he had to say.

"We've decided to make a change," O'Connell said. "Would you mind taking over the team until we get back home?"

"Okay," I said. "Whatever you want to do."

When we got back to Boston a week later, O'Connell called me over to his box seat next to our dugout at Fenway Park and said he wanted me to manage the team for the rest of the season and sign a contract for next year as well. He asked me if I wanted to bring in any coaches, but I said, "let's wait until after the season."

Walt Hriniak had played for me in Salt Lake City, and I knew him to be a good baseball man who loved and knew the game. So I hired him as my bullpen coach. He later took on the duties as Red Sox hitting coach and passed on many of the hitting principles that he learned from his mentor, Charlie Lau, who was considered one of the best batting instructors of all time. I didn't have a real hitting coach. The job just kind of evolved. Some of my players gravitated to Hriniak and others went to Johnny Pesky. I didn't care.

Years later, Hriniak's technique—in which hitters seemingly took their upper arm off the bat at the last instant before contact—came under a lot of criticism. That exaggerated, goofy one-arm swing I think was misinterpreted. Guys weren't hitting one-handed. They took their hand off *after* they hit the ball. Fisk and Evans in particular were Hriniak guys. Rice went to Pesky. Like I said, I didn't care as long as they were getting the help they needed. Hriniak lasted 16 years in the big leagues as a hitting coach and got a record salary for a coach from the White Sox when he left Boston, so he had to have been pretty good.

We played a little better over the second half of '76, 42–34, to finish third, a distant 15 ½ games behind the Yankees. But Lee was lost for pretty much the rest of the season after the fight, and two of my other veteran starters, Rick Wise and Ferguson Jenkins, struggled. Only Tiant, who won 11 of his last 13 decisions to finish 21–12, lived up to pre-season expectations. In addition, neither Lynn nor Rice came close to matching their sensational rookie seasons.

I was looking forward to a new beginning in 1977 and having my own staff in spring training. But the death of Mr. Yawkey created a power struggle among the Red Sox ownership and uncertainty for me about my future with the club. The Yawkey estate put the team on the block and it wound up being purchased by Mr. Yawkey's widow, Jean; Haywood Sullivan, the former Red Sox catcher who had worked in the club's scouting and player development departments; and Buddy LeRoux, who had been the team trainer from 1966–74.

There was a lot of criticism in the media about how the sale went down, especially since Sullivan and LeRoux weren't believed to have had put much of their own money into the deal. Nevertheless, they became the joint managing general partners, and that only meant problems for both the club and me.

Among the first things the new ownership group did was to fire O'Connell and his two chief assistants, John Claiborne and Gene Kirby, in October, leaving me out there alone as the only remaining high-level O'Connell man in the organization. I wondered where I stood, and then out of the blue I got a call from Buzzie Bavasi, who had left the Padres and was now running the California Angels for Gene Autry.

"Would you like to manage the Angels?" he asked.

I didn't know what to say. I had a contract for 1977, and even though I knew I wasn't Sullivan's and LeRoux's man, I wasn't sure I should be having this conversation with Buzzie.

"Are we doing something against the rules here?" I said to myself.

"How do you stand over there?" Buzzie persisted.

"I got one year," I said.

"Well, I'm in a position to give you three years."

"You're not gonna pay me the same paltry salary you gave me in San Diego, are you?"

"No," he said. "We've got a lot of money here."

Now I really was getting worried that this was a case of tampering and that I could get in a lot of trouble. I told him I'd have to think about all this, but before anything, I had to find out where I stood with the Red Sox.

Two hours later, my phone rang and it was Haywood Sullivan. He began by making a lot of small talk, asking me if there was anything I needed.

"By the way," he then said, "I talked to your old boss yesterday."

"I got a lot of old bosses," I said, playing dumb.

"Buzzie," he said. "He called me to ask for my permission to talk to you about managing the Angels."

"Well how do I stand here?" I asked.

"You stand better than you did before," Sullivan assured.

He didn't specify but that was good enough for me. I called Buzzie back and told him I was okay in Boston and that I wasn't interested in leaving.

"That SOB Sully!" he screamed. "He said I could talk to you!"

A few days after that, Sully called me again and asked me what I wanted as far as a contract was concerned. Well, I had already talked to Peter Bavasi, who had given me some advice in the past on contract negotiations, and he gave me an idea—which I decided to throw out to Sully as long as he was telling me I was in such good shape with the Red Sox.

"I'd like to have a rollover deal," I said. "In other words, every time I start a new season, I'm guaranteed a contract for the following season, so I don't ever have to go into a season not knowing if I have a job beyond that year."

After talking it over with Mrs. Yawkey, Sully agreed. So when I ultimately was fired in 1980, I still had 1981 coming from the Red Sox. Buzzie's call didn't hurt, of course, but Dick O'Connell and Haywood Sullivan had treated me as great as any general manager ever did.

Once I got my contract situation straightened out, I went about lining up my coaching staff. I had read the Mets were firing all of the coaches who had been with them since 1968 when Gil Hodges brought them there. These were the same coaches Gil had in Washington when I played for him there. I especially wanted to hire Eddie Yost, their third base coach, and my old Dodger teammate, Rube Walker, their pitching coach. I called Yost and he was delighted to join me, but at the last minute, the Mets decided to keep Walker. So now I had everyone except a pitching coach. Later that winter, I happened to be over at the Mets' instructional league camp in St. Pete, not far from my house in Treasure Island. I was talking to Whitey Herzog, who was their farm director at the time, and he asked me if I had hired all my coaches.

"Everyone but a pitching coach," I said. "You know anyone?"

"Sure do," said Herzog, pointing up to a black fellow in the tower that overlooked all four practice fields. "Al Jackson. He's our minor league pitching coach and a good one, but if you're gonna give him a major league job, we'd give you permission to hire him."

That's how I hired Al Jackson, who proved Herzog right in his assessment of him. Unfortunately, I lost him a couple of years later when he got caught up in the front office turmoil between Sullivan and LeRoux.

At the December '76 winter meetings, Sullivan made his first trade and it stirred up a lot of controversy with the Boston media. He sent Cecil Cooper, a real promising young hitter, to the Milwaukee Brewers for another first baseman, George Scott, who had led the American League with 36 homers in 1975 but had slumped to just 18 in '76. Perhaps as a means of defusing a lot of criticism from the fans on the deal, Sullivan, at my urging, also got '75 World Series hero Bernie Carbo back from the Brewers. Carbo was a bit of a head case, but I liked his bat.

With Scott now added to a lineup that already included Lynn, Rice, Fisk, Evans, and Yastrzemski, I knew I wasn't going to lack for the longball in 1977. When I got to spring training, however, I realized I had yet another budding power hitter in Butch Hobson, the former Alabama quarterback under my old friend Bear Bryant who had showed promise in a half-season at third base in '76. The problem was the incumbent third baseman, Rico Petrocelli, was one of the most popular players ever to wear a Red Sox uniform.

It didn't matter that Petrocelli, at 33, was clearly at the end of the line, having hit just .212 in 85 games in '76. Red Sox fans don't like to let go of their heroes and I was suddenly in the position of having to make them. Probably the toughest thing I ever had to do as a manager was going to Sullivan before the start of the spring training games and saying: "I think it's best to play Hobson at third all spring because if Petrocelli is with us, they'll all be yelling for us to get him in there every time Hobson makes an error." Sullivan agreed to release Petrocelli, and I told him I'd handle the face-to-face dirty work. That's part of the manager's job.

I called Rico into my office and confessed to him: "I'm gonna do something that's killing me."

"Wait a minute, Zim," he said. "I'll make it easy for you. I know you want to play Hobson, and if I'm there, it's a problem. Don't you worry. I'd do the same thing if I were the manager."

I don't think I ever had more respect for any player than I did that day for Rico Petrocelli and the way he handled being released.

As soon as the news got out, I had my life threatened by people in Boston. I sent the death threat letters to the commissioner's office. One guy said I'd be shot getting off the plane at Logan Airport when we came home from spring training.

For the rest of that spring, I had a couple of plainclothes detectives following me around. When we got home to Logan, I said to Jim Rice as the plane landed, "You get off first."

"My ass!" Rice said. "You get off first. I'm not taking no bullet for you."

Fortunately, the death threats proved to be just that—threats—and nothing more ever came of them.

Once I realized no one was going to shoot me, the '77 season proved to be a truly fun year for me. The Boston media quickly began to call us the "Crunch Bunch" because of all our home run hitters. Rice hit 39, Scott bounced back from his off season in Milwaukee with 33, Hobson hit 30, Yaz 28, and Fisk 26. We led the majors with 213 homers—the sixth highest all-time total by a team. The fans loved it, too. We drew 2,074,549 to Fenway Park that season, a Red Sox record.

As late as August 18, after an 11-game winning streak, we were in first place by 3 ½ games, but in the end were done in by a lack of consistency, particularly from our pitching. We won 16 of 18 games in June, only to go on a nine-game losing streak late in the month into July, and another 11-game losing streak in late July–early August. Tiant was my biggest winner, and he won only 12 games. Wise, Lee, Jenkins, and Reggie Cleveland had respectable seasons record-wise, but if it wasn't for the contributions I got from three rookies—Mike Paxton, Don Aase, and Bob Stanley—I know we wouldn't have taken the Yankees right down to the end of the season. We wound up in a second-place tie with the Orioles, two games out.

My old Dodger roomie, Johnny Podres was our roving minor league pitching instructor, and he kept calling me with pitchers he insisted could help me. The first was Stanley, who won eight games filling in as a starter and reliever and went on to pitch 13 years in the big leagues. Next was Paxton, who wound up winning 10 games. The last one was Aase, who struck out 11 batters in his debut against the Brewers and went on to go 6–2. Because of the makeshift starting rotation I had all year, I had to rely heavily on my bullpen and there's no question that was the strength of the ballclub that year. Over the winter, we had signed Bill Campbell as a free agent from the Twins for $1 million, and he proved to be worth every penny of it, winning 13 games in relief and leading the league with 31 saves. Both Campbell and Tom Burgmeier, my lefthanded set-up man, were real professionals.

After the season, in which we won 97 games, I told the media: "We finished two games out with Bill Campbell. I don't know where we'd have finished without him." That was the truth.

I also got my full indoctrination to George "Boomer" Scott that 1977 season. I love Boomer to this day. He was a terrific fellow, but boy, could he drive a manager nuts. We were in Toronto for a big five-game series the first week of September, trailing the Yankees by one game. Boomer was in a terrible slump. I mean the man was hitting nothing. I had no choice. He had been hitting fourth and fifth in the lineup most of the time, but I felt I had to drop him down to sixth. He was lucky I was still writing his name in the lineup.

Nevertheless, after he batted sixth in the first game of a double-header against the Blue Jays, my third base coach, Eddie Yost, came into my office between games and said, "Your first baseman can't play the second game."

"What's wrong?" I asked.

"He says he's mentally unprepared," Yost replied.

Mentally unprepared? This was a new one on me. I'd never heard that term in baseball.

Now, after the second game Boomer pops off to Larry Whiteside, the *Boston Globe* beat man, saying he's no sixth-place hitter. His quotes were all over the Toronto newspapers the next day when I spotted him sitting in the lobby of our hotel.

I prepared myself for a confrontation and walked right up to him.

"What's your problem, Boomer?" I asked.

"Ah, Skips," he whined. "I'm an RBI man."

"No kidding?" I said. "Do you think I don't want to believe that? That I wouldn't want you in the No. 4 spot? Look at how you're going right now!"

"Aw, I know, Skip," he said, almost apologetically. "But I need to be able to drive in runs."

"Well," I said, "are you mentally prepared to play tonight?"

"Oh yeah," he said eagerly. "I'm okay now."

"Good," I said. "You're hitting eighth."

For all of his silly statements and nutty thinking, Boomer was okay to deal with, mainly because he was at heart a good person. I had different kinds of problems with my veteran pitchers, Bill Lee, Ferguson Jenkins, and Rick Wise, all of who were mean-spirited in their criticisms of the way I handled them. Lee was the ringleader, but the other two willingly joined in with him as clubhouse lawyers. In the case of all three, they were previously effective major league pitchers who were generally pitching lousy and blamed me for their inability to get hitters out anymore.

They called me names like "Gerbil"—that was Lee's favorite and he got a lot of mileage out of it—and "buffalo head" because, as Jenkins explained, "a buffalo is the dumbest animal on earth."

Jenkins took a lot of shots at me, which is okay. The man is in the Hall of Fame. I only wish he'd been a Hall of Fame pitcher for me. We were in Baltimore once during that 1977 season, and I had taken Jenkins out of the rotation and put him in the bullpen. I called down there one day and they told me they couldn't find him.

"What do you mean you can't find him?" I demanded. "Where the hell is he? Find him!"

They did. He was sleeping in one of the trucks parked behind the bullpen.

All I've ever heard about Jenkins is that he was a great player like Ernie Banks, and isn't it a shame neither of them ever got to play in a World Series. I can only say one thing about that. If Ferguson Jenkins had won just a couple of more games—in Boston in 1977 and in Texas when I managed him there in 1981—he might have gone to at least two World Series. I had to take him out of the rotation in 1977 because he couldn't win for us. In 1981 at Texas, we were 33–22 on June 11, a half-game behind Oakland in the AL West as the season-splitting strike was about to take place. We were playing the Brewers in Milwaukee and we staked Jenkins to a 3–1 lead into the sixth inning. He couldn't hold it and the Rangers lost the game. Had we won, we'd have moved ahead of Oakland by a percentage point as the strike took effect. That was the year they split the season in half and awarded playoff spots to the teams that were in first place after each half.

The fact is, Ferguson Jenkins was a great pitcher who pitched away. In Fenway Park especially, you have to pitch in. "If you don't pitch in here," I repeatedly told my pitchers, "you're gonna get your asses kicked because hitters are forever gonna be jumping at outside pitches, trying to hook them over the left field wall."

After we traded Jenkins to Texas for a non-prospect minor league pitcher in December 1977, he ripped me for sending him to the bullpen. He said, "I got shoved into the bullpen by a fat, ugly, bald man who doesn't know anything about pitching."

My response to that was: "He's right on three counts. I am fat, I am bald, and I'm ugly, and he may be right on the other count, too. But if he was left in the rotation, I would have been fired."

Jenkins' best pitch was a slider on the outside corner, and he simply couldn't adjust to pitching in Fenway Park. When we traded him to Texas after the '77 season, he won 18 again. But he couldn't win in Boston and he blamed me for his problems there. Ironically, years later, the winter after he got fired as Cubs pitching coach, I ran into him at a golf tournament and asked him what happened to cause him to lose his job with the team he was most associated with.

"The biggest problem I had," he said, "was that we had an entire starting rotation of righthanded pitchers and I just couldn't get them to pitch inside."

It was obvious after the 1977 season that the one thing the Red Sox needed to do to close the narrow gap with the Yankees was to upgrade our pitching. Tiant was finally starting to show his age. Lee just wasn't the same pitcher as before Nettles broke his shoulder, and Wise and Jenkins just couldn't win for us anymore. So in the off-season Sullivan made two significant moves to rectify the situation. He signed Mike Torrez (a 17-game winner with the Yankees and A's in '77) as a free agent, and in spring training executed a six-player deal with Cleveland that landed us the Indians' top starter, Dennis Eckersley. We sent Wise, Mike Paxton, catcher Bo Diaz, and a kid named Ted Cox over to the Indians for Eckersley and my old catcher with the Padres, Fred Kendall. At the time of the deal, we got criticized by the media for giving up Cox, a DH-outfielder type. Ted Williams had made a statement that Cox was one of the best hitting prospects he'd ever seen, and all of a sudden it was as if we had given away the next

Rogers Hornsby. It turned out Cox, who was 6-foot-4, 210 pounds, hit only ground balls between first and second. In barely five years in the majors, he hit .245, while Eckersley was my best pitcher in '78, winning 20 games. A few years later, Eckersley re-invented himself as a relief pitcher with the Oakland A's and became one of the greatest closers in baseball history. When Eckersley goes to the Hall of Fame, Ted Cox can at least tell his grandchildren he was once the indispensable player traded for him.

With Eckersley and Torrez bolstering the rotation, I felt very optimistic about the '78 season. On paper this was by far the best team I had ever managed. And combined with a rash of injuries suffered by the Yankees, we got off to a great start and were able to take command of the American League East race early. By July 8 we had a 10-game lead on second-place Milwaukee, and on July 18 we were ahead of the Yankees by 14 ½ games. Then all of a sudden we just stopped hitting.

Before we began to go into our slump, I had one of my last verbal run-ins with Bill Lee—over, of all people, Bernie Carbo.

As I said before, Carbo was a bit of a screwball, but he had tremendous power to leftfield and I liked him as an extra outfielder. I was the reason he was a Red Sox in the first place. I had managed him at Indianapolis when he was in the minors with the Reds. I recommended him to Darrell Johnson after I became a coach, and the Red Sox acquired him from the Cardinals prior to the 1974 season. After his homer in the sixth game of '75 World Series, Carbo became one of the most popular players in Boston.

But the following season, Carbo was repeatedly coming to the park late, and Darrell had his fill of him and traded him to Milwaukee. Alex Grammas, a longtime friend of mine, was the manager of the Brewers and he told me later Carbo wasn't there 10 days when he'd had his fill of him too. So after I took over from Darrell as Red Sox manager, I knew I could get Carbo back if I wanted to, and it was that winter I asked Sully to get him included in the Cooper-for-Scott deal.

In spring training of 1977, I called Carbo into my office and told him the way it was.

"You know why you're here, don't you?" I said.

"Yeah, Poppa," he said (he always called me "Poppa"), "cuz you got me here. I appreciate that."

"Good," I said. "Remember what you're saying now."

"Oh, I will," he said, patting me on the back. "I'll do anything you want."

"Remember that," I repeated, "because if you don't, I'll be the first guy to run your ass out of here again."

If Carbo was hitting, he was fine, but if he went into a slump and you didn't have him in the lineup, he would start to become a problem, showing up late for batting practice. That's what began to happen in June of '78, and again I had to call him aside and remind him of his promise to me. He straightened out for about four or five days and then he showed up late again. This time, I didn't say a word to him. Instead, I called upstairs to Haywood and told him to "get Carbo out of here."

Haywood wasted no time, selling Carbo to the Indians the next day.

Well, this set off Lee, who had adopted Carbo as one of his fellow free spirits on the team. As soon as the announcement was made that Carbo had been sold, Lee ripped the front office as "gutless" and announced he was staging a walkout in protest of the sale of his pal. At the time, Lee was already in the midst of a horrible streak of pitching in which, after a 7–1 start through May 26, he went 3–9 over his next 14 starts (including seven losses in a row).

After Lee's outburst, Haywood came to me and said, "Lee's quitting."

"Good," I said. "I hope he means it." That's what I thought of Bill Lee by this time.

To the surprise of no one, Lee came back to the team a day later and accepted a fine of a day's pay. But when I finally took him out of the rotation in Oakland, August 19, after his seventh straight loss, he started in again with all his verbal attacks on me.

Bill Lee was a good pitcher from 1973–75 when he won 17 games each year. Then he hurt his arm in that fight with the Yankees and he was no longer a good pitcher. He was also not a good person. He's the only man I've ever known in baseball who I wouldn't let in my house, and I don't care who knows it. There was nothing funny

WEDDING BELLS: If Soot wasn't sure what a baseball life was going to be, she sure found out on this day, August 16, 1951, when we were married at home plate in Elmira, New York. Our "honeymoon" was the ballgame right after the ceremony. I played. Soot watched.

BEGINNING OF A GREAT RIDE: I was some hot potato that day, in my white suit and tie with my new bride. Here we are being chauffeured off the field in a Cadillac convertible. I changed right into my uniform. A lot of people thought the ballclub gave us the Caddy as a wedding present. I only wish.

A FAMILY GROWS IN BROOKLYN: This picture of Soot and I, with Donna (age 18 months) on her lap and Tommy (age 3) on mine, was taken in 1955 at the house we lived in on Fort Hamilton Parkway in Brooklyn. This was my first full season with the Dodgers. NICK SORRENTINO (New York Daily News)

MEETING THE KING: One of the unexpected added "spoils" of winning the American Legion baseball tournament in Hollywood in 1947 was getting to meet Clark Gable. I've never been much of a movie buff, but I always admired Gable. That's my close friend Glenn Sample on Gable's left, and Jim Frey wearing the letter sweater. I'm peeking between them.

MAKE WAY FOR POPEYE: Here I am working out at Vero Beach in one of my first springs with the Dodgers. I look pretty good in my Dodger-blue duds, no? Do you think Pee Wee was worried? (Photofile)

BLIND MAN WALKING: Here I am being escorted out of Long Island Hospital by Soot (left) and a nurse, 10 days after my beaning by Hal Jeffcoat. My retina was nearly detached from the beaning, necessitating the use of these protective "pinhole" glasses. (AP Wirephoto)

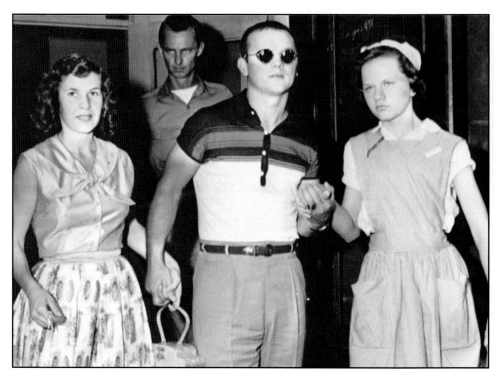

A WELCOME SIGHT: This was after my first beaning. I was in a coma for six days and nearly died. I was on the road to recovery here, about to finally be discharged from White Cross Hospital in Columbus. Soot, as always, was at my side. She had to teach me how to talk and walk again.

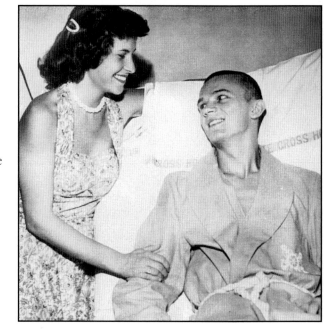

PICKING A WINNER: Herbie Scharfman, the longtime "in-house" Dodger photographer and dear pal to all of us, took this publicity shot of Pee Wee Reese, hoisted on my shoulders, picking a grapefruit at spring training in Vero Beach in 1955. It's an appropriate picture, I'd say, in that I was seemingly destined to be Pee Wee's caddie. HERB SCHARFMAN

WHAT DO I HAVE TO DO TO PLAY SHORTSTOP HERE? This picture was taken in just one of my springs in Vero Beach when I knew I had no chance of displacing Pee Wee Reese as Dodger shortstop. Choking him obviously wasn't enough. Pee Wee was indestructible.

CHAMPS AT LAST!: This was part of the celebration scene after the Dodgers finally beat the Yankees in the 1955 World Series. I'm not quite sure why Jackie Robinson and Roy Campanella are lifting me up there in triumph while fellow Hall of Famer Duke Snider looks on from behind. I've always said my biggest contribution to the '55 championship was being taken out of Game 7 so Sandy Amoros could go in and make the saving catch off Yogi Berra.

COMPARING ASH: Gil Hodges and I were having a laugh here talking about hitting. I know from the angle this picture was taken that my bat looks a lot bigger than Gil's. Believe me, it wasn't. (UPI Telephoto)

THE BROW HOLDS COURT: That's Charlie "The Brow" DiGiovanna, the Dodgers' longtime clubhouse chief, with the cigar and his feet up on the desk, presiding over a bull session in one of the Dodger Stadium offices. This was during our first season in Los Angeles. That's Sandy Koufax with his back to the camera. Carl Furillo and Don Drysdale are on the other side of the table, and that's me and Ed Roebuck on the right.

PRISONERS OF THE GAME: This was the recreation league prison softball team I played with during the winters of 1956 and '57. In case you can't tell, I'm the one wearing the Dodger cap. The SRD, I think, stood for "State Road Department." I was happy to play only road games with this team.

CUBAN DANDY: Here I am in January 1953 when I played winter ball in Cuba for the Marianao team. I got traded to Marianao from Cienfuegos late in the season. Back then I played baseball the year round. The pay was good, and in the winter, especially, it beat working for a living.

MR. MET: Because I lived nearby, the Mets asked me to come over to their spring training headquarters in St. Petersburg for the unveiling of their new uniforms in February 1962. I was the first to wear a Mets uniform. My son, Tommy, helped. (AP Wirephoto)

BROOKLYN REUNION: In forming the expansion Mets in 1962, the team execs went out of their way to bring in as many familiar faces as they could for the New York fans. Here's Casey Stengel addressing the ex-Dodger contingent: (Sitting left to right) Gil Hodges, Clem Labine, Cookie Lavagetto, Roger Craig. (Standing) Myself and Charlie Neal. JAMES D. McCARTHY

HOME AT LAST: After 11 years in the Dodger organization, two more with the Cubs, and a brief stay as an original Met, I finally got to play for my hometown team, the Cincinnati Reds. The uniform looked nice on me, but I only got to wear it for 63 games before they traded me back to the Dodgers. (Cincinnati Reds)

SENATOR ZIM: In 1963 I got my first taste of American League ball when I was traded to the Washington Senators. Here I am in my new Senators togs giving Tommy some batting tips. DON WINGFIELD

TOUGH COMPANY: I look like a pretty mean All Star here, don't I? As team captain of the Cubs, I got selected to the 1961 National League All-Star team along with my teammate George Altman (right). That's Mike McCormick (far left) and my buddy Don Drysdale on the other side of me.

RED SOX ROYALTY: You can't find much more select company than this. In my first year as manager of the Red Sox, I'm standing here at spring training in Winter Haven flanked by Hall of Famers Ted Williams and Joe Cronin.

CUB QUINELLA: Here's Jim Frey and me in front of the ivy-covered outfield wall at Wrigley Field when he was Cubs GM and I was his manager. Jimmy was not only a great boss, but also one of my dearest friends in life. I'd like to think we were a great team for the brief time we were given in Chicago. DON LANSU

THE THRILL OF VICTORY: This was the greatest moment of my baseball life—when my 1989 Cubs won the National League East title. Nobody gave us a chance, and I confess that after a 9–23 spring training, I didn't either. That '89 Cubs team—the "Boys of Zimmer" as they called them—was simply magical. Everything they did went right. What a season!

RUBBING SHOULDERS WITH THE CLIPPER: I got to know Joe DiMaggio through the years and spent a lot of time with him at the racetrack in San Francisco when I coached there in 1987. This was taken in 1986 at Old Timers Day at Yankee Stadium when I was a Yankee coach. JACK POKRESS

GIVING JETER LUCK: I don't know what Derek Jeter would do without me. He gets his kicks out of teasing me, and when he's not doing that he's rubbing my head or my stomach for luck before he goes up to hit. He thinks it works. I think he's a little wacky. MICHAEL ALBESE (NY Yankees)

FRIENDS IN HIGH PLACES: What's a .235 lifetime hitter doing shaking hands with the President of the United States? One of the benefits of winning a world championship was the Yankees' getting invited to the White House by President Clinton after we won the 1996 World Series. (Official White House Photo)

LATE NIGHT WITH ZIM: Since coming back to New York and sitting next to Joe Torre through all these world championships, I've gotten to know a lot of showbiz people. David Letterman's asked me to appear on his show a couple of times, and it's always fun being around him. (Time & Life)

TORREADORES:
I wouldn't want anyone to get the wrong idea here, but I love Joe Torre. Ever since I agreed to come back to the Yankees in 1996 as Joe's bench coach, we've had a very special bond. This is one of the great things about baseball. There's this common bond that makes people in it like brothers. As a player, for me it was Pee Wee. Now it's Joe.

FAMILY PORTRAIT: Here we are, on the dock at Treasure Island—the Zimmer family, my real support system, without whom I have nothing. That's Tommy and Soot to my right in the first row, and Donna to my left. The back row, left to right: Tommy's wife, Marian; their sons, Lane, Ron, and Beau; Donna's daughter, Whitney; and Donna's husband, David Mollica. (Maddock Photographers, St. Petersburg, Fla.)

about the things he said about people. They were hurtful and mean-spirited. I saw later that dumb remark he made in a magazine about putting marijuana on his pancakes. It was a typical remark from the jerk that he was.

It was after the All-Star break in '78 when we started to go into our slump. For one thing, we were banged up a little. Burleson was bothered by a bad ankle, Jerry Remy, our second baseman, had a cracked wrist, and Hobson had bone chips in his elbow which he had to continually rearrange between pitches. I got a lot of criticism for keeping Hobson in the lineup every day because he was committing a lot of throwing errors. But the man hit 17 homers and knocked in 80 runs. Who else was going to do that?

We lost 11 of 14 right after the All-Star break but were still seven games in front. At the same time, though, the Yankees were getting healthy again and starting to play like the defending champions they were. We managed to hold our own through late July and August, but then we lost 14 of 17 from August 30 through September 16. In the middle of that streak, we were playing a three-game series in Baltimore when my old boyhood pal, Jim Frey, who was coaching first base for the Orioles, casually asked George Scott what the hell was going on with us.

"Some of these guys are choking, man," said Scott.

Boomer. He was a beauty. If anything, he was going the worst of our hitters and it wasn't because of injuries. He was a good guy, very intelligent, and loved to play. Weight was his problem. He just couldn't control it. He'd come out early every day wearing a rubberized jacket and would run laps around the field and take water pills. But everything he'd sweat off wasn't real weight, and by 7 P.M. it was all back. In the meantime, all the running and sweating had made him weak and he could hardly swing the bat. He wound up hitting just .233 with 12 homers in '78, and in mid-season of '79 we traded him to Kansas City.

For whatever reason, all of our hitters went through bad stretches in '78. All of them, that is, except Jim Rice, who had one of the greatest seasons by any hitter in the history of baseball. Rice was voted Most Valuable Player that year in a landslide over Ron Guidry (who was 25–3 for the Yankees), and to be perfectly honest, it should have been a landslide. Taking nothing away from Guidry, who was a great pitcher for the Yankees every five days, Rice was a great player for the Red Sox every single day of 1978. He batted .315 and led the league in hits (213), triples (15), homers (46), RBIs (139), total bases (406) and slugging (.600). He remains today the only American League player since 1937 to amass more than 400 total bases in a season and is the only player in history to lead the league outright in homers, triples, and RBIs in the same season.

I'm not a big guy on stats and trivia, but when I'm asked about who should be in the Hall of Fame, I say unquestionably Jim Rice. And certainly not just for that 1978 season, either. For 12 years Jim Rice was one of the most dominant and feared hitters in baseball. And from 1977–79 he did something nobody in the history of baseball ever did—have three straight seasons of 35 or more homers and 200-plus hits. You can also add a .300 average and 100-plus runs in each of those years.

I remember a few years ago, when I was a coach with Colorado, I was having this discussion with Jerry Royster, another of our coaches. That was the year Dale Murphy was finishing up his career with the Rockies, hoping to get to 400 homers. It wasn't going to happen. He was through. But I asked Royster: "Dale Murphy? Hall of Famer?"

"Oh yeah," he said without any hesitation. "First time out of the box."

I thought a minute and then said: "Okay, how about Jim Rice?"

"No way," said Royster.

So we went into the manager Don Baylor's office and got out the encyclopedia and checked the records, Murphy against Rice. Royster was dumbfounded. It isn't even close. Rice hit over .300 seven times (to Murphy's twice), and had a .298 lifetime average to Murphy's .265. Rice had 1,451 RBIs to Murphy's 1,195, and 1,249 runs to Murphy's 1,197. The only category where Murphy beats Rice is in homers, and there by only 12 (398–386).

A couple of years later, I had the same conversation in Joe Torre's office at Yankee Stadium with Red Foley, the longtime official scorer in New York, and Leonard Koppett, the former *New York Times* baseball writer who's now a member of the Hall of Fame Veterans Committee. Again, I asked each of them if they thought Murphy should be in the Hall of Fame.

"Possibility," Koppett said.

"What about Jim Rice?" I asked.

"No way," Koppett said.

As soon as I heard that, I came to the conclusion that the Hall of Fame is nothing more than a popularity contest. I know why these people would immediately say yes to Murphy and no to Rice. Because Murphy was a terrific and obliging guy with the press, and Rice was not. Jimmy's problem with the press goes all the way back to his rookie season in 1975 when a couple of writers in Boston misquoted or twisted around something he said. After that, he just stopped talking to all the writers. When I became manager the following year I called him aside and said, "Jimmy, I understand how you feel about those guys who got what you said wrong. But you can't take it out on everyone in the media. At your age you're going to be around this game for a long time, and you're a big man on this team. You're only hurting yourself if you blow off the media. If you're upset by what a couple of guys wrote, blow them off, but don't take it out on everyone. The media can only help you."

I wish he had taken my advice, but I guess he felt he just couldn't. It's a shame, because I'm sure if Jim Rice had been as obliging to the media as Dale Murphy was, he'd be in the Hall of Fame by now. And he wasn't just a great hitter. He wore Johnny Pesky and me out hitting balls to him in left field at Fenway and also became an excellent outfielder. He really learned how to play that left field wall. In 1983, he had 21 assists, the only Red Sox outfielder since 1944 to have more than 20.

I confess I'm prejudiced when it comes to Jim Rice, and I make no apologies for that. In 1979 we suffered a tough 7–6 loss in Kansas City when the Royals' Willie Wilson hit a ball off Rice's glove in left in the 10th inning for what was ruled a three-base error, and Steve Braun followed with a game-winning homer off our reliever, Dick Drago. On the way up the runway to the clubhouse, I was walking a few steps behind Drago when I heard him mutter something like "What, are they allergic to fly balls out there?" Well, when we got into the clubhouse I lit into Drago (who, by the way, I really liked) in front of everyone. There was no question the ball should have been caught. Rice simply misjudged it. But I wasn't about to have one of my players criticize one of their teammates. I started in on Drago before the clubhouse attendant even had a chance to escort the writers back outside.

"I don't ever want to hear someone in here criticize another player," I screamed. "Nobody on this ballclub plays his ass off harder than Jim Rice!"

It was one of those unfortunate situations where a pitcher hangs a slider, it gets hammered and he's looking for someone else to blame for losing the game. I understood Drago's frustration, but he was wrong to blame Rice. The funny thing about Drago was that he was not a great pitcher in all the places he played, but for me he did a real good job, especially in 1978 and '79 when he won a combined 14 games and had a 3.03 ERA over those two seasons.

By September 7 of '78, our lead had been shaved to four games by the Yankees as they came into Boston for a four-game series. We were reeling, but I refused to lose faith in this team. The Yankees pounded us 15–3, 13–2, and 7–0 in the first three games, and for the fourth game I had Bobby Sprowl, a rookie who had pitched only one other game, as my starter. There was a hue and cry from Lee and his supporters for me to start him, and when Sprowl failed to get out of the first inning, I was blamed for letting personalities get in the way of winning. Believe me, my decision to start Sprowl had nothing to with personalities. I didn't throw him out there on a "hope". Podres had told me Sprowl had big league stuff, and I had confidence the kid could give us five or six innings. If I didn't, I'd have started a relief pitcher.

It turned out I was wrong, but there was no reason to think Lee would have done any better. In his last seven starts before I had to take him out of the rotation in mid-August, he gave up 54 hits, 16 walks, 27 earned runs and struck out only nine in 41 ⅔ innings. In other words, he couldn't get anybody out.

The writers called the Yankee sweep (which brought them into a first-place tie with us) the "Boston Massacre." I guess you could say it was, but the funny thing about it was the Yankees hit only two home runs in the four games. They pretty much singled us to death.

After that, we lost five of the next six games as the Yankees took over first place from us. Then, the strangest thing happened. We started winning again, beginning with salvaging the last of a three-game series in New York in which Eckersley won, 7–3. We lost the next game at Toronto, then ran the table by winning the last eight games of the season.

But as we were winning every day down the homestretch, so too were the Yankees, and on the final day of the season they still held a one-game lead on us. I had Tiant pitching for us in Boston against Toronto, and the Yankees had Catfish Hunter going for the clincher for them in New York against Cleveland. Needless to say, there was a lot of scoreboard-watching going on in both ballparks that Sunday afternoon. It turned out to be one of the most satisfying days I ever had in baseball. While Tiant was pitching a vintage 5–0 shutout, the Indians pounded Hunter, 9–2, behind an unsung lefthander named Rick Waits. As the day ended, a message flashed across the outfield scoreboard in Fenway Park: "Thank you, Rick Waits."

There would be a one-game playoff for the division title the next day, and how great was that going to be? I know there were an awful lot of people in Boston who never thought it would come to this after that Yankee sweep of us earlier in the month. People may not believe this, but through all the tough times we went through those last two months of '78, I never thought we were going to fold. I always believed we'd somehow right the ship, and we did.

Monday morning, October 2, I got out to Fenway Park early and immediately sought out Joe Mooney, our groundskeeper. Mooney is a crusty, hard-boiled guy on the outside who has been known to be particularly gruff with the media and opposing players. (In 1999 he kicked the Yankees off the field as they were celebrating beating the Red Sox in the ALCS!) To me, however, Mooney was one terrific person, one of my best friends in all of baseball. Even though it was a beautiful, 75-degree October day, I wanted to get his input because, as any American League umpire will tell you, there is no better weather forecaster anywhere in New England than Joe Mooney. Usually in October, it's chilly and the wind is blowing in. On this day it appeared to be blowing out a little, and while Mooney said that would probably remain the case all afternoon, I wasn't overly concerned.

The Yankees had a rested Guidry for their starter, and I countered with Mike Torrez, who was our second-highest winner behind Eckersley, with 16. We scored a run off Guidry in the second and another in the sixth, and Torrez was pitching a strong shutout into the seventh when he gave up one-out singles to Chris Chambliss and Roy White. That brought to the plate the No. 9 man in the order, Bucky Dent, the Yankees' shortstop who had batted just .243 with four homers in 123 games during the regular season.

After fouling the second pitch from Torrez off his foot, Dent went back to the bench to shake it off and took a new bat from the batboy. The whole delay lasted nearly four minutes. It was later revealed that Mickey Rivers had given him the bat because the one he had been using was a little chipped. During the long interruption, Torrez chose not to stay loose by throwing a few pitches—a decision he later admitted to regretting. I don't know if it would have made any difference. When Dent finally got back into the box, Torrez threw him an inside fastball that he golfed into the air to left.

My first reaction watching from the dugout was, *Good. That's an out.* Then I watched Yastrzemski start backing toward the wall, only to turn around. "Okay," I said to myself, "it's off the wall. No real harm done."

Finally Yaz started looking up, and as I remembered how the wind was blowing out, the next thing I knew the ball was in the screen above the left field wall and the Yankees were ahead 3–2. I know this will always go down in history as the Bucky Dent game, but what I'll always remember as the play that really decided the game was something nobody ever talks about.

In the sixth inning, we had runners at first and second with two out and Fred Lynn at the plate against Guidry. In Fenway Park the normal defensive strategy is to bunch your outfielders toward center in order to cut off the gaps, and when Lynn hit a drive toward the right field corner I said to myself: "That's extra bases and two more runs for us." I just hoped it didn't bounce into the stands for a ground rule double.

But as I leaped up and craned my neck out of the dugout I was dumbfounded to see Lou Piniella run over and catch the ball. I couldn't believe he was able to get to that ball. Instead of having two more runs in, a 4–0 lead and Lynn on second or third, the inning was over.

As it turned out, we got two more runs in the eighth to cut the Yankees' lead to 5–4 and we went down to the last out in the ninth with a legitimate chance to win the game. With one out in the ninth, Burleson drew a walk from Guidry's successor, Goose Gossage, and Remy hit a liner to right that Piniella lost in the sun. Somehow, though, Piniella was able to keep the ball in front of him and he was able to recover it on the bounce, preventing what might have been a bases-clearing double or triple. That left us with Rice and Yaz to drive in the tying run, and I'd have taken that situation anytime. When Rice flied out, Burleson was able to make it over to third, 90 feet from tying it up on even a passed ball or wild pitch. As Mr. Yawkey would have said, however, it just wasn't meant to be, and Yaz popped out to Nettles at third to end the game and our season at 99 wins.

I've never really discussed it with Yaz, but I have to believe that was probably the most disappointing at bat of his Hall of Fame career. Before I got to Boston, he had the reputation of being a pampered player, who if a manager fined him, would merely have it paid by Mr. Yawkey. That may be true, but Yaz was a matured player when I had him—a very, very tough player.

There would be times when I'd go to him and ask him if he wanted to DH instead of play left field and he'd say: "Whatever you want. It doesn't matter. I've got all winter to rest." We had a great relationship and it was a privilege to manage him.

I was really kind of numb after his final out. It was hard to believe our season was really over. When I got back upstairs into the clubhouse, I closed the door to the media and gathered the team in the middle of the room.

They were crying, and for the first time in my baseball life, I was crying right along with them. Then I gained my composure and let them know what I'd been thinking and feeling all through that eight-game winning streak at the end of the season.

"There is not one man in this clubhouse who should even think about dropping his head," I said. "I couldn't be more proud of this ballclub and the way you guys played those last 20 games of the season. Everyone in this town gave up on you but yourselves and me and I just want you to know it. This is something we just have to live with. It's baseball."

When I went into my office and the media all came in, nobody said a word. I guess they didn't know what to ask me or how I felt so I told them myself.

"Frankly," I said, "everybody knows I love the horses and betting them. I've been in many photo finishes, but this is the toughest one ever."

Later, after everyone started clearing out of the clubhouse, some of the Yankees came over to offer their congratulations on what really had been a great season. As I looked out of my office, I spotted Piniella and I called him in.

"I've just got to ask you this," I said. "Why in the hell were you playing so close to the line in the sixth inning to make that catch off Lynn?"

He said, "I thought 'Gator' had lost some of his good stuff, so I shaded Lynn three or four steps closer to the line."

To me, that's why Piniella is managing today and is one of the better managers in the game. Ordinarily with a hard thrower like Guidry, you don't ever figure anyone is going to pull the ball off him. But Piniella was smart enough to sense Guidry had gotten tired. He didn't need the manager or an outfield coach to position him. He used his own ingenuity, and in my opinion that, as much as Bucky Dent's home run, is what won that playoff game for the Yankees.

Driving home to Florida the next day, the game is spinning around in my mind and all I can think is *Bucky Dent, my ass*. It was my same sentiments as after that first game, the 11–0 loss to the White Sox in the '59 World Series, only this time there were no more games left to rally and win. But if it broke my heart, I wouldn't be here. Like I said to my players, it was something that just happened. You go on. Ralph Branca plays golf at Westchester every day and has lived a fulfilled life for 50 years after giving up Bobby Thomson's home run. It's baseball.

Just the same, five years later when I became a coach with the Yankees, they traded Bucky Dent to Texas and I wound up renting his house in New Jersey. Just what I needed. Everywhere in the place, on every wall, was all this memorabilia, all of it different pictures of that damn home run. I turned every one of 'em around and left 'em that way for the rest of my stay there.

On Opening Day 1979, we were playing the Cleveland Indians. I'll never forget the look on the face of Indians manager Jeff Torborg when I came out to home plate to exchange lineup cards. The boos from the Fenway Park crowd were so loud I'm sure you could hear them all the way to Cape Cod.

"Wow!" Torborg exclaimed. "This is one tough audience. You win 99 games and go to a playoff and they boo you like that? I'd hate to ever work in this town!"

I wish we could have picked up in 1979 where we left off in '78 with a resolve to get that one more win to put us in another World Series. Instead, after a real good start in which we went 20–8 in June and were 56–32 at the All-Star break, two games behind the first-place Orioles, injuries and the collapse of our pitching did us in.

Over the winter, we signed free-agent righthander Steve Renko, who had been 6–12 with the A's in '78, as a fifth starter. He essentially replaced Bill Lee, who we traded to the Expos for a utility infielder named Stan Papi. I'd have taken a utility garden hose for Lee, but I was glad to get a useful player. We also picked up Bob Watson from Houston to replace Boomer Scott at first base, and Watson had a helluva year, hitting .337 with 13 homers and 53 RBIs after joining us June 13.

As it turned out, I never really had five dependable starters and Renko, who was 8–3 at the All-Star break, was really my No. 4. In the second half of the season, I decided to go with a four-man rotation of Eckersley, Torrez, Bob Stanley, and Renko, but it didn't work out. Renko stopped winning. Eckersley, after winning eight in a row, developed a sore arm and won only one game after August 14. Torrez won only three games after August 3, and the various kids we brought up from Pawtucket—John Tudor, Win Remmerswaal, Joel Finch, and Allen Ripley—simply weren't ready.

The injuries began taking their toll when Remy, my only speed guy, tore up his left knee sliding into home against the Yankees, July 1. Fisk was already on the shelf with a sore elbow that limited him to 35 games behind the plate all season. (It's perhaps a measure of how important he was to the Red Sox that we won 25 of those games.)

Yaz was plagued by Achilles tendon problems the whole second half and hit just .233 with five homers after June. He did provide me with yet another baseball thrill on September 12 against the Yankees when he became the 15th player in history to achieve 3,000 hits.

Lynn, at least, had a season almost equal to his '75 debut. He hit .333 to win the batting title and tied Rice for the club lead in homers with 39. He also knocked in 122 runs and won his third Gold Glove, but it just wasn't enough. We simply didn't have the pitching or enough able bodies to keep pace with the Orioles who won 102 games to take the division title going away. Our under-.500 performance the second half and subsequent third-place finish, 11½ games back at 91–69, predictably had a lot of people calling for my head. By now I was pretty used to this. I felt, to win 91 games we did as good as we could under the circumstances, and I know I did as good as I could.

At the end of the season, Buddy LeRoux, who seemed to be sharing the duties of running the club with Sully, came down to my office and informed me they were going to make a change.

"What's that?" I said, thinking he meant me.

"We're going to fire Al Jackson."

"I don't think that's fair," I said. "Al Jackson's a good man. He's done a good job as my pitching coach. The injuries and the problems our pitchers had this year weren't his fault."

"Maybe not," LeRoux said, "but we're firing him anyway."

"You're putting all the blame on one man," I persisted. "It's not fair."

"Well, that's the way it is," LeRoux countered. "You can find a new pitching coach in the organization."

In that respect, I was fortunate that Podres was there, working as the roving minor league instructor. But it was never my intention to replace Jackson with him, even though that's the way it got reported in a lot of the newspapers. I didn't want to lose Al Jackson, but as it turned out, he was a victim of front office politics.

I was aware that Tommy Harper, who had played 15 years in the big leagues, including 1972–74 with the Red Sox, was working in the front office and was tight with Buddy. As soon as I named Podres my pitching coach, LeRoux informed me he was naming Harper to my staff as well. I didn't mind. If that's what they wanted to do, I had no problem with taking Harper. But as the 1980 season went on, Harper always had something else to do when I'd invite him out with the other coaches on the road. I don't know what was on his mind, but he kept aloof. He would never throw batting practice, and he'd always be down in the right field corner before games leaning on a fungo bat.

Harper, who is black, later sued the Red Sox for racial discrimination after he got fired. A few years later, he was working for the Expos when I was with the Cubs and he came over to me one day and said: "I want to apologize to you. I wasn't a very good coach for you and I'm sorry about that."

Maybe it was my fault too. I didn't hire him. Buddy LeRoux did, and I didn't know what to do with him so I left him alone. He was a class act and, I guess, as much a victim of circumstances as Jackson.

Opening Day 1980 proved to be an omen for the entire season when I got thrown out of the game by home plate umpire Marty Springstead. Eckersley was pitching for us, and the first three pitches he threw—all of which appeared to be in the strike zone—were called balls. On ball three, Eckersley starts off the mound and Springstead hollers at him: "Get your ass back on the mound and throw strikes!"

I ran out of the dugout and got in Springstead's face. "What's going on here?" I asked. "This man never complains about pitch-calling!"

To that, Springstead waved his pinky and shouted, "You're outta here!"

I'd been thrown out of more than a hundred ballgames in my career, but never before on Opening Day.

As I said, that was pretty much a harbinger of the tough times to come for me that 1980 season. In June we were in Anaheim, and I went to the ballpark early as usual and was sitting in the dugout all by myself when Jack Rogers came up to me.

"I've got some bad news, Skip," he said. "Your dad died."

My dad, Harold, had been in bad shape for quite awhile and every time I got a phone call from home, that was always the first thing I thought had happened. Rogers asked me if I wanted him to get me on the first plane out of Anaheim.

"No, Jack," I said. "My dad wouldn't want me to leave without managing the game."

I left the next morning, and all the way home I thought of how much of my baseball career I owed to my dad. He had taught me how to play the game, and bought me my first glove when I was eight years old. He encouraged me to follow my dream and turn pro instead of going to college, and made all those trips to be with me in the hospital in Columbus after the Jim Kirk beaning. It was going to be a terrible void in my life not to be able to call him and share my experiences with him. I'm grateful for all the ones I could share with him, and I'd like to think I made him proud.

Meanwhile, LeRoux's decision to blame Jackson for the team's inability to challenge for the division title in '79 was proven to be baseless when, in 1980, we had more of the same pitching problems. Sully gambled that Eckersley, Torrez, Stanley, Renko, and Campbell could anchor our staff in 1980, and as a result, he made few changes over the winter. His one primary pitching acquisition was Skip Lockwood, a free-agent righthanded reliever who had been the Mets' principal closer in '76, '77, and '78. We gave Lockwood a two-year contract worth nearly $1 million. I was told he was a very useful, workhorse reliever, but to be honest, I never got to find out because I could never seem to get him into a game. All through spring training, he had some sort of injury or ailment, and that continued into the regular season. Finally, after one of his long layoffs, Lockwood told me he was ready to pitch.

"Good," I said. "We'll activate you and I'll probably get you into a game tomorrow."

The next day, he came into my office and said he couldn't pitch because he'd hurt himself stepping on a rake. I'll say this: Fifty-two years in baseball I never heard of a player, before or after, going on the disabled list for stepping on a rake.

Among our starters in 1980, only Eckersley won in double figures, and he was only 12–14 and missed over a month with a sore arm and sore back. Aside from a hot streak we had in August in which we won 21 of 28 to get back into contention, it was an overall disappointing season.

I remember after one particularly bad loss in which our pitchers had walked a bunch of people and we just played lousy, I was about as exasperated as I've ever been as we boarded a commercial plane for a short flight to Cleveland. I'm not much of a drinker, but as soon as I got into my seat, I turned to Joe Giuliotti, the *Boston Herald* beat man, who happened to be sitting next to me.

"What's a good drink?" I barked at him.

"I don't know," he said. "I like vodka."

"Good," I said, hailing the flight attendant. "Let me have three vodkas!"

I proceeded to throw down the vodkas, one by one, while our meal arrived. Halfway through the meal, I decided to have some coffee. I like cream in my coffee, and I grabbed the little white plastic container and poured it into my cup. But as I started to drink it, Giuliotti tapped me on the shoulder.

"If I were you, Zim," he said, "I wouldn't drink that."

"Why?" I said, defiantly.

"Because that was salad dressing you just poured into your coffee."

That was the last time I ever tried to drink away a bad loss.

In late August Yaz suffered a broken rib running into the left field wall at Fenway, and Lynn broke his foot fouling a ball off it. Both were lost for the season. In addition, Hobson's shoulder problems worsened and I finally had to replace him at third base with rookie Glenn Hoffman, who hit .285. Also, Remy blew his knee out at the All-Star break, and we brought up Dave Stapleton, who did a good job, hitting .321 at second base.

Another bright spot in an otherwise disappointing year was veteran Tony Perez, my old '75 World Series nemesis. He signed with us as a free agent over the winter, and proved he still had thunder left in his bat by hitting 25 homers with 105 RBIs in 151 games at first base. Looking back, I was really lucky in Boston to have managed three first basemen like Boomer Scott, Bob Watson, and Perez, and I was especially proud of Perez getting elected to the Hall of Fame in 2000.

Overall though, the injuries (especially the ones to Yaz and Lynn) and the pitching did us in, and we wound up 83–77, in fourth place, 19 games behind the Yankees. We also had a losing record at Fenway Park for the first time in 14 years, and by late September the writers were really getting on Sullivan and LeRoux. Whenever I'd see them I'd kid them about stealing all of my heat, but I knew it was only a matter of time before that heat was going to be deflected to me. Even though I had never been fired before in my life, I knew that's what managers were hired for.

We began our last homestand of the season losing three straight to the Orioles, and as I was sitting in my office early the next afternoon, the phone rang on my desk. It was Sully.

"What are you doing?" he asked.

"Nothing," I said. "Just sitting here."

"I'll be right down," he said.

A few minutes later, he comes into my office, shuts the door, and starts pacing back and forth in front of my desk. I looked up and there was this sheepish look on his face like on one of our kids when they've done something wrong.

I said, "Sully, what's wrong? We're both baseball men. I know what you're here for."

He said, "Aren't you and Soot tired of all the heat you're getting here?"

I said, "The heat's off me. It's all on you and Buddy. They're not even on me now."

He kept pacing. Finally I said, "Sully, this isn't so tough."

He looked at me sadly and shrugged. Then he turned and walked out the door, saying nothing.

He just couldn't do it. I told Soot that night, "The man came into my office to fire me and just couldn't bring himself to do it."

The next day, Sully called me at home and asked me if I could come down to the ballpark.

I told him I would, but there were some things he needed to do first. I said: "Get the publicity director, Bill Crowley, to call a press conference in the morning in the press room and get it out of the way. I don't want to be there when the players get to the park. We'll get it done and over with in twenty minutes."

This was Sully's first firing, and here I was instructing him how to do it.

We held the press conference in the pressroom that morning, as I had asked. Sully started off by saying how he'd never fired anyone before and that I was his friend. Then he turned it over to me and I took some questions and went home. I later found out what had happened behind the scenes to make Sully so upset and guilt-ridden.

Haywood Sullivan was like a son to Mrs. Yawkey, and under the new management arrangement, they had always voted together against LeRoux on all club matters. But after my firing, Sully and Mrs. Yawkey had a falling out, and I was told it was because Sully had voted with LeRoux—and against Mrs. Yawkey—to fire me.

Nobody ever wants to be fired, but at least mine had its benefits. Remember, I had gotten Sully to agree to that rollover contract, and the Red Sox were therefore obligated to pay me for the next season. Even though I got myself another job, they paid me in full. I guess that was a leftover sentiment from Mr. Yawkey.

People don't believe me because of all the criticism I took, but those seven seasons I spent in Boston were the most enjoyable of my life. The reason I say this is because the most important thing in baseball is to have something to play for in September, and we did in five of those seven years. I loved the town of Boston, and Sully and Dick O'Connell were two of the best people I ever worked for. The Yawkeys were as good to me as it gets. Plus there were all those great players I had—Rice, Yaz, Fisk, Lynn, Burleson, Tiant, Eckersley—and, of course, Fenway Park.

My one regret is that we didn't win a championship in Boston, especially for Mr. Yawkey. I still get a rush every time I go up the tunnel in that old ballpark and look out at the Green Monster and the red seat in right field where Ted Williams hit the longest home run.

If Bucky Dent doesn't hit his homer I might still be there.

8

A Real
Texas Gusher

I had been home in Treasure Island a couple of weeks, wondering where or if I would have a job for 1981, when the phone finally rang. It was, of all people, George Steinbrenner, who I had gotten to know through the years. George lived in Tampa and would frequently show up at Derby Lane, the dog track in St. Pete, or Tampa Bay Downs. We'd compare horses or dogs together, and I really got to like him. The one thing about George is, for all his money, he's just as comfortable around the common folks as he is with his billionaire friends. Anyway, it seemed George was upset over the Yankees losing the AL playoffs in three games to the Royals in 1980, and he wanted to replace Mike Ferraro, the third base coach for his manager, Dick Howser. Apparently George had already leaked word of this out, and when Howser read it, he made some remarks about how he would have liked to have been consulted before having a new third base coach hired on him. As far as I was concerned that settled it for me. As much as I liked George, I couldn't go to work for him unless his manager really wanted me.

Then, a few days later, I got a call from Eddie Robinson, the general manager of the Texas Rangers. I had read the Rangers had been interviewing a bunch of guys for their managerial vacancy, which was created when they fired Pat Corrales after a 76–85, fourth-place season in '80. Eddie was a longtime baseball man, a strapping 6-foot-2 Texan, who had had a real fine playing career as a first baseman with the Indians, White Sox, Athletics, Orioles, and Yankees in the '40s and

143

'50s. I suspect being general manager of the Texas Rangers was a dream job for him in that it was his home. I would soon find out, however, that dream could become a nightmare.

"We have a manager vacancy here," Robinson said over the phone. "Would you be interested?"

"Sure," I said. "Would you like me to come to Texas to talk about it?"

"Let's do it this way," Robinson said. "I don't want a lot of publicity around who I'm interviewing for this job anymore. You fly into Dallas and I'll meet you at the airport. We'll go to my house, talk, have dinner, and then I'll put you back on a plane the next morning."

Robinson had a beautiful home on a golf course in Fort Worth, and I immediately could see why he loved it so much there. Naturally, during the course of our conversation Robinson discussed the team owner, an 70-year-old billionaire oilman named Eddie Chiles. I knew nothing about Chiles except stories I heard that he had license plates on his car that said "I'm Mad." That was supposedly his motto.

As we continued to talk through the afternoon, I could see Robinson felt comfortable with me and was ready to offer me the job. At one point he said, "No matter who I hire here, I can't offer more than a one-year contract."

"Well," I interjected, "I guess there's no point in talking anymore. I'm not interested if that's the case."

I thought about it later that afternoon, however, and said to myself, "What difference does it make? If you don't do well, you're gonna get fired anyway."

Once we seemed to get past that hurdle, Robinson all of a sudden pulled out a sheet of paper from his briefcase with a bunch of questions on it for me. At first they were pretty routine, questions like "Why do I want this job?" and "What's my style of managing?" But then he starts asking me all these questions about in-game strategy, and I started to laugh.

"Eddie," I said, "I don't even know who we're playing here! How can I answer these questions? Who's pitching? Who's hitting? You know there are all different circumstances when it comes to strategy!"

"I understand," he said, almost sheepishly.

But that wasn't the end of the quizzing I got. I have to say, to become manager of the Texas Rangers I had to answer some of the strangest questions I could ever imagine being asked.

"I understand you gamble," Robinson said.

"Excuse me?" I said.

"I understand you gamble," he repeated.

"I'm not sure what you're talking about, Eddie," I said, "but if you're talking about betting on horses and dogs, I suppose I do gamble. But I don't know what that's got to do with managing a baseball team."

"Well," he said, "I'm not sure if that's a good thing for a manager to be doing, hanging out at the racetrack all the time."

"Let me ask you something, Eddie," I said. "Have you ever made a bet on the Dallas Cowboys or the Cotton Bowl or the Super Bowl?"

He hesitated a moment and his face began to redden a little.

"If you did," I continued, "I wonder if you know that's illegal. Betting football games is illegal. Betting horses and dogs at the track is legal. I'm not gonna lie to get this job. That's how I live my life, and I think you should know that as soon as I fly back to Tampa, I'm going to Derby Lane in St. Pete and bet all 13 races. If that has anything to do with my ability to manage a baseball team then I'm probably not the right guy for you."

I knew where Robinson was coming from, why he felt he had to ask me all these questions that had nothing to do with managing the Texas Rangers. He did too. He was only covering himself with an owner who was on his case about everything, and he couldn't afford to hire the wrong guy (in the owner's mind) as manager.

As the day went on, I could feel Robinson was comfortable with me and we eventually got around to contract terms. He threw a figure—$100,000—at me. I said that was okay, but I wanted a Texas credit card and an expense account to take my coaches out to dinner.

"I can't do that," Robinson said.

"Okay," I sighed, "If that's going to be a problem, then make my salary $95,000 and give me a $5,000 expense account."

This was a few days before the annual winter baseball meetings, which were to be held that year at the Anatole Hotel in Dallas. Once we agreed on the contract terms, Robinson suggested I take a room at the Anatole and stay over through the meetings. It turned out Corrales was still on the Rangers' payroll as a scout, and they had him staying at the Anatole as well.

On the day before the meetings were supposed to begin, Corrales and I were sitting in the hotel lobby when I was paged to the phone. It was Robinson.

"C'mon upstairs to our suite," he said. "Mr. Chiles is coming in and he wants to meet you."

I got up there to this suite where there was this big round table in the middle of it. Eddie was smoking a cigar and he offered me one. We were sitting there at the big table, smoking cigars, when there was a knock at the door. Eddie damn near broke his leg, knocking into a chair as he rushed to open the door.

In comes this little white-haired man, about 5-foot-6, with a briefcase and a frown on his face. He brushes right past me and throws his briefcase down on the table. Then he turns around and sticks out his hand.

"Mr. Manager," he says, "nice to have you around." Next, he pulls out this stack of papers and casts his eyes on Robinson.

"Eddie," he says, "this is directed at you." For the next 10 minutes he proceeded to bury Robinson with criticism and abuse, and all the while he was talking, poor Eddie sunk deeper and deeper into his chair until he looked almost as small as Chiles. He didn't want to lose this job because it was home, and so he just took it. I figured this wasn't the first time he'd been berated by Eddie Chiles.

Finally, when Chiles got through dressing down Robinson, he turned to me.

"Mr. Manager," he said in the same commanding manner, "this is directed to you."

I said to myself: "This ought to be good. What's he gonna scream at me about? I haven't even done anything for him yet."

After taking another stack of papers out of his briefcase, Chiles began.

"I'm a very successful oilman," he said. "I started out from scratch, with nothing, and founded the Western Oil Company of North America in 1939. I started out with three employees, two trucks and $10,000 in debt, and built it into a $500 million corporation with 5,000 employees. I did it despite the government continually trying to interfere in my business. I don't really like baseball the way it is now. I think it needs a lot of improvements, but I'm gonna run my baseball team the way I run my oil company.

"Now, you're getting top dollar to be my manager, and as such, you will live in the metroplex area like all of my other employees."

"What's that?" I said.

"You will live here in the metroplex area full time," he repeated.

At that point, I got up from my chair, snuffed out my cigar and said to him: "Mr. Chiles, I respect everything you've done. You're a very successful man, and I'm sure you're successful because you've done things your way. I'm also sure you probably have some good ideas on how to improve baseball, but as of right now, the one thing you don't have is a manager."

With that, I started walking out the door. The two of them, Chiles and Robinson, came running after me, shouting, "Wait, Don! Wait! Come back to the table."

"There's nothing more for us to talk about," I said. "I'm not moving to the metroplex. I live in Treasure Island. That's my home and that's where I go every year as soon as the baseball season is over."

Finally, Chiles kind of shrugged and said: "You know, Mr. Manager, I'm a man of my word. If this is the way it is, we'll try it."

"Mr. Chiles," I replied, "as long as I manage Texas that's the way it will be."

Later, as I thought about this whole conversation, I realized I was gone before I even started this job. I also realized this was going to be anything but a smooth sailing job. Mr. Eddie Chiles was unlike any owner I had ever worked for. He was sure no Walter O'Malley or Tom Yawkey.

Meanwhile, I felt embarrassed for Eddie Robinson. He'd done just about everything in baseball before he came to work as GM of the Rangers for Chiles. It seemed everywhere around the club offices there were these charts and reports, because as the party line went, "That's the way we do it at Western Oil." Robinson, I could tell, was uncomfortable dealing with all of this, but he obliged the old man because he had to.

One day, Robinson came down to my office in the clubhouse and had with him a stack of these index cards.

"This is what Eddie wants done," he began, plopping the cards on my desk. "He calls this 'formalized goal-setting.' What he wants is for you to meet with your coaches and evaluate every player on the team. After you get done evaluating each player, he wants you to write on these cards what you all feel that particular player will do over the next three weeks. You know, how many hits, how many homers, how many wins, hits, runs, and homers allowed for the pitchers . . . all of that."

I looked at him in astonishment.

"What is this, Eddie?" I asked. "I mean, is this some sort of joke? You can't be serious. This is nuts!"

"This is what he wants," Robinson said, looking down. "And then, when you've made your evaluations on the cards, you're to call the players in one by one and have them do the same thing, evaluating themselves."

This whole thing was so goofy I didn't know what to say. After he left, I just started laughing. "How could a baseball man like Eddie Robinson bring something like this to me?" I said to myself.

Nevertheless, we did our best to accommodate Mr. Chiles and his formalized goal-setting. My coaches and I started calling the players in, with predictable reactions from them. Buddy Bell was the first one.

"You want me to tell you how many homers I'm going to hit in the next three weeks?" he asked.

"Uh, huh," I said, trying to keep a straight face.

"And how many hits? And runs scored?"

"Uh, huh."

After a few moments of looking at the cards, he burst out laughing.

"You've gotta be kidding," he said, prompting me to start laughing along with him. Billy Sample later told me that he wanted to revise his numbers downward after looking ahead at the schedule, and figuring out Dave Stieb and Jack Morris would be facing us.

This went on for a couple of days until I had finally had enough of all the nonsense. I called Eddie Robinson and told him the joke was over. "We're supposed to be telling the player what we think he's going to do," I said. "How can we do that? What if we put on the card we think he's gonna hit .199? The player sees that and says: 'Is that all you think of me?' I fail to see how any of this can motivate a player."

When I got done venting on Robinson I called all my players together in the clubhouse.

"Fellas," I said, "you've all had your chuckle, but now we're getting back to baseball."

With that I threw all the cards in the garbage pail. I don't know if Eddie Chiles ever asked to see the cards. I didn't care. I only wish that had been the end of his running of his baseball team like he ran his oil company. A couple of weeks later, I came into the clubhouse and saw all these nutrition charts on the wall, detailing what to drink and eat to combat the summer heat in Texas.

The 1981 season was the year in which the players' strike cut the season in half. You might say the Texas Rangers had two distinctly different halves as well. I thought the day the strike hit we were the best team in baseball. We were 33–22, and would have been in first place in the American League West had Ferguson Jenkins been able to hold a 3–1 lead against the Brewers in the sixth inning of the final game before the strike.

We wound up losing that game and finishing a half-game behind Oakland in the first half. If we had won that game, and subsequently the first half, we'd have gone to the playoffs—although I don't know how we would have done, because we were not nearly as a good a team the second half, especially our hitters. At the top of the order, Mickey Rivers and Bump Wills were hurt a lot and just not getting on base enough, and because of that, the RBI production from Al Oliver and Buddy Bell fell off.

In the first half of '81, we had led the majors in team batting average and runs scored, despite not being a real power club. We dropped to sixth in the league in runs by the end of the season, while Bell limped through the last five weeks with a back injury and a pulled groin muscle. The second-half slump left us at 57–48, in second place, five games behind Oakland, which won both halves.

As I said, we were not a power club—we hit only 49 homers that year. And over the previous winter we had made a big trade with Seattle in which we sent our No. 1 power hitter, Richie Zisk, to the Mariners in exchange for pitcher Rick Honeycutt and a shortstop named Mario Mendoza. Mendoza, who couldn't hit a lick, batted .229 as my regular shortstop in '81, which was actually 10 points higher than his eventual lifetime average. He was a stylist, who for the first month of the season looked like the second coming of Luis Aparicio. Then he started missing the easy plays, and I found out I had a flashy-fielding shortstop who couldn't hit or be relied upon to make the routine plays. Today, at least, Mendoza holds a special place in baseball infamy in that whenever a player is hitting less than .200, it's said he dropped below the "Mendoza Line." I seem to recall I was there a few times myself.

In September I moved Jenkins out of the rotation and replaced him with knuckleballer Charlie Hough, who had been mostly a relief pitcher the previous 11 seasons with the Dodgers. In five starts for me at the end of that season Hough was 4–1 with 37 strikeouts in 39 innings, and went on to pitch 25 years in the big leagues, winning 216 games. One reason for Hough's success was that he was able to hold runners on. Usually you can run wild on knuckleballers because of how slow their pitches take getting to the plate. But he had a knack of stepping off the rubber and then quick-pitching to keep the runners honest. I've always felt very good about making Hough a starter. He was a terrific guy to have on your ballclub, and he made me look real smart.

Another guy who made me look smart in 1981 was Steve Comer, a righthanded relief pitcher who had been a pretty good starter for the Rangers a few years earlier before hurting his arm. Comer, as the saying goes, couldn't break a pane of glass with his fastball, but he knew how to pitch: He threw strikes and had a great changeup. The closer I inherited was Jim Kern, but for some reason he just couldn't get the job done.

It was sometime around the middle of the season I had brought Kern into a tight game and he couldn't get the ball over the plate, walking the bases loaded. I had Comer in the bullpen, and when Kern went 2–0 on the next hitter, I brought him in.

"Boss," I said to Comer, "just try to throw four balls down the middle."

On the next pitch, Comer got the batter to hit a grounder to first that should have been the inning-ending out, except our first baseman booted it and we lost the game. Still, Comer showed me something, doing the job he did in that situation where there was no margin for error, and I began using him as my closer from that day on.

Comer was a little crazy, too, which doesn't necessarily hurt in baseball, especially if you're a closer. One time, in what was probably one of the worst days of his life, he was standing behind the batting cage when a ball hit by the Twins' Tony Oliva ricocheted off the cage and caught him in the mouth, cracking a couple of teeth. That night, we were in the airport waiting to fly out for the start of a roadtrip. I'm glad I didn't see this, but later some of the players told me Comer was at the bar and ordered one of those screwball flaming drinks. When he went to drink it, he spilled it on his face and set his beard on fire!

All I know is, Comer did a helluva job for me that year. He got into 36 games, was 8–2 and had six saves. He may not have been your prototypical closer, but he was good enough for me.

After the second-half disappointment in '81, Chiles told his front office people he wanted changes made, and Robinson and his chief assistant, Paul Richards, set out to overhaul our lineup in an effort to get more punch into it. One position where they felt we could upgrade our offense was first base where Pat Putnam, the regular there since 1979, hit .268 with only eight homers in '81. In mid-January we signed Lamar Johnson, who had been a pretty good-hitting first baseman for the White Sox from 1977–80 before getting hurt in 1981. Even though he'd reportedly had some problems with White Sox manager Tony LaRussa, I found him to be a delight. Then, when we got to spring training in Pompano Beach, Robinson and Richards really swung into action.

On March 26 they sent Bump Wills to the Cubs for lefty reliever Paul Mirabella, who I wound up getting into 40 games in '82. Wills was a real enigma. It was his father, Maury, who ultimately got me traded away from the Dodgers by taking command of the job as Pee Wee Reese's official shortstop successor in 1959. When Bump first came up, a lot of people thought he'd be as good a player as his dad. In his first four seasons in the big leagues, he was one of the better offensive second basemen in baseball, hitting .270 with about 35 stolen bases per year. I wish I had seen that player, but I never did.

When I took over as Rangers manager in 1981, I told Bump, "You're my leadoff man. Steal as many bases as you can."

For some reason, however, he just stopped stealing. Finally one day, I went to Al Oliver, who hit second and third for me, and asked him, "Does it bother you when Wills steals?"

"Hell no," he said. "I love it. Gives me more of an opportunity to knock him in. Not only that, but it opens up the right side of the infield for me 'cause they have to hold him on."

So I went to Bump and asked him why he'd suddenly stopped running.

"Scoop [Oliver] doesn't want me to," he said.

Now I had to get the two of them together in the same room with me to straighten this out. Oliver reiterated that he liked it when Wills was running. It didn't change anything, though. I later heard Wills was in the last year of his contract and he didn't want to risk hurting himself. If that was the case, he took away from himself his best weapon for getting rich. If he had stolen 50 bases in 1981 and not just 12, he'd have gotten himself one big contract. Instead, he got himself traded, and he wound up finishing his career in Japan.

Five days after we traded Wills, we sent Oliver to the Montreal Expos for Larry Parrish and a minor league first baseman named Dave Hostetler. Although Parrish was primarily a third baseman, and we had an all-star in Bell there, he could also play the outfield. The main reason we made the deal was because we wanted a righthanded hitter with power. Parrish had been hurt a lot in 1981, but two years earlier he'd hit 30 homers for the Expos.

Oliver did a good job for me and was a fun guy to have on the ballclub, but he was lefthanded and more of a line drive hitter. We just felt we needed more power in the middle of the lineup.

Robinson and Richards still weren't finished, however. They felt they needed one more hitter to make our lineup set. On April 1— fittingly, April Fool's Day—I was sitting in my office in Pompano Beach when I got a call from Robinson telling me to come down to the executive trailer where he and Richards were working.

After I sat down, Robinson said: "We can make a trade right now for a leadoff hitter who can steal bases, hit for some power, play center field, left field, or first base—all the things you're looking for— but we've got to give up two of our young pitchers."

"What's the trade?" I asked.

"We can get Lee Mazzilli from the Mets for Darling and Terrell."

Ron Darling was a kid we'd taken No. 1 in the draft and given $100,000. At Yale he'd been the best college pitcher in the country in 1981. I could see he was going to pitch in the big leagues and probably be a real good one. Walt Terrell was a big husky righthander who we had taken in the 33rd round of the 1980 draft. He didn't have the same great stuff as Darling, but I felt he could be a Bob Stanley workman-like major league pitcher who would get his share of hitters out. There was no doubt in my mind that both of them were genuine big league pitching prospects.

Robinson was right. We didn't have a real leadoff hitter, but they wanted me to give my opinion of this trade right there.

"What do you think?" Robinson persisted.

"I can't help you," I said. "I don't know Lee Mazzilli. I've never seen him play two games in my life. I'm not sticking my neck out on a player I've never seen. Pitching is the name of the game, and you just gave $100,000 to this guy."

"I know," Robinson said, "But Paul doesn't think Terrell will ever pitch in the big leagues."

By now I'm saying to myself, "They've already made this deal. They're just trying to get me to make it unanimous for them."

This, I wasn't about to do. I told them to make the trade if they want, and I'd support them from an organizational standpoint, but it was their trade, not mine. It turned out to be a disastrous deal for the Rangers. Both Darling and Terrell went on to have long careers as frontline starting pitchers in the major leagues. Darling was a two-time all-star and won 136 games in the big leagues, including a 15–6 season for the Mets' '86 world championship club. Terrell, who Richards thought would never pitch in the big leagues, won 111 games, including back-to-back 15-win seasons for the Tigers in '85 and '86. The Rangers, on the other hand, went all through the '80s in constant need of pitching.

Meanwhile, Mazzilli just never did anything in Texas. As it was, I had a young kid in center field, George Wright, who'd had a great spring and had earned a place on the club. He was an excellent defensive center fielder, and he also had good speed. So right away, Mazzilli was going to have to play left. He wasn't at all happy about being traded from his hometown, New York, to Texas—and unfortunately, his play showed it. I was already gone when on August 8 the Rangers traded him back to New York, this time the Yankees, for of all people, Bucky Dent! Mazzilli had been hurt and was hitting only .241 with 17 RBIs at the time of the deal. Neither the Rangers or the Yankees were very good right then, but I couldn't help but laugh at how I came so close to actually having Bucky Dent on my ballclub.

Despite all the trades that seemingly made us a better team, at least offensively, we got off to a poor start in 1982, at one point losing 12 in a row from April 22–May 6. Toward the end of that losing streak, Tim Kurkjian, one of the rookie newspaper beat men, came into my office and said: "This is too much for me."

"Too much for you?" I said. "You're young. You've got your whole life ahead of you. I'm old, I'm fat, and I've got metal buttons in my head, and I've got this team!"

We just never seemed to recover from that losing streak. The primary victim of our early-season struggles was Parrish, who was trying to adjust to contact lenses and was hitting just .160 in late June.

When we acquired him, we thought we were getting the big, strong righthanded hitter we so desperately needed; and I've got to say, even through all his early problems, Parrish was a great guy to have on the ballclub. But he was swinging and missing at balls by two feet, and I couldn't help but wonder if he had something wrong with his eyes. He absolutely stunk, and I couldn't believe this was the same hitter we thought we had acquired from the Expos. It wasn't long before the Texas fans began really booing him.

Needless to say, Chiles was the first to start asking questions about what was wrong with this guy and why did we acquire him. I kept telling him what a good guy Parrish was, but I could tell Chiles' patience had worn pretty thin. I finally decided to sit Parrish down for the last two games of a homestand in early June.

"We're going to the West Coast in two days," I told him, "and I'll play you there. But right now, I want to give you a break from all the booing they're giving you."

Chiles was tired of it, too, but he wanted to just release Parrish.

"I'm sick of listening to this," he told me after I had again tried to defend Parrish. "I'll bite the bullet with this guy—pay him off the $1.3 million we owe him."

I said, "I know someone will pick him up, Eddie. Hold off a day or two."

Just before we left for the West Coast, I called Billy Martin, who was managing the A's.

"Would you have any interest in Larry Parrish?" I asked him.

"Hell yes," said Billy.

"Would you claim him on waivers?" I persisted.

"I'm sure we would," Billy said.

Well, all I could think of then was trying to save Eddie Chiles $1.3 million. I told Eddie Robinson that Billy Martin was ready to grab Parrish as soon as we released him.

"Okay," Robinson said. "We'll hold off. You can take him to the West Coast, but don't play him."

"Hell yes, I'm going to play him!" I asserted.

"No, no!" Robinson pleaded. "The old man is tired of seeing him!"

When we got to Oakland, Martin told me that Parrish was just too rich for the A's. Ironically, that night Parrish hit a home run and a double. The next night he hit another homer, and all of a sudden he got on fire. He wound up second on the team in homers and RBIs, with 17 and 62 respectively, and went on to have five more highly productive seasons with the Rangers, including two 100-RBI years. I felt good for Parrish, and I felt good that I had saved Mr. Chiles $1.3 million, although I wasn't surprised he never thanked me.

Unfortunately, Parrish's bat revival wasn't nearly enough to get us back into contention. Jim Sundberg, my all-star catcher, went into a bad mid-season slump, and Buddy Bell played all year with a bad right knee. The rookie switch-hitter Wright played extremely well in center field but struggled from the left side of the plate. One player who proved to be a real surprise—at least for a brief period of time— was Dave Hostetler, a big, hulking 6-foot-4 first baseman who put on an unbelievable power show for about six weeks.

Hostetler had come over as the extra player from the Expos in the Oliver-for-Parrish deal, and during that six-week period he hit home runs over houses and into parking lots. He had 22 homers in his first 72 games, and it looked like a sure thing he'd win Rookie of the Year honors. He was the rage of the whole American League. Then, all of a sudden, he stopped hitting. It was like the lights just went out. He didn't hit another homer after August 17, and two years later he was back in the minors.

While our overall hitting improved somewhat in '82, especially after Parrish got going, our pitching all but collapsed. Rick Honeycutt mysteriously lost his sinker and fell to 5–17 after going 11–6 in '81. Veteran lefthander Frank Tanana, who we signed as a free agent over the winter, led the league in losses with 18, but to be fair, pitched in a lot of hard luck. Tanana was one of the few pitchers in baseball I ever knew to be able to make a successful transition from a power pitcher to a finesse pitcher. With the Angels in the '70s, he was one of the premier power pitchers in baseball, three times striking out over 200 batters in a season. Then he hurt his arm and became a junkballer. I had been the one who recommended we sign him. Robinson and Richards both felt he was finished.

"The man may not throw the way he used to," I said, "but he knows how to pitch."

Like Charlie Hough, Tanana went on to a long and successful second career after I had him. The Rangers eventually traded him to Detroit where he won 59 games from 1988–92. He finished up with 240 wins in the big leagues.

By the second week in June, before Parrish started hitting, it had started to become pretty obvious we weren't going to have a good season, and I had an inkling Chiles was getting ready to fire me. On June 10, an off day, I decided to drive over to New Orleans and go to Louisiana Downs with Randy Galloway, the *Dallas Morning News* baseball beat writer, and our wives. Galloway and I were sitting in the front seat of the car, and as we were driving, I said to him: "I've got a feeling I'm getting fired today."

"No way!" Galloway said.

"We'll see," I said. "I hope you're right, but I have this feeling. A guy usually knows when they're getting ready to fire him in baseball."

As we pulled up in front of Louisiana Downs to the valet window, a cop came up to the car.

"Are you Mr. Zimmer?" he said. "You have a very important call."

I looked at Galloway and winked.

"Have the wives go upstairs to the dining room and get the table for lunch," I said. "You want to come with me? This won't take long."

I went to the office and took the phone call. Sure enough, it was one of Chiles' executive assistants.

"We've decided to make a change," he said. "We need you to get back here right away. Mr. Chiles' private plane will take you back."

"What's going on?" I asked.

"We've fired Eddie Robinson."

I was momentarily dumbstruck. I wound up leaving the three of them at the track and took Chiles' plane home to attend this nothing, 20-minute press conference. There was no need for me to be there, but that's what the man wanted.

Two days later I was in my office at Arlington Stadium, and I get a call from Chiles.

"I'm coming down there with Joe Klein and Paul Richards," he said.

Joe Klein had been the farm director, and the reports were he was going to be elevated to take over most of Robinson's GM duties. I couldn't imagine what this meeting was going to be about. I just hoped it wasn't to revive the formalized goal-setting project.

When he came into the room, Chiles started right in throwing questions at me.

"What is the job of a general manager?" he asked.

"I don't know," I said.

"Well, as of today I'm the general manager of this ballclub," Chiles said, "and I will be until the end of the season!

"Now let me tell you: Starting today, there will be nobody brought up from the minors unless you okay it. There will be no trades unless you okay them. You got that?"

"My god?" I said to myself. "For a guy who two days ago thought he was about to be fired, I just got big!"

"Then," Chiles continued, "when we start next year, you will be responsible for this team. Is that fair enough?"

"That's fine with me," I said, my head still spinning.

Right after that meeting, we went out on a 12-game roadtrip to Toronto, Boston, New York, and Detroit and lost 10 of them. When I got home to my apartment on Sunday night, my wife, Soot, said,

"The Rangers called earlier. You're to be in Mr. Chiles' office at 10 o'clock tomorrow morning."

I went to his office, as instructed, and he was sitting behind his desk waiting for me.

"Mr. Manager," he said, "we're gonna make a change. We're gonna make a manager change."

I didn't know what to say. All I knew was I never got to approve one move in my role as the all-powerful manager who answered only to the owner! Chiles said nothing about that. Instead, he began spelling out how I was to be departing the organization.

"Here's what I want you to do," he said. "I want you to manage the club Tuesday and Wednesday, and we'll announce it on Thursday."

"No way," I said. "Thursday's an off-day and I plan to play golf. I'm not spending my off-day at a press conference to announce my firing."

Here I was telling him the way it was, and I'm already fired! But he's still paying me, and he wants me to manage the team two more days, so I told him he could announce it after Wednesday night's game. The next night, Joe Macko, our team trainer, approached me as I was standing in the dugout by the camera cage.

"Zim!" he said. "It just came over the radio that you're fired! Is it true?"

"Does it look like I'm fired?" I asked. "I'm managing, aren't I?"

Obviously, I couldn't tell him what was going on, and I added: "And I'll be managing tomorrow night, too."

By the time Wednesday night came, it was all over the airwaves and the newspapers that I was fired. Nevertheless, I went to the park thinking that by now he can't make me manage the team tonight. When I got to my office, Chiles called. I figured he was going to tell me it was all over, but instead, he says: "Okay, everything is right on schedule! You manage tonight and we'll announce it after the game."

I couldn't believe it. By this time there was no point in me telling him that it had already been announced by everybody in the city except him. So I made out the lineup card, and when I took it out to home plate I got a standing ovation. Everybody in the ballpark knew I was fired. That's how dumb a baseball man this guy was.

After the game, I was in my office when Macko came running in.

"What are you doing, Zim?" he said frantically. "They're waiting for you in the lunch room!"

Nobody had bothered to tell me where my firing was supposed to take place, so I wound up being a little late for it. When I walked into the lunchroom, there was this podium set up and all these TV cameras and media crammed in around it. The room was so small there was no room for any of the players.

Chiles was standing behind the podium, and as I joined him he began my dismissal speech.

"You know this guy sitting next to me is a good man and a good friend," he said, "and he's been nothing but a good manager."

"So why are you firing him?" somebody from the media shot back.

Well, Chiles started getting real hot now, and began to fluster.

"Some day you'll understand," he stammered. "We did it for personal reasons."

"Personal reasons?" I said to myself. "What the hell is that supposed to mean?"

When it was my turn to speak I said, looking straight at Chiles: "I never murdered anyone and I never robbed a bank, so whatever personal reasons you're talking about, I don't know what they are."

Right afterward, Chiles went on the radio and told a bunch of lies about how the organization had been run and why it was necessary to fire me. The whole thing turned out to be an embarrassing public relations disaster for Chiles. I didn't care. I figured maybe I'd set some sort of record for most games managed after I'd already been fired. Looking back at all the goofy doings working for Eddie Chiles, my firing was right in step with them.

I found out later Chiles hadn't made up his mind who he wanted to replace me. He had narrowed it down to two of my coaches, Darrell Johnson and Fred Koenig. But when he went down to the clubhouse to interview them, he came across Koenig who had bumped into a door a couple of days earlier and had a black eye. Chiles decided that wouldn't play well on TV, so that's how Johnson supposedly got the job. The only thing was, he didn't know who Johnson was. As he walked around the clubhouse, Johnson happened to be standing in front of the locker of Wayne Terwilliger, another of my coaches. The story was Chiles went up to Johnson, assuming he was

Terwilliger, and asked him where he could find Darrell Johnson.

That night, after my firing, I went over to a restaurant down the street from the ballpark called "Mr. Catfish" where I was joined by Joe Macko and a bunch of the Texas beat writers. We were sitting around the table, telling stories, when all of a sudden this guy with a drink kind of lurches up to us. It was Brad Corbett, the previous Texas owner who had sold the team to Chiles. Corbett's term as Rangers owner had been just as turbulent as Chiles' in that he was always firing people, making bad trades, and signing a lot of big-money free agents who didn't pan out.

As he approached our table, he said, "This guy Chiles is even making me look good! There's no way you should have been fired."

He sidled up next to me and glanced at my watch, which was this old beat-up thing I'd worn for years.

"Let me see your watch!" Corbett said, adding, "That's no watch for you. Here, look at this one."

He pointed to his own watch, which was this huge gold Rolex. Had to be worth easily $10,000. The next thing I knew he was taking it off and handing it to me.

"Here," he said, "let's make a switch. You take mine."

My farewell party as manager of the Texas Rangers turned out to be a pretty raucous affair, in which definitely no tears were shed. I would miss the players and the baseball writers like Galloway, Jim Reeves, Paul Hagen, and Phil Rogers who I'd worked with there. But I sure wasn't going to miss the organization or working for Mr. Eddie Chiles. A few years later it came out that he'd been diagnosed with Alzheimer's disease, and he died in 1993 at 83, four years after selling his majority share of the team for $46 million to a group headed by George W. Bush, the future Texas governor and President-elect in 2000.

Looking back, I'd have to say Chiles wasn't at all a bad guy. He just didn't know anything about baseball, and was misguided enough to think he could run his ballclub like an oil company. I guess you could say that's my formalized goal-setting assessment of Eddie Chiles. I might add that a year later, when Larry Parrish was en route to a 26-homer, 88-RBI season with the Rangers, I wrote him a note that said: "Sure, you get me fired and then you start hitting. Great."

9

Billybrawl and Two Reunions

After I parted company with the Rangers and Eddie Chiles, I got a call from Billy Martin, who was still managing the A's. Billy and I had known each other ever since those great Yankees–Dodgers World Series of the '50s, and he was always appreciative of my testifying for him in the Jim Brewer incident.

"Would you have interest in coaching third base next year for me?" Billy asked.

I told him I didn't know what other offers might come my way but, certainly, if no one had a managing job I'd be interested.

It turned out, George Steinbrenner called me right after the '82 season and again offered me the Yankees' third base coaching job. This time, Clyde King was still Yankees manager, but there were all kinds of rumors that Martin was going to be let out by the A's so he could go back to managing the Yankees for George again. For that reason, I didn't bother contacting King to find out if he wanted me on his staff. I figured if Billy was going to be the manager, he would be comfortable with me since he'd already offered me the job in Oakland.

A little aside here about Steinbrenner: As I said, I had gotten to know him through the years in Tampa when we'd run into each other at the track. The first time I ever met him, however, was when I was managing the Red Sox. We were in Yankee Stadium one day, and as usual I was at the park early. When I went out to the dugout, I saw this guy on the mound throwing batting practice to some kid. I asked one of the groundskeepers, "Who's the guy throwing BP?"

"That's the boss!" he said.

"The boss?" I asked.

"Yeah, the boss! Steinbrenner!"

When he was done throwing, Steinbrenner came over to the dugout and we started talking. I was impressed at what a down-to-earth guy he was. I never did find out who the kid he was pitching to was. It wasn't one of his own. I wouldn't be surprised if it had been the son of a cop killed in action. George has always been doing things for the families of New York cops and firemen, and he has a foundation that helps pay for the education of the kids whose fathers were killed in the line of duty.

That December, the winter baseball meetings were held in Hawaii and Steinbrenner asked me to go as part of the Yankees' delegation, even though Billy had not yet been named to replace King as manager. It wasn't until after the meetings that Billy officially was named Yankees manager for the third time. If only I knew his third tour of duty for George was going to be even stormier than the first two!

Throughout the '83 season, when Billy and George weren't at odds with each other, they were allies-at-odds with the umpires and the league office. It started right from the get-go when George got himself in trouble in spring training, complaining about a call made by National League umpire Lee Weyer against the Yankees in a Grapefruit League game. A reporter quoted George as calling Weyer "a National League homer," and for that he got slapped with a $50,000 fine from baseball commissioner Bowie Kuhn.

In May, George got himself suspended for a week by American League president Lee MacPhail after criticizing AL umpire Derrel Cousins for throwing Dave Winfield out of a game. Winfield had been brushed back by a pitch from Oakland's Mike Norris and started to mix it up with the catcher, Mike Heath. That brought players rushing from both benches, and when order was restored, Winfield was ejected but Heath was allowed to stay in the game.

George was only sticking up for his player, but by now the league office had lost any tolerance for him blasting the umpires. It was the same thing with Billy, who was suspended twice that season, leaving me both times the interim manager.

Billy was involved in a heated argument with umpire Dan Morrison in the Yankees' season opener in Seattle, and 10 days later he got ejected at Yankee Stadium by Vic Voltaggio, prompting MacPhail to fine him $5,000 and warn him he'd be suspended if his behavior didn't improve. It didn't.

Just eight days after the Voltaggio ejection, Billy got into three arguments in one game in Texas. After the third one, which resulted in his being tossed out of the game by Drew Coble, he kicked dirt all over the umpire's shoes. For that, he was suspended three days by MacPhail.

We were in Kansas City and then on to Minnesota when Billy's suspension began, and in handing the reins over to me, he told me he was going to go fishing with a friend of his named Howard Wong. "Don't worry about what I might do," he said. "You do it your way."

One thing I knew was that Billy and our catcher, Rick Cerone, didn't get along too well. Billy always batted Cerone seventh, and in the lineup I made out for the first game, that's where I had Cerone. But as the team was taking batting practice, I was called off the field to take a call from Billy.

"What's your lineup?" he asked.

I told him and he suddenly snapped: "Dammit! I want Cerone hitting eighth!"

No problem, I said, and I simply changed it. I never knew what Billy's reason was for wanting to make the change. One of the writers speculated that Billy wanted Cerone to think Billy had more confidence in his hitting ability than other people—such as me—did. I preferred to think Billy just didn't remember where he was hitting Cerone. All I cared about was that we won all three games while Billy was on that first suspension, and I was able to hand the team back over to him without having lost any ground.

By mid-June, however, the team was treading water around .500 and tensions were mounting between Steinbrenner and Martin. They came to a head in a weekend series in Milwaukee, which began with Billy skipping an off-day workout that George had ordered. Steinbrenner probably would have never found out if Billy hadn't gotten the media on his case by carrying on with his girlfriend during the entire series. At one point during the Sunday afternoon getaway game, Billy was sitting outside the Yankee dugout against the fence that separated the field from the box seats. The writers reported he was passing notes back and forth to his girlfriend who was sitting in the first row of the box seats.

Needless to say, this touched off a furor in New York, with rumors flying all over the place that Yogi Berra was going to replace Martin as manager. From Milwaukee the team went to Cleveland, where Steinbrenner was waiting. Nobody knew what was going to happen—there were TV cameras and reporters all over the lobby of the Stouffer's Hotel where the team was staying. Then everything seemed to get resolved—sort of—after Billy and his lawyer had a meeting with Steinbrenner at the Pewter Mug restaurant in the Cleveland stadium. The resolution was that Billy was staying, but his pitching coach, Art Fowler, was going.

We didn't know until we got back to New York the following Friday what a toll that took on Martin. Yogi and I were sitting together by our lockers in the Yankee clubhouse early that Friday afternoon when this attractive young woman representing *The New York Times* came in. The word was she was conducting some sort of survey about the upcoming All-Star Game.

The woman headed to a table in the back of the clubhouse where a few of the players were congregated. She was still there when Martin came in about a half-hour later. We'd heard he'd been out on the town all night with Fowler, and from his hung-over appearance, that looked to be an accurate rumor. Almost as soon as he spotted the *Times* woman, Martin got embroiled in an argument with her. Heated words were exchanged, mostly by Martin, and as Billy walked past relief pitcher George Frazier and myself on the way to his office, he turned and hollered at her: "You can kiss my f—ing dago ass!"

We played the game, beating Milwaukee 7–2 that night, and went home. The next morning, I'm driving to the ballpark and I hear on the radio, "Billy Martin will be fired as Yankees manager today and replaced by Jeff Torborg."

Here we go again, I thought, only now it was Torborg, another of Billy's coaches, who was supposed to be replacing him. I didn't know what to expect when I arrived at the clubhouse. When I walked in, there was Billy, sitting in his office, and as far as I could see, it was business as usual. After the game, I was taking my shower when one of the clubhouse kids came to me and said, "The lawyer wants to see you upstairs."

I had no idea what he was talking about, and since I had never been upstairs in the Stadium, I told the kid he'd have to take me up there. When we got to the receptionist area, I was instructed to go through the door into Steinbrenner's office—another place I had never been in my life. There was George sitting in a chair behind this big round table.

"Let's talk a little about what happened down in the clubhouse yesterday," he said.

"Oh shit," I said to myself. "I'm in a mess now."

"Did Billy Martin tell this woman to kiss his dago ass?" Steinbrenner asked.

I didn't want to lie, and I was thankful he put it that way.

"Yes," I said.

Had Steinbrenner asked me if Martin had said, "kiss my f—king dago ass," I don't know what I would have said. Thank goodness he didn't ask it that way.

He wasn't finished, though.

"Now," Steinbrenner said, "I have to ask you something very important. Do you think we can win this thing with Billy Martin managing this team?"

I got up out of my chair and headed for the door. "George," I said, "you're asking the wrong man."

I wasn't about to get into that. No matter what I thought, Martin had hired me. I wasn't going to be a part of his getting fired.

I know Martin didn't like Torborg. A lot of it had to do with the fact that Torborg had been given this seven-year contract by Steinbrenner to pass up a college coaching job at Princeton and be the Yankees' bullpen coach, and Martin resented that. Overall, Martin was very tough on coaches, although he was more than decent to me. We did have one very public blow-up that season which, when it was over, was more comical than anything else.

We were playing the Tigers in Detroit, August 12, and as usual there was a lot of stuff going on with Martin and the umpires, especially the pine tar business, which I'll get to later on. The old Tiger Stadium had dugouts in which the benches were so low you could barely see the tops of the players' heads from the field. It was especially hard for the third base coach to see the manager flashing signs. Because of that, Billy decided before the game to change the signs, especially the squeeze, which he said he'd put on by leaning against the support pole in the middle of the dugout.

I didn't think anymore about it until the eighth inning when Dave Winfield broke a 5–5 tie with a double that put runners at second and third with one out. Graig Nettles was the runner at third, and Ken Griffey was the batter with Don Baylor on deck. It looked like it had the makings of a big inning—with one run in, two runners in scoring position, and two of our best hitters coming up.

But as I looked over to the dugout, I saw Billy leaning up against the pole.

I sauntered over to Nettles, who was one of the slowest runners on the club, and mumbled, "Get ready, you're going."

"I'm what?" he said.

"You're going," I repeated. "We're squeezing here."

"Is Billy nuts?" Nettles protested.

"Don't ask me," I said. "I'm just the messenger. The man has the squeeze on."

On the first pitch, Nettles took off for home and was tagged out by five feet as Griffey missed bunting the pitch, which was high and almost at his head. Griffey, who seldom had ever been called upon to bunt, then flied out to end the inning.

All the while, Billy is waving his hands and screaming, telling everyone on the bench what a dummy I am. As I ran in from third base, he was waiting for me on the top step of the dugout.

"What the hell are you doing out there?" he screamed. "Who's the manager here? You just ran us right out of the inning!"

I just let him have his say as everyone in the dugout looked on in confusion. Finally, after I'd had enough I said: "I'm not trying to manage your team. I'm trying to be the best third base coach I can for you. I'm only doing what you said."

"What do you mean?" he said. "I never gave you the squeeze!"

"Billy," I said, "you leaned against the damn post."

"Oh my god," he said, his face reddening. "I forgot."

Another time that season, I was involved in a similar incident, only this time indirectly related to Martin. We were in Chicago and

Billy had gotten thrown out of the game. As he passed me in the dugout on the way down the tunnel, he didn't say anything, so as far as I knew, someone else was running the club.

When I ran out to the third base coaching box and looked into the dugout, I realized that that someone was Lee Walls. Walls and I had been teammates briefly in Los Angeles with the Dodgers, but we didn't have a whole lot in common. Martin had brought him in as one of his coaches for '83, and it was an accepted fact that Walls and Art Fowler were Billy's guys and the rest of the coaches were not part of his inner circle of after-hours "running mates." That was fine with me. Billy's and my relationship was strictly business. When the games were over, we went our separate ways. I didn't like going out drinking every night.

Besides being one of Billy's drinking companions, Walls thought of himself as a sort of "discipline" coach—or at least that's the impression he tried to give. He had shaved his head and he would often walk around the clubhouse with a nightstick in his hand, giving him a sort of "General Patton" look. The players jokingly called him "Echo" in reference to the fact that he had a habit of repeating everything Billy would say. As the outfield coach he used a towel to wave and direct the outfielders. Otherwise, he kept the towel wrapped around his neck, which I suppose he thought further added to his enforcer image.

Butch Wynegar had led off the inning with a single when I saw Walls standing on the top step of the dugout pointing at himself. I took that to mean Billy had assigned him to be the manager for the rest of the game. However, I quickly came to realize Billy had stationed himself in the runway, out of the sight of the umpires, and was giving Walls the signs to relay to me. Being that Wynegar was about the slowest player on the team, I was expecting Walls to give me either the sacrifice or the hit-and-run. Instead, to my astonishment, he flashed the steal sign.

I shook my head, figuring that he'd made a mistake, but he persisted. He began pointing at himself again, as if to remind me that he was in charge, and he was giving me the sign. Again he flashed the steal sign. This time I just waved my hands in the air as if to say, "Forget it. Do what you want!"

By now, everyone in the White Sox dugout had become aware of the chaos going on, and they were laughing out loud, watching

Walls frantically flashing the steal sign and me waving him off in disgust. After the inning, Walls started in on me as soon as I got to the dugout.

"What the hell are you doing waving me off?" he screamed. "I'm giving you the signs and you're ignoring me! I'm trying to win a game here. Where do you get off not obeying my signs?"

I let him rant while all of our players were also laughing now, and finally I cut him short.

"You're trying to win the game?" I said. "Is that why you wanted Wynegar stealing?"

"I didn't have him stealing," Walls protested.

"That's the problem," I retorted. "You're in charge and you don't even know our damn signs."

The sign screwups were nothing, however, compared to the brouhaha I got involved in on July 24, against the Kansas City Royals at Yankee Stadium. On that day one of the most controversial and explosive incidents in baseball history occurred, and I'm not proud of the fact I was the primary cause of it. Before the game, I happened to notice that George Brett, the Royals' future Hall of Fame third baseman and three-time batting champion, had excessive pine tar on his bat. Under the rules, pine tar—which is used to give the batter a better grip—can only extend 18 inches up the handle of the bat. In the case of Brett's bat, it was a couple of inches beyond that.

I said to Martin: "Look at all that pine tar on his bat. That's illegal."

"That's good," Martin said. "But don't say anything about it. We'll protest it when the time is right."

The time came with two outs in the ninth inning. Trailing 4–3, the Royals stayed alive when U.L. Washington singled off reliever Dale Murray, prompting Martin to bring in our closer, Goose Gossage, to pitch to Brett. Sure enough, if Brett doesn't hit a home run into the right field seats to put the Royals ahead, 5–4.

Brett had just finished circling the bases and was heading to the Royals dugout when Martin went out to home plate umpire Tim McClelland and lodged his protest about the bat. After examining the bat, McClelland called the other umpires over and crew chief Joe Brinkman measured the pine tar against the front of home plate.

After a few minutes of deliberation, the umps concluded the pine tar had extended beyond the legal length and signaled Brett out. This, in turn, touched off one of the most famous player rages ever seen in baseball, before or after, as Brett came charging out of the dugout like a wildman and had to be forcefully restrained from attacking the umpires.

It also touched off a three-week media circus in which everyone, from the judges and the politicians, to Bowie Kuhn and Lee MacPhail, got involved. I guess you could say it was not unlike a presidential election process in Florida.

The Royals, naturally, protested the game, and I didn't think they had a chance of having it upheld. After all, it was a rule, wasn't it? But four days later, MacPhail overturned the umpires' decision, saying they hadn't acted in "the spirit of the rule," and ordered the game resumed from the point of Brett's restored homer. It was completed on August 18, the Royals flying all the way from Kansas City to get three outs from the Yankees. For his part, Martin showed what he thought of the whole crazy deal by putting Don Mattingly at second base and Ron Guidry in center field, then trying appeal plays (of the Brett homer) with the new umpiring crew—at first, second, and third base.

It was certainly not one of baseball's finest hours. At the end of the season, Kuhn, in one of his final acts as commissioner, fined Steinbrenner a record $250,000 for his critical comments about MacPhail, as well as for his efforts in preventing the game from being resumed. I wished I had never opened my mouth about Brett's bat. To this day, though, I still don't understand why if there's a rule in the books it isn't enforced.

That was pretty much Martin's point a few days after the Pine Tar Game when he was chased from a game at Comiskey Park in Chicago for arguing that Wynegar hadn't been given enough warm-up throws after replacing Cerone as catcher. The Yankees rallied to win the game, but when everyone came back into the clubhouse, Martin was still raging about home plate umpire Dale Ford, who had ejected both him and Cerone. He said something about Ford not knowing the rule book (regarding the number of warm-up tosses a replacement catcher is entitled to) and went on to say the umpire might as well use it for toilet paper when he goes hunting. Then he called Ford a "stone liar" which resulted in his second suspension of the season.

It was that kind of year. I never saw so many goofy things go on in one season as with the Yankees in 1983. The height of goofiness may have been Steinbrenner and Martin taking the umpires' side in arguing with the league president over the pine tar ruling!

Throughout the entire season, Martin was under tremendous stress, although most of it was self-inflicted. One time, after a real wild game at Yankee Stadium, which we'd lost, the media was all in Billy's office. George called and lit into Billy with everyone standing right there. After they left, I walked into the office, and Billy was sitting at his desk, his head buried in his arms. I just put my arm around him. He was sobbing.

Like I said, Billy unfortunately put himself under most of his stress. Steinbrenner is a tough owner for any manager to work under, but with Billy it was often open warfare between the two. Nothing was ever hidden. It was right out there in the open for everyone to read and hear about.

I will say this, though: For all his personal demons, Billy Martin was a helluva manager. He really knew how to run a ballgame. It was all the other stuff, away from the field, that did him in. That stuff took its toll on everybody around him.

One time, in August, he had decided he was going to platoon Don Baylor at DH. He just couldn't tell Baylor himself and, instead, asked me to do it. So I went out to right field where Baylor was shagging flies before the game and said, "I'm the messenger boy. I've come to tell you you're platooning now."

By September I had made up my mind I wasn't coming back to the Yankees, no matter what George decided to do with Billy. Other than my wife, the only two baseball people who knew my intentions were Jim Frey, who was coaching for the Mets, and Gene Mauch, who was now working as an advisor under Buzzie Bavasi in the Angels' front office. It wasn't that Martin had mistreated me. It bothered me the way he treated others. It was like a firecracker going off in the clubhouse every fourth day, and I just had had enough of it.

I never officially said I wasn't coming back. Then on the last day of the season, Dick Young sat down next to me in the dugout.

"Why didn't this team win?" he asked me.

"I don't know," I replied. "Why are you asking me?"

"Why are you leaving?" Young persisted.

"Dick," I said, "I'll answer you the same way I've answered everybody else."

"Ah, c'mon," he said. "You can tell me, Zim. Off the record."

I said, "I'll say it on the record if I want to say anything."

What I didn't tell Young was that I had always wanted to work in Anaheim. It was an area of the country I liked because of the weather. The Angels had a nice stadium, and there wasn't a better owner in baseball to work for than Gene Autry. Both John McNamara, the Angels manager, and Mauch said to call as soon as the season was over; that the third base coaching job would be mine for the asking.

The Yankees finished the season in Baltimore and I had told all the reporters, Young included, that if they had any questions for me they had better ask them before the game, because after the game I planned to be showered, dressed, and out of the clubhouse in five minutes. Soot had instructions to pull the car up right to the press gate with the engine running.

In the sixth inning I ran up to the gate just to check everything out, and discovered a bus standing there blocking my car. I got the bus removed, and as soon as the game was over, Soot and I were the first car out of the lot and on the road to Florida. The next day I found out Young had written an article in which he said: "Don Zimmer is going to California as third base coach, but he will become the manager." He went on to say McNamara was having some contract problems and that's why he wouldn't be the manager much longer.

"Oh shit," I said. "I've got to get a hold of Johnny Mac." When I couldn't find him, I called Buzzie and told him my problem.

"I can't take that coaching job now," I said. "I couldn't work for Mac under those circumstances and all that speculation."

"Oh, don't be silly," Buzzie said. "It'll all be forgotten in a week."

"No," I said. "I can't come there now."

Finally I was able to get Johnny Mac on the phone and I said to him: "You'll never know how badly I wanted to coach third base for you, but I just wouldn't be comfortable with it now."

"Why don't you sleep on it," he said.

"Things aren't going to change," I said. "I have to pass."

Now I had no job. The next day I got a call from Frey, who had some interesting news.

"You never know what might happen here," Frey said. "I might be managing the Cubs."

He had just been interviewed by Dallas Green, the Cubs' president.

"Wow!" I said. "What a great thing that would be!"

The next day, Frey was sitting in Green's office at Wrigley Field when he called me again.

"Well," he said. "I'm the manager of the Chicago Cubs. How are you doing? You okay in California?"

"Not really," I said. "I have no job."

"What?" he said. "I thought you were going to the Angels?"

When I explained to him what happened, Frey started to laugh. "Hold on a minute," he said. A few seconds later he was back on the phone and said: "You want to coach third base for me?"

Disappointed as I was not to be able to go to Anaheim, I couldn't be happier going to work for an old friend.

The 1984 Cubs were not a good club coming out of spring training. Jim Frey had never been to Arizona, but I had and I knew how the elements there could play tricks on you as far as being able to truly evaluate your team. I told Jim, "Don't judge your ballclub on Arizona. The high sky and the wind in particular make it very tough." Combined with that, we had Leon Durham in left field, Mel Hall in center, and Keith Moreland in right. None of them would ever be confused with a Gold Glove outfielder at their position, and as a result balls were dropping in all over the place. Nobody could catch the ball out there.

Finally at one point Frey said to me: "I remember that crap you laid on me about the high sky, and the wind out here, and how I can't judge my outfielders on what happens here. Well, I'm getting awfully sick and tired of all these goddam fly balls dropping in all over the damn place. Screw you and your high sky!"

Apparently Dallas Green felt the same way. On March 26 he executed a trade with the Phillies in which the Cubs got left fielder Gary Matthews and center fielder Bob Dernier for Bill Campbell, my old closer with the Red Sox, and minor league catcher-first baseman

Mike Diaz. It turned out to be the trade that turned around our entire season. Frey immediately installed Dernier as his leadoff man. After hitting over .400 for the first month of the season, Dernier went on to steal 45 bases and score 94 runs, while making all the plays in center field. At the same time, Matthews, who had earned the nickname "Sarge", became a leader for the Cubs. He hit .291 with 14 homers and 82 RBIs in left field, and enabled Frey to move Durham to first base, where he was much more suited.

If we didn't make that trade, we were dead. Dernier and Matthews transformed us from a slow-footed, bad defensive team into a complete team. That '84 Cubs team was also the best I ever saw for relaying signs from second base to the batter. They excelled in stealing signs from the catcher.

When the season got underway, we suffered two key losses to our pitching staff that could have been disastrous, as both Dick Ruthven and Scott Sanderson went down with injuries. Green resolved those problems by acquiring Dennis Eckersley from the Red Sox for Bill Buckner—a longtime Wrigley Field favorite who had lost his first base job to Durham—and Rick Sutcliffe from the Indians for Hall and Joe Carter. Carter had been a No. 1 draft pick, and was the most highly regarded prospect in the Cubs organization.

I remember the conversation we all had about Carter that spring. Frey had never seen him play. All he knew about him was what other people in the organization had said. But when he asked them, "Is there anyone here who can tell me Carter can play left field on Opening Day?", nobody spoke up. Carter went on to have a great career, knocking in over 100 runs eight times with the Padres, Indians, and Blue Jays; but without Sutcliffe, the Cubs would have never won in 1984. Frey told me after the season: "When we got Dernier and Matthews, I felt we had become a decent team. When we got Eckersley and Sutcliffe we became contenders." That was a fact.

Sutcliffe had been only 4–5 with the Indians, but had lost 18 pounds after undergoing root-canal surgery. When he came over to us, he'd regained his stamina and was virtually unbeatable. He went 16–1 with a 2.69 ERA and won the Cy Young Award going away. I later found out only three other pitchers in baseball history had ever won 20 games in a season in different leagues, and that the last one to do it was Hank Borowy with the 1945 Cubs—ironically the last Cubs team to make it to the World Series.

As it turned out, we didn't make it to the World Series in 1984, but we came damn close, and were the first Cubs team to finish first and make it to the postseason since that 1945 club.

Eckersley was 10–8, Steve Trout, a screwball lefthander, had his best season with a 13–7 record, and Lee Smith saved 33 games for us. Offensively we were led by Ryne Sandberg who won the National League MVP award and came within one triple and one homer of being the first player in history to collect 200 hits, 20 triples, 20 homers, and 20 stolen bases in one season. He had that kind of a season and played a fantastic second base, where he committed only six errors all year.

I really thought we were going to go to the big one, but after winning the first two games of the National League Championship Series against the Padres, we lost the next three in San Diego. The final game was especially disappointing, in that Sutcliffe carried a 3–2 lead into the seventh inning when a sharp grounder by Tim Flannery went through Durham's legs for an error that tied the score. The Padres scored three more times that inning to do us in. I didn't look at that defeat the way everybody else did. I felt it had been a terrific season. We did what no other Cubs team had done in nearly 40 years. Sure I was disappointed, but it didn't come close to the disappointment I felt in 1978.

As is so often the case in baseball, you can be on top of the world one year and at the bottom the next. That's what happened to the Cubs in 1985. We went from a first-place team, 96–65, to a distant fourth, 77–84. Mostly it was injuries that ruined our season, as all five of our starting pitchers—Sutcliffe, Trout, Eckersley, Sanderson, and Ruthven—went down for extended periods. In addition, Matthews underwent knee surgery, Dernier foot surgery, and our catcher Jody Davis was in the hospital with a stomach disorder. Somebody in the media computed that the five pitchers missed 60 starts, and that 11 players spent a total of 14 stretches on the disabled list. As a result Frey was juggling constantly to field a competitive team, and used 101 different lineups that season.

For me, one of the lowlights of the season was getting nearly killed by the big, beefy umpire, "Cowboy Joe" West. There had been a close play at third base, in which I was trying to get into position to tell my baserunner to slide. West was also trying to get into position to make the call. As he did, he literally threw me backwards to get me out of his way. Naturally, as soon as the play was over I was up on my feet and in his face. I was steaming—and also really hurting.

"What the hell is wrong with you?" I screamed. "You could have broken my neck!"

West just laughed. He had fooled around as a pro wrestler, and he thought it was no big deal to try his act out on the baseball field. He did it routinely, tossing people around whenever there'd be a brawl in a game he was umpiring. I was told Bill White, the National League president, reprimanded and fined him for his actions.

My other big run-in that season came with one of our own players, Larry Bowa, who had been a helluva shortstop for a lot of years on artificial turf with the Phillies, but who lost his job in 1985 to Shawon Dunston. Actually Bowa had shown signs of slowing down a couple of years earlier after he came over to the Cubs from the Phillies. He had been a very outspoken player with the Phillies, often criticizing the front office. The story goes, Bill Giles, the Phillies' owner, was so determined get rid of Bowa that when Dallas Green asked for one extra player in a straight swap of shortstops—Bowa for Ivan DeJesus—Giles didn't hesitate an instant in saying, "You got him." That player was Ryne Sandberg.

Anyway, in the spring of '85, it was apparent to everyone that Dunston, who had been the Cubs' No. 1 draft pick in 1982, was ready to assume the No. 1 shortstop job. He had one of the strongest throwing arms I've ever seen on a shortstop; and he also had good range, a good bat, and could run. As the season got underway and Bowa was in the lineup once every two or three weeks after averaging 150 games a season since 1970, he began to start sniping at Frey. I dressed just a few lockers away from Bowa in the Wrigley Field clubhouse and I'd watch how he worked the media the previous year. When he'd have a good day, he'd say stuff like "Us veterans know how to win and we'll pull this thing out." But any time he'd have a bad day he hid in the trainer's room. I'm thinking, *What is it with this guy that he only shows up when he's playing good?*

In both '84 and especially '85, I felt Chris Speier, who the Cubs purchased from the Expos in mid-August, should have been playing over Bowa, but Jimmy didn't think so. So now it's the next season and Dunston is playing over both of them all spring.

One morning in Arizona, I got up and went to breakfast, and as I'm reading the paper I see this article that says "Bowa blasts Frey." In it are all these comments by Bowa questioning why Dunston should be taking his job. I folded up the paper and headed out to the ballpark, and I was seething. I was so pissed off I actually wrote down a bunch of things on a piece of paper I was going to say to both Bowa and the media, because I didn't want to leave anything out. In my opinion, this was bullshit—this guy Bowa blasting Frey every other week after Frey had given him every opportunity to keep his job the year before by playing him every day.

The fact is Bowa, for all his defensive records, shied away from balls at second base rather than preventing them from going into center field. I said that and a lot of other things to him, including calling him selfish and self-serving, and I have to say it was pretty tough for me to go to the ballpark the next day. But I meant every word of it. I knew, too, there would be a meeting. Jimmy summoned me to his office, and I confirmed to him everything I had said to Bowa.

"I wish you hadn't said all that," he said. "But I know that's you. Still, I can't let this go. I've gotta call both of you guys in here together. Bowa says he thinks it's horse shit for a coach to be going off on players."

I said, "I agree with you 100 percent, but I still think this situation is bullshit, and I have nothing to apologize for. I regret nothing of what I said. You take it from there."

When I left the ballpark that day I decided I was going home. "I don't need this anymore," I said to myself.

I was packing up my stuff to leave the next day, and had already called Soot to tell her I'd be home in Florida that night, when there was a knock on my door. It was Jimmy and Billy Connors, our pitching coach.

"What are you doing?" Jimmy demanded.

"I'm going home," I said.

"What do you mean?"

"Just what I said. I'm going home. I've had enough."

It took about a half-hour, but the two of them talked me out of leaving and I came back to the ballpark. I still hadn't changed my feelings about Bowa, however. For all he'd done in the past (he set the major league records for highest fielding percentage by a shortstop, both lifetime and single season, and also played more games than any National League shortstop in history), he was no longer a good shortstop and was now a clubhouse lawyer. Bowa finished his career with over 2,000 hits, and I was surprised to learn he'd been dropped from the baseball writers' Hall of Fame ballot after just one year. I can only imagine that too many of the writers remembered him from how he played shortstop on grass with the Cubs rather than all those years on turf with the Phillies.

I remember a meeting we'd had in Dallas Green's office late in the '84 season when it was apparent we had a real shot at winning. Dallas asked Jimmy: "What can I do to help you down the stretch?" and I replied: "Get a shortstop!"

"That's a lot of crap," Dallas yelled. "Bowa can play."

We didn't talk for eight or nine days after that. Then one morning he came up to me and said, "We had a disagreement. I'm not mad at you." To which, I replied, "I wouldn't have said anything if you hadn't asked us."

Bowa wound up getting released in August of '85, and by then the Cubs were long out of the race. We were just too crippled up and we just couldn't compete, although we did set a Chicago attendance record that year.

Unfortunately, the injury-plagued, dismal '85 season carried over to '86. I should have had a premonition of this in spring training when I nearly killed myself. We were standing around the clubhouse in Fitch Park, our minor league training headquarters in Mesa. I was having this conversation with Ned Colletti, our media relations director, when I leaned against a piece of exercise equipment that gave way on me. The next thing I knew I was lying on the floor with the team doctor, Jake Suker, standing over me. I had fallen right on my head and knocked myself out cold. Everyone knew about all the screws and soft spots in my skull, and they were scared I was going to die right there.

"Zim!" I heard Dr. Suker yell, "can you hear me?"

He had given me some smelling salts and I was starting to come to.

"Zim!" he repeated as I opened my eyes. "How many fingers can you see?"

I could see two fingers and I knew I was okay.

"Two," I said.

"Okay," he said, "what are your kids' names?"

"Tommy and Donna," I responded.

"Fine," he said. "Now, who's the President of the United States?"

"Ah, c'mon, Doc," I said. "That's a trick question. I didn't know that before I fell!"

It was apparent as we broke camp that Sutcliffe's shoulder was about shot and he just couldn't win consistently anymore. Eckersley and Trout also struggled, and we got off to a really bad start. By June 1, we were 19–27 when we went on a 10-game roadtrip to Cincinnati, St. Louis, and Pittsburgh. We went 2–8 on the trip, and there had been stories that Jimmy might be fired. John Cox, Dallas's right-hand man, was on the trip as an observer. On the last night, Cox got a call from Dallas instructing him to tell Jimmy there was to be a workout at Wrigley Field at 12 noon the next day.

Now Frey had to tell the players this, and needless to say, it didn't sit too well with them.

"F—ing Frey!" I heard them saying in the trainer's room. "Where does he get off calling a workout on our day off?"

I couldn't take it any longer. I walked into the trainer's room and said, "All you guys who are pissed off at Jimmy Frey better call Chicago and talk to the big gray-haired man. He's the one who called the workout."

The next day at the workout, Yosh Kawano, our clubhouse man, informed me I didn't have to put my uniform on, which made me start to wonder what was going on. As I was sitting on a chair looking into my locker, John Cox came by and stood next to me, not saying a word. Finally, after a few minutes, at 10 minutes to 12, he said to me: "Dallas wants you up in his room."

As I was going out the back door of the clubhouse to the stairway leading up to the club offices, I ran right into Frey.

"Where are you going?" he asked.

"To Dallas's office," I replied.

"Me too," he said.

When we got up to the office and sat down in the reception area, the secretary said: "Mr. Frey, you can go in to see Mr. Green."

About 10 minutes later, Jimmy came out and walked right past me, saying nothing. Now it was my turn to go in. As I sat down, Dallas looked at me and started scratching his head.

"This can be a tough game at times," he began.

"Yeah, I know," I said.

"I just had to let the manager go," he said.

"Well," I said to myself, "that's baseball." As I was getting ready to say it out loud, Dallas continued: "And being as you're so close to Jimmy, we're letting you go, too."

"Wait a minute," I protested. "How can you let a guy go for being too loyal? Why not let Vukey (John Vukovich, another of Jimmy's coaches) be the manager and me be his coach?"

"I didn't give that a thought," he countered.

Although Green denied knowing anything about it, I really believe the reason he also fired me was because someone informed him I had told the players it was he, and not Frey, who had ordered that workout. It turned out Green had already decided to bring in Gene Michael as manager. Michael had been coaching third base for Lou Piniella with the Yankees. In the press release, they said something about Michael being hired because of his familiarity with the National League. I couldn't quite figure out where they got that from, being that Michael had been working for the Yankees for nearly 10 years.

At any rate, Jimmy and I were both out, and now I went to look for him, only to be told by Yosh that he'd packed up his stuff and driven home. I had to get another ride home, and when I arrived at our apartment, Soot was all upset.

"I just talked to Jimmy's wife," she said, "and she told me Jimmy got fired, and that you're probably going to take over the club. What's going on?"

"What did you say?" I asked.

"Jimmy says you're taking over the club," she repeated.

"Jimmy's wrong," I said. "It's a quinella. They got us both."

The next day Steinbrenner called me.

"What are you doing?" he asked.

"I'm packing up," I said.

"Would you like to come over with us again?" he asked. "Lou needs a good third base coach."

"I'd have to talk to Lou first," I said.

"You don't have to bother," Steinbrenner said. "Lou said he wants you."

The end of 1986 with the Yankees turned out to be a lot like the beginning of the season with the Cubs. Piniella was at odds with Steinbrenner and was rumored to be on the way out as Yankees manager. Nobody seemed to know for sure what was going to happen. On the last day of the season Lou said to me, "Look Zim, I wish I could tell you I'd have a job here for you next season, but I really don't know anything right now."

"That's good enough for me," I said.

Five days later, Roger Craig called me and asked me to coach third base for the Giants in 1987.

This was a prime example of the true and lasting friendships I've been so fortunate to develop through my seven decades in the game. Craig had been a Dodger teammate in the '50s, but as I discussed earlier, I'd replaced him with Johnny Podres as my pitching coach with the Padres in 1972. It was a completely amicable parting, with Craig actually reminding me that he'd been there years earlier when I'd promised Podres a pitching coach job whenever I got a big league managing job. So now, here I was without a job and Craig immediately came to my rescue.

In the weeks leading up to spring training 1987, I was having trouble with my neck. It got so bad that when I'd get up in the morning in Treasure Island I couldn't walk. The doctors had to operate to relieve the nerve pressure on my vertebrae, and they used 20 clamps, instead of stitches, to close up the back of my neck. So I was at home, unable to move, and now I was going to be late for spring training—with a new team—for the first time in my life. I felt terrible—a new coach and I wasn't going to be there for Craig. When I finally got the clamps out, I put 'em in the envelope and mailed them to

Roger. When I got out to Arizona at last, I had to wear a towel around my neck for the first week I was in camp. I felt like Lee Walls without the billy club!

For the first half of 1987, the Giants were a pretty mediocre ballclub, and were 39–40 on July 4 when general manager Al Rosen swung into action, making a big seven-player trade with the Padres. He sent third baseman Chris Brown and pitchers Mark Davis, Mark Grant, and Keith Comstock to San Diego in exchange for third baseman/outfielder Kevin Mitchell and pitchers Dave Dravecky and Craig Lefferts. Mike Krukow, the Giants' best pitcher that year who would go on to finish 20–9, later said "We became a real team on July 4," and he was right.

Although Davis went on to win a Cy Young Award two years later with the Padres, Mitchell finished with 22 homers and 70 RBIs in 1987, and would win the NL MVP in 1989 by leading the league with 47 homers and 125 RBIs. Lefferts provided the Giants with a valuable lefthander in the bullpen, and Dravecky went into the rotation and was 7–5 the rest of the season after being just 3–7 for San Diego. The trade was also a sort of "addition by subtraction" chemistry deal for the Giants, in that Brown had worn out his welcome with both the San Francisco fans and Giants management. A great talent, Brown was always hurt and his dedication and desire had repeatedly come into question. He lasted barely one more season in San Diego, and was out of baseball by '89.

With improved pitching and attitude—plus two more separate trades with the Pirates by Rosen that brought in veterans Don Robinson and Rick Reuschel to further fortify the pitching—the Giants went on a strong second-half surge and won the NL West by six games over the Reds. Robinson, who came over from the Pirates July 31 for a catching prospect named Mackey Sasser, was installed by Craig as his closer and notched a career-high 19 saves. A week later, Rosen tapped the Bucs again for the veteran Reuschel, who wound up 13–9 and tied for the NL lead in complete games with 12. I've got to say, in all my years in baseball I never saw a general manager put together the pieces of a championship team in such short order as Rosen did that year. I know Craig was grateful to have a boss like Rosen, who went out and got him everything he needed to win the division.

Rosen really was a master trader. Two years earlier he had traded a backup catcher, Alex Trevino, to the Dodgers for outfielder Candy Maldonado. Maldonado had barely hit .250 with a total of 10 homers in two seasons with the Dodgers, and they obviously no longer considered him a prospect. But with the Giants he suddenly began to blossom and was a driving force on the '87 team, hitting .292 with 20 homers in 118 games.

While the 1987 Giants set a franchise record with 205 homers, they were by no means a super team. The closest to any potential superstar on the club was Will Clark, who in only his second year in the majors hit 35 homers, the most by a Giants first baseman since Willie McCovey's 39 in 1970. Another guy who made a big contribution was outfielder Jeffrey Leonard, who hit 19 homers and drove in 70.

Leonard was a big, tough guy with a gruff demeanor. He was scary looking, and his teammates gave him the uncomplimentary nickname "Penitentiary Face." But inside that fearsome image was one of the sweetest guys I ever knew in baseball. When I got to spring training, Leonard was distant and true to his image as someone you might just want to leave alone. Then one day I walked into the clubhouse in Scottsdale with my neck wrapped in the towel, and as Roger was showing me around, all of a sudden I heard someone mumble, "Who the hell is this guy?" It was Jeffrey Leonard.

I thought to myself, *I'll pick my spot here to deal with this guy.* The next day I walked up to him and got right in his face.

"You got a problem with me?" I said.

"Huh?" he said.

"Because if you do," I continued, "I'll knock you right on your ass!"

He looked at me, this bald, chubby old man some four inches shorter than he was, and cracked this big smile.

From that day on, we were best buddies.

Leonard hit four homers in the first four games of the '87 NLCS against the Cardinals to help the Giants take a 3–2 lead in games. But the Cardinals came back to shut the Giants out in Games 6 and 7 to advance to the World Series. There was disappointment but few regrets around the Giants, since they'd come so far to have such an unexpectedly successful season. I really got to like that team, and I especially liked San Francisco. After the season, I said to Soot, "I'd like to stay here. This is a great town."

"Good," she said. "I'm tired of moving around."

Still, I wanted a little security. I had never in my life as a coach worked with a two-year contract, but I had made up my mind I was going to ask for one when the time came. About two weeks later, the phone rang at my house in Treasure Island.

"Don Zimmer?" the voice on the other end said. "Al Rosen here. I'm getting ready to send out the contracts for next season, but I always like to talk to a guy first."

I didn't say anything and after the long pause, Rosen spoke again. "Are you there?" he said.

"Yeah," I said. "Am I allowed to say anything here?"

"Absolutely," Rosen said.

"Well, I want a raise and a two-year contract."

"You got it," he said, without even offering any resistance.

I figured everything was all set, and I was ready to finally settle down in my career, working in a great city with two great people in Craig and Rosen. Then a few days later, I was playing golf at Seminole Country Club with George Bamberger, who had coached with Frey under Earl Weaver for the Orioles in the '70s, and Billy Connors, who had been Frey's pitching coach with the Royals in 1980.

We were about to tee it up when Connors said to me, "Did you hear the news?"

"What news?" I said.

"Dallas Green resigned and Jim Frey is the new general manager of the Cubs."

After being fired by Green in 1986, Frey went the way of previous Cubs managers Charlie Grimm and Lou Boudreau, and stayed with the organization by going upstairs into the broadcasting booth. Now in a wild turn of events, he was back in power.

Connors didn't stop there, though.

"You got to get on the phone and call him, Zim," he said.

"What?" I said.

"You got to call him, Zim, right now," Connors persisted.

"I'm not calling Jim Frey. I'd never do that," I said. "I'll call him to congratulate him after he names a manager."

The next day ESPN, in announcing that Frey was taking over the Cubs, began speculating on whom he would select as manager. I was getting increasingly aggravated when they kept saying I was the No. 1 candidate because I went to school with him. *That's a helluva reason for hiring a guy to manage your ballclub*, I thought.

The fact was we were childhood friends, but some of the things I pulled on Frey back then would more likely have made him not hire me. One time in high school I convinced him to join me in taking a plane geometry class. I didn't even know how to spell plane geometry, much less understand it, but the teacher was this Mr. Ehler, who was known to give easy grades to athletes. The first few weeks of school go by, and I was doing just fine, sitting in the back of the room and making my B's. Then one Saturday night, Mr. Ehler dropped dead. I heard the news on Monday morning, and my first thought was, *Uh-oh. I ain't got a chance now.*

This young woman took over the class for Mr. Ehler, and on her very first day she called on me to solve a problem she'd written on the blackboard.

"Mr. Zimmer?" she said. "Do you want to solve this?"

I didn't even want to try and fool her.

"No ma'am," I said. "I can't."

I sat right down. I didn't want to embarrass myself. And as soon as the bell rang, I ran down the hall to the principal's office and got myself a transfer out of plane geometry into wood shop. For years afterward, Frey always told the story about how he wound up struggling through plane geometry while I was making lamps!

Now, of course, all the writers from Chicago started calling, and none of them believed I was telling the truth when I told them I hadn't spoken to Frey since he got the GM job, not even to congratulate him. Finally, I'd had enough and decided I was going to go to Las Vegas for a few days just to get away from it all. I instructed Soot not to tell anybody where I was, but if Jim Frey called, she could tell him.

The next night I was eating dinner at a place called Michael's in Las Vegas, where coincidentally, there were a lot of Cubs fans hanging out. I went back to my room at Bally's and saw the red message light on. It was from Frey, instructing me to call him.

The first time I called, he wasn't home. An hour later I called again, and this time he answered the phone.

"You want to manage the Cubs?" he said.

"Who wouldn't?" I replied.

"Well here's what you do," he said. "See what kind of flight you can get on for a noon press conference in Chicago tomorrow. I'll have Peter Durso, our traveling secretary, pick you up and take you to your hotel."

I got on the first flight to Chicago the next morning. All the while, however, Frey never said anything about salary or length of contract. Here I am flying to Chicago to be a manager again and I don't even know what I'm making! When I got to the Westin Hotel, Jimmy and John Madigan, the Cubs' board chairman from the Chicago Tribune Co., which owns the team, were waiting for me. The three of us got into a limousine and drove up to Wrigley Field. There was a lot of small talk during the ride but, again, still no mention of any terms of my contract.

After the press conference, we had a meeting in Frey's office, and I told him I wanted Joe Altobelli and Chuck Cottier as my coaches. I also knew Dick Pole, the Cubs' minor league pitching coach, from when he pitched for me with the Red Sox. I said I'd take him, too; and the Cubs were thrilled to give him a chance to be a major league coach. It wasn't until the next day, over dinner, that Jimmy told me he was giving me a two-year contract. Years later he always told the story about how loyal a guy I was not to even ask how much money or how many years on a contract I was getting to manage the Cubs.

10

My Kind of Town

T he Cubs team I took over in 1988 was in transition from the veteran team Frey had managed to the NL East title four years earlier. Of that '84 team, only Ryne Sandberg at second base and "the Hawk," Andre Dawson, in right field, were still around as regulars. We were breaking in some real promising young players—Rafael Palmeiro in left field, Mark Grace at first base, Damon Berryhill at catcher, and a 22-year-old righthanded starting pitcher named Greg Maddux.

Maddux's rookie season in 1987 had been a rude and rough baptism for him: He was 6–14 with a 5.61 ERA. But over the winter he had pitched in the Caribbean under the tutelage of Dick Pole, and I could tell right away when I saw him in the spring of '88 he was going to be a good pitcher. Maddux already had the stuff. Pole taught him what to do with it, and that season he emerged as the ace of the Cubs staff. At 18–8 he was my only starter to win more games than he lost. Rick Sutcliffe, who was still battling shoulder problems, was my No. 2 starter at 13–14.

Maddux is without question one of the greatest competitors of any pitcher I ever managed. The reason he's become the Hall of Fame–bound pitcher he is, winning four Cy Young Awards (not to mention nine Gold Gloves), is because he studies hitters tirelessly. While you'll see so many other pitchers today sitting in the clubhouse in a lounge chair, watching the opposing team's hitters on TV or videos, Maddux is always right there in the dugout watching them live. Anybody who tells you they can learn more about a hitter off TV is full of it. Maddux is a student of pitching who pitches as much with his head as with his arm. I've known him to throw ball three on a 2–2 count just to get to a 3–2 changeup because everyone is expecting a fastball!

Grace's emergence as the Cubs' first baseman for the next decade and beyond was the result of Leon Durham being out of shape and basically playing himself off the ballclub. Durham had been the Cubs' regular first baseman since 1981 and had hit a career-high 27 homers in 1987. But when he came to spring training in '88, he was overweight and I went up to him on the first day he reported to camp and said, "Man, you've got to lose that!"

"Don't worry, Skip," he said. "I'll be in shape by Opening Day."

"Okay," I said, "but I've got a young player ready to take your job."

Grace had played only two seasons of minor league ball, winning a batting title at Class A Peoria his first year, and leading the Double-A Eastern League in RBIs his second. The intention was to send him to Triple A for one more year of minor league seasoning in '88, even though most of our people felt he could make the jump right to the big leagues. He was that good.

I watched Durham carefully all spring and didn't like what I was seeing. He'd do the obligatory eight wind sprints in the outfield after games, but never any extra. It was clear he wasn't losing any weight. With a week to go in spring training, I told him, "What you've done here in the past is what's earned you a place on this club to start the season. But from here on in, it's up to you to keep it."

We sent Grace out to Iowa and Durham began the season at first base. He just couldn't move over there, and I didn't see that work ethic I had seen from him back in '84 and '85. I liked him, but he was barely hitting over .200 after the first 24 games, and it got to a point where in a game against the Giants I played Manny Trillo, a righthanded-hitting utility infielder, against a righthanded pitcher instead of the lefthanded-hitting Durham.

Frey called me after the game and said, "Is Durham hurt?"

"No," I said. "He just can't play. I suggest you get Grace here tomorrow."

Frey obliged, trading Durham home to Cincinnati. Grace came up and hit .296, and he was there hitting .300 year after year through the 2000 season, when he finally gave way to a couple of rookies and moved on to Arizona. He was a good first baseman when he joined us, but my coach, Joe Altobelli, deserves all the credit for making him an excellent first baseman who went on to win four Gold Gloves. Before Altobelli started working with him, he couldn't throw the ball to second base. They put in hours of practice together, and Grace got to be able to make that throw as good as any first baseman in the game.

Grace was a contact hitter who wanted to learn every aspect of the game. I'd have him squeezing, hitting-and-running—everything—and if he'd pop the ball up or swing at a bad pitch, he'd come in to me and say, "It's okay, Skip. Just keep putting it on. I'll get it right." The one thing Mark Grace wanted to do was win.

Because we were pretty much a work in progress in 1988, Frey didn't make many moves. His only in-season trade of consequence was sending center fielder Dave Martinez, another promising young player, to Montreal for Mitch Webster. Webster was a switch-hitter who really only hit lefthanded. He gave me a little more versatility and a good lefthanded bat (with limited power) off the bench. Otherwise, the '88 season, in which we finished fourth, 77–85, was mostly about our kids. Besides Maddux's and Grace's breakthroughs, Palmeiro hit .307 to finish runner-up to Tony Gwynn in the batting race; Berryhill wrested the No. 1 catching job from veteran Jody Davis; and Jamie Moyer, a hard-luck 25-year-old lefthander, had a 3.48 ERA despite winning only nine of his 24 decisions.

Frey's one prominent free-agent signing of the offseason was Vance Law, a 31-year-old third baseman who had previously had a couple of good seasons with the White Sox. Law did a real good job for me, hitting .293 with 78 RBIs—19 more than his previous career high.

The thing I suppose I'll most remember about the 1988 season was the introduction of lights to Wrigley Field after 82 years of the ballpark's existence. The historic occasion took place August 8—or at least it started to take place that night. The Cubs were leading the Phillies 3–1 in the fourth inning when thunderstorms and heavy showers hit Chicago. After a 2 hour 10 minute wait, the umpires called the game. The "official" first Wrigley Field night game was then switched to the following night against the Mets, which we won 6-4 after breaking a 2–2 tie with four runs in the seventh inning. I, for one, kind of welcomed the instituting of night baseball at Wrigley. It felt pretty good to sleep in till 10 o'clock for a change. I don't buy the theory about the Cubs never winning because of the toll all those day games took on them. They never won for one simple reason: They weren't run well.

Phil Wrigley, the chewing gum heir who owned the Cubs all those years from the 1930s into the '60s, was a nice man who simply didn't know anything about baseball. He ran the Cubs on a tight budget, especially when it came to scouting and player development, and he didn't seem to mind if they never won. The Cubs were just a hobby to him, and he was content to see Wrigley Field filled with happy fans every afternoon for day baseball. One time, Billy Connors and I were having this conversation about why the Cubs were continually so bad all those years. "All you have to do," said Connors, "is look at their No. 1 draft picks for the last 15 years."

With that, he went into the manager's office and got out a Cubs press guide. I was astounded as he reeled them off. In order, from 1965–80 the roll call of No. 1 Cubs draft picks was: Rick James, Dean Burke, Terry Hughes, Ralph Rickey, Roger Metzger, Gene Hiser, Jeff Wehmeier, Brian Vernoy, Jerry Tabb, Scot Thompson, Brian Rosinski, Herman Segelke, Randy Martz, Bill Hayes, Jon Perlman, and Don Schulze. I'm sure they all came from nice families, but other than Metzger, I never heard of any of them. Metzger was the only one who ever spent any significant time in the big leagues—and that was in Houston where he was traded after playing one game for the Cubs. They say even a blind squirrel can somehow find one acorn, yet in 15 straight years the Cubs' scouting and player development department was 0-for-15. You tell me why they had one losing season after another?

It wasn't until Dallas Green and his top player development man, Gordon Goldsberry, took over in 1981 that the Cubs finally began to mine some considerable homegrown talent. I was the first beneficiary of that with the development of Shawon Dunston, Maddux, Palmeiro, Grace, Moyer, Berryhill, and in 1989 Jerome Walton and Dwight Smith.

A prime reason for our inability to compete in 1988 was the absence of a closer. Frey and I had hoped we'd rectified that problem with his acquisition of Goose Gossage from the Padres in February in exchange for veteran outfielder Keith Moreland and catcher Mike Brumley. It was my idea to get Gossage. I'd remembered him from 1983 with the Yankees when he won 13 games and saved 22 before moving on to the Padres as a free agent. Unfortunately, there was a reason the Padres let Gossage go to us. He was now 36 and no longer had that overpowering fastball and slider that had made him the most intimidating closer in baseball from 1977–85. I knew we weren't getting the Goose of 1978, but as I kept going to him in save situation after save situation, it was distressing to see he simply couldn't get the job done anymore. It got so bad that as soon as I'd get him up in the bullpen, fans started booing. I would bring him in anyway, and then we'd have to walk back to the dugout together, both getting booed, after I had to take him out. It didn't bother me that I was getting booed. It bothered me for him because he'd been such a great pitcher.

One day Goose made a statement in the newspapers directed at me, something about the way he was being used. The next day he came to me to apologize. I accepted his apology and chalked it up to frustration. Then a few days later we lost a game to Houston, 7–4, and once again I had to go out and get him. When I got to the mound, he flipped the ball to me instead of handing it over. Now I was angry with him. When I got back to the dugout, he was standing there instead of having gone up the stairs into the clubhouse. We got into a really heated argument that began with him shouting, "If you had a little more confidence in me, I'd be a better pitcher."

"Confidence?" I yelled back. "I've brought you into every save situation a man could be brought into!"

At that point Chuck Cottier, one of my coaches, interceded.

"You're out of line, Goose," he said.

After Gossage went up to the clubhouse, I said to Cottier, "After the game, he's gonna want to apologize, but I've had enough of his apologizing."

Sure enough, he was waiting by my office door after the game ended. I told him to go to his locker, that we were having a meeting. I was still seething at the meeting with my coaches. I said in all my years in baseball the one thing I wouldn't tolerate is a pitcher flipping me the ball when I came to take them out.

I fined Goose $500 for his actions but continued to use him as our closer the rest of the year, mainly because I didn't have anybody else. We hardly spoke after that incident with Houston, and the following spring we released him. For years after, we ducked each other. Despite what had happened, though, I didn't think it was right for us to be this way. I understood his frustration. This was a proud man with a Hall of Fame resume, and it wasn't easy dealing with the fact he couldn't dominate hitters anymore.

Then in the spring of 1994, I was coaching for the new expansion team, the Colorado Rockies, who trained in Tucson, and Goose was trying to make the Mariners, who were training in the Phoenix area and managed by his old Yankee teammate, Lou Piniella. Our paths hadn't crossed in over five years when the Mariners came to Tucson for an exhibition game. There was an American Legion game going on prior to our game, and while we were waiting to take the field, everyone from both clubs was mingling on the sidelines. All of a sudden I spotted Goose about two feet away from me. I wanted to get this thing straightened out once and for all, and apparently so did he. He came over to me and said, "We've got to have a talk."

I told him, "I felt I had a right to say the things I said to you. I was that pissed off. But at the same time, I understand what you were going through."

He said, "Zim, I acted like a jerk. I know you gave me every opportunity. I was just horseshit and I didn't deal with it very well."

I felt really good after that talk, because despite everything that happened I always liked Goose. I thought down deep he was a good person and in his day he was a great pitcher. I only wish he could have still been a great pitcher for me in 1988. Ever since that day in Arizona, we've been the best of friends. I've looked forward to seeing him at spring training with the Yankees when he comes to camp as a special coach, and I even more look forward to seeing him someday getting his deserved plaque in Cooperstown.

I had one other problem with a player in 1988, although not nearly as highly charged as the thing with Goose. Jody Davis had been the Cubs' No. 1 catcher since 1982, but he had started to slip a little, and with the emergence of Berryhill there was increasing talk about him getting traded. Like Gossage, he didn't handle his situation well, and every day it seemed he'd be making cracks to other players like "What team am I going to today?" As he kept it up, I started getting really tired of listening to his crap. Then one day he put a calendar up on his locker with a picture of a bear on it. He inscribed on it: "Thirty days till hunting season." I thought that was really weak, but I also knew he wasn't going to be with us the following year so I let him have his good time. If I thought he was going to be a member of the Cubs in 1989, I'd have never allowed it.

Jody was a big favorite with the fans at Wrigley Field and he did a good job for four or five years. Every time he'd come to bat, they'd start chanting "Jo-dy, Jo-dy." When the season started I was told he'd caught too many games in the past couple of years and that's why he wore out. So I told him, "I'm gonna catch you five games a week and Berryhill two."

"Great," he said. "That's fine with me."

But he wasn't catching or hitting very well, and Berryhill just took advantage. By midseason Berryhill was No. 1 and Davis couldn't handle that. He started taking a lot of it out on Frey.

I didn't want this to happen, but there was nothing I could do. Berryhill simply outplayed him. Finally, with three days to go in the season, we traded Davis to the Braves for two minor leaguers who never became major leaguers. It was all we could get for him, but if he thought we were wrong in our decision about him, the Braves apparently felt the same way. He was the backup catcher for them too in 1989 and hit just .169. A year later his career was over.

After the season, Frey and I sat down and assessed our needs for 1989, and we both agreed a closer had to be our No. 1 priority. When we got to the winter meetings in Atlanta, the Texas Rangers approached our chief scout and point man, "Uncle Hughie" Alexander, with a trade proposal. They would give us Mitch Williams, a hard-throwing, 24-year-old lefthanded reliever who had saved 18 games for them in 1987. Williams was known to be wild at times, but all of our scouts agreed he had closer stuff. In exchange for him, however, the Rangers wanted Rafael Palmeiro. Everybody knew Palmeiro was going to be a consistent .300 hitter for years to come. But he had no power and wasn't a run-producer. He'd get his hits it seemed when nobody was on base. That was then, when he was only 24. Today, of course, he's one of the best overall hitters in baseball. With Palmeiro and Williams as the principals, we put together a 10-player deal with Texas.

Baseball historians may look back on it and ask how we could have traded a hitter of Palmeiro's potential, but the fact is we won a division title with that deal, and there's no way to measure what that meant to the city of Chicago. It took a couple of more years before Palmeiro began to combine power and production with his textbook .300 stroke. For us in 1989, Williams saved 38 games and led the league with 76 appearances.

The first day of the season, against the Phillies at Wrigley Field, I got to find out just what to expect from Mitch. I brought him into the game with one out in the eighth inning after Mike Schmidt had hit a home run to bring the Phillies to within 5–4. He managed to get the last two outs of that inning, but not before issuing two walks and a balk. Now came the ninth, and the first Philadelphia batter, Bob Dernier, hit a broken-bat single to center. The next batter, Tommy Herr, hit a line-drive single to left. With Von Hayes up, the Phillies put the sacrifice on, but Mitch got ahead in the count 0–2. Forced to swing away, Hayes hit a grounder to deep short that went for another base hit. Bases loaded, nobody out. Terrific.

I figured there's no way he gets out of this mess, but who am I going to bring in? This is the guy we got to be our closer. I can't pull the plug on him on opening day. So I sat there and squirmed as Mitch proceeded to strike out the next three batters in a row, starting with Schmidt! After the game the writers all came in and started talking about how Mitch was overpowering but was also overthrowing. I said, "Bullshit, overthrowing. That's the way he always pitches."

Not long after that, they started calling him "Wild Thing," which was the nickname that stuck with him the rest of his career. I said to myself after that first game, "I'm not gonna let this guy bother me with ball one, ball two. Nevertheless, I found myself on the edge of my seat almost every time I called him into a game and he'd throw one pitch after another further out of the strike zone. I never could figure out how he could throw three balls in a row so far out of the strike zone and then come back and throw three straight strikes. That was his style, though. He wasn't a Mariano Rivera by a longshot, but he pitched us to the playoffs. Every time he'd save a game that year he'd come into my office and say, "Did you lose any more hair tonight?" I know I did.

Coming out of spring training, I could never have imagined the kind of season we were going to have. We looked absolutely horrible all spring, going 9–23 in the Cactus League.

When we got off to a 1–5 spring training start, I called my old pal John Vukovich, who had coached with me under Frey in my first term with the Cubs and was now coaching for the Phillies.

"How's it going?" Vuke asked.

"We're right on schedule," I replied, "winning one out of every six."

The Saturday night before we were to break camp, Frey and I had dinner to commiserate with each other.

"Any way we can win 81 games this year?" Frey asked me.

"Are you nuts?" I answered.

"Well, if we do," Frey said, "you and I will walk down Michigan Avenue arm-in-arm celebrating."

After the first 35 games of the season we were 17–18, and I was tickled to death. Everybody in the world had thought we'd wind up last and here we were at least holding our own. In early June we actually found ourselves in a three-way tie for first place with the Mets and Expos. A month earlier the Expos had made a controversial trade with Seattle in which they sent their No. 1 pitching prospect, 6-foot-10 lefthander Randy Johnson, and two other young pitchers, Brian Holman and Gene Harris, to the Mariners for Mark Langston. Although they gave up Johnson, Langston was an established winning pitcher in the major leagues, and this was supposedly the deal that would win the pennant for them. Instead, the deal completely backfired on them. They went 20–37 over the last two months of the season, and then Langston walked as a free agent, signing a five-year deal with the Angels. Johnson, of course, more than lived up to his potential and became one of the most feared and formidable pitchers in baseball with the Mariners over the next eight years, before moving on the Astros and Diamondbacks.

We lost seven in a row at the end of June, and then things started coming together for us. An 18–9 July got us back into first place, and suddenly everyone started thinking we might really have something here. Williams had 22 saves by the All-Star break, Maddux was well on his way to a tremendous 19–12, 2.95 ERA season, and Shawon Dunston came into his own at shortstop, making only one error after

July 1. Another big performer in our July surge was Jerome Walton, our rookie center fielder, who put together a major league-high 30-game hitting streak from July 21–August 20.

The first time I saw Walton in the spring, he tried to bunt with two strikes and fouled it off. I didn't like that but I left him alone, and as the spring went on, he started getting more and more hits, a lot of them with two strikes. I could see he had talent. He could hit, run, and cover all the ground in center field. He wound up hitting .293 with 24 stolen bases in '89 and was named Rookie of the Year after the season. Unfortunately, he was never the same player after that, for reasons I never could understand.

The following spring, I couldn't help but notice Walton moping around. When we started playing the exhibition games, I knew I wasn't seeing the same guy who had been so important to our championship run the year before. He wasn't hustling and wasn't going after fly balls the same way and was mostly in a funk. Finally I called him into my office and asked him if there was a problem.

"Yeah," he said, "But it's not your problem. It's got to do with my contract. They didn't treat me right."

I never wanted to know anything about players' contracts because so often there are performance clauses in them that can be affected by the manager. Without asking him to be more specific, I said to him, "Did you sign it?"

"Yeah," he said.

"Well," I said, "the right thing to do is to go out and live up to your end of it so that next year you can go back to them and tell them what you want."

He just wouldn't do it, though. A couple of years later, the Cubs flat out released him, and he bounced around from team to team, never approaching that first season. It was a real shame.

The '89 season was truly a collective effort. I was never part of a team that executed better than the '89 Cubs, or had so many different people give peak performances. You manage according to your team, and they were a team that could run and do all the little things it takes to win ballgames. With the Red Sox I didn't have any speed, so I had to always manage for the big inning. The '89 Cubs were a totally different ballclub, and I couldn't believe their success ratio in executing all the plays I kept putting on. Managing is a lot like the horse track. You get on a lucky a streak for a couple of weeks and then all of a sudden everything turns to garbage. The Cubs that year had a lucky streak the entire season. It got to a point where the media started calling me a genius, which was really embarrassing to me. Finally I had to call a meeting with my players to set the record straight.

"I don't want you guys paying any attention to all this 'genius' bullshit they're writing about in the papers," I said. "I ain't done nothing here. We're succeeding because you guys are doing it all. Squeeze, hit-and-run. You've done it. I'm getting too much credit here. I'm not managing any different than when I was in San Diego, losing 100 games a season. All I can do is put the plays on. If you guys don't execute them, they're worthless."

Good players always make the manager. I'm not taking anything away from Joe Torre, but he'd be the first to tell you there was a reason he became a championship manager with the Yankees after getting fired by the Mets, Braves, and Cardinals.

We also had a lot of guys come out of nowhere to make big contributions in '89. Berryhill was disabled from Opening Day with a bum shoulder, and for a long period of time we had to make do with a pair of rookies, Joe Girardi and Rick Wrona, who despite their inexperience combined to do a great job in handling the pitching staff. There were at least three games where Wrona got a big hit with a man on third base. Three other times I squeezed with him on 1–2 counts, and all three times he laid a perfect bunt down the first base line.

Over the winter Frey had picked up a righthanded-hitting bench player, Lloyd McClendon, from the Reds. McClendon could catch, too. He also could play first base and the outfield, and he filled in at all of those positions while hitting .286 with 12 homers and 40 RBIs in just 92 games. For a guy I knew nothing about when we got him, Mac turned out to be a manager's dream. And in 2000 he became a manager himself when the Pirates promoted him from batting coach to replace my pal Gene Lamont.

Another bench guy I hadn't figured on was Dwight Smith, a left-handed-hitting outfielder who we called up from Iowa on May 1 to platoon in left field with McClendon. Smith proved to be the biggest surprise of all. He was a little shaky in the outfield, but he could flat-out hit. He batted .324 in 343 at bats, the highest average for a Cubs rookie since 1922.

There's no question our farm system really provided us with a lift in '89. Another farm product, righthanded reliever Les Lancaster, came up on June 24 and did a tremendous job setting up Williams— although I've got to say it was purely by necessity, since neither Frey nor I wanted any part of him. Lancaster had been up early in the season, and besides not getting anybody out, he had what I felt was a bad attitude. He was kind of a wise guy who'd either come in late or just walk around like he had everything made. When I finally sent him down to Iowa early in the season, he made a big stink about it. Once down there, I found out he was continually knocking Frey and me, and had even gotten himself a dartboard with Frey's and my picture on it which he used for his recreation in the clubhouse.

A couple of weeks after he'd been sent to Iowa, the Cubs had an exhibition game scheduled there. As it happened, the Iowa team had been on the road and we got to the ballpark that afternoon before they did. Somebody told Frey and me about the dartboard and suggested we check out the Iowa clubhouse. Sure enough, there it was, with a hundred or so little holes in it from Lancaster and his pals throwing darts at our faces. Well, Frey was livid, and I was really pissed too—not just at Lancaster but even more at the Iowa manager, Pete Mackanin, for allowing this in his clubhouse. I mean, Frey was Mackanin's boss!

I looked at the dartboard and said, "Isn't this beautiful?"

Frey said, "Make sure the clubhouse guy puts this thing on our plane. I'm taking this back to Chicago."

But when we got on the plane, the dartboard wasn't there. Someone must have gotten wind of what was going on and stole the dartboard back. Meanwhile, Frey had aired out Lancaster, telling him, "You will never pitch for the Chicago Cubs again."

Well, come mid-June we started having all sorts of pitching problems with guys getting hurt, and it coincided with us losing six of eight. We put a call in to Iowa for a relief pitcher, and then Pat Perry, another reliever, developed arm trouble. Now we were really in a bind, and Frey asked me what I wanted to do.

"I don't care," I said. "Send me anybody. We need a body. In fact, send me Lancaster if you have to."

"Are you crazy?" Frey said. "That'll never happen."

I said, "At least he's pitched in the big leagues and has a little experience. If he doesn't do the job, we'll just send him back. At this point we've got nothing to lose."

I wish I could say I could believe what happened when Lancaster came up, but I still can't. He was nothing short of unhittable, at one point setting a Cubs record by pitching 30⅔ consecutive shutout innings of relief. I used him mostly as a set-up man to Williams, but one time Mitch went nuts when I brought Lancaster in to finish one of his games for him. There's just no explaining Lancaster's turnaround, but his attitude changed too, and he later thanked me for giving him another chance. He got a huge raise the next year, and even after the Cubs released him in March 1992, he wound up making over a million dollars with the Cardinals.

Then there was Mike Bielecki, a 30-year-old righthander who Frey acquired from Pittsburgh in May of the previous year. In three undistinguished seasons with the Pirates, Bielecki bounced back and forth from starting to relieving, and was 10–14 overall when they gave up on him. Going into spring training, I wasn't sure Bielecki would even make our staff. But after pitching just so-so for me in 1988, he went to winter ball and, like Maddux the year before, hooked up with Dick Pole, who taught him a split-fingered fastball. Bielecki started the season in the bullpen, but it wasn't long before he pitched himself into the rotation and wound up as our No. 2 winner behind Maddux with an 18–7 record and 3.14 ERA.

If there was one position where we simply couldn't get any production in 1989, it was third base. After the fine season he gave me in 1988, Law went backwards in '89 and really struggled with the bat, hitting .235 with only seven homers. A few days before the last trading deadline, on August 31, Frey came to me and asked what I needed. I told him I could use a third baseman and another extra player with some speed.

On the morning of the deadline, Frey called and said he'd made a trade with San Diego. He sent Darrin Jackson, a promising backup outfielder, and Calvin Schiradli, a righthanded pitcher we'd gotten from Boston the year before, to the Padres in exchange for third base-man Luis Salazar and outfielder Marvell Wynne.

I loved Darrin Jackson, a tremendous kid who later made a coura-geous comeback from cancer. But he'd had a tough season with the bat in '89 and looked like he was going to need more time in the minors. We were trying to win now and couldn't afford to wait for him. While he later had some good seasons with the Padres and White Sox, the trade couldn't have worked out better for us. Salazar was everything and more I could have wished for at third base that final month of the season, with one timely hit after another. In just 26 games for us, he hit .325 with 12 RBIs. One time, however, he popped up to lead off an inning, and as he came in to the bench, everybody started shaking his hand. I'm thinking, "What's going on here? Am I missing something?"

The next inning he sat down next to me and said, "Thanks, Skip. I just got a $30,000 bonus for that at bat."

You'll forgive me if I state here, for the record, this is a part of baseball I can't relate to. When I was playing, I was happy just to *get* an at bat.

Salazar knew how to play, though. With a man on second base, you could always count on him hitting the ball to right field. You didn't need any signs for him. He knew what to do.

The following winter, I was home in Treasure Island when I received this box in the mail. Inside it was a miniature TV. It was a gift from Luis Salazar with a note thanking me for giving him the opportunity to be part of a playoff team. In all my years in baseball I'd never gotten a gift from a player. I felt like he'd given me a mil-lion dollars.

But as much as Salazar, Walton, McClendon, Smith, Bielecki, Girardi, Wrona, and Lancaster contributed, I wouldn't want to give the impression that we won the 1989 NL East title entirely with over-achieving rookies and former humpties. Ryne Sandberg had a little bit to do with our success, too.

By 1989 Sandberg had more than given Phillies owner Bill Giles regret over making him the "throw-in" player in the Bowa-for-DeJesus trade in 1982. He'd had seven sensational seasons with the Cubs. In 1984, our division championship year under Frey, he led the league in triples with 19, runs with 114, and stole 32 bases to be named National League Most Valuable Player in only his third full year in the majors. He followed that up by hitting .305 with 113 runs scored in '85, and won Gold Gloves at second base every year from 1983–88.

Early in the 1985 season, before a game, Sandberg was standing next to the batting cage, waiting for his turn to hit when Frey walked over to him. I was hitting fungoes to the infielders and I heard Frey say to him: "Hey, Ryno, you know how you can really help me win some games?"

"No, how?" Sandberg answered.

"I know you can hit the ball up the middle and to right field," Frey said. "I'm not trying to make you a home run hitter, but when you get a count in your favor, 2–0, 3–0, or even 3–1, I want you to look for a fastball in the middle of the plate and hit a home run into the left field seats."

Wouldn't you know? Sandberg wound up hitting 26 homers in '85, and from that year on was regarded as a rare power-hitting second baseman. In 1989 he hit .290 with 30 homers and 76 RBIs, and led the league in runs again with 104. He should have won another MVP Award, and probably didn't only because of all the other people we had working together at winning the NL East.

I've got to say this: If Sandberg isn't a Hall of Famer, then I'm a baseball dummy. All this guy ever did was hit, hit for power, steal bases, and play the hell out of second base. He never made more than six or seven errors a year! In 1985 he became the first National League second baseman since Rogers Hornsby in 1925 to lead the league in homers, and he also set a record with 123 consecutive errorless games. I've heard about the reputation he had for not diving for balls. Well, there are guys who simply can't leave their feet. Junior Gilliam couldn't dive either, but how does that make him a bad second baseman?

Sandberg was a quiet player, just like the Hawk. And also like Dawson, he played hurt. You'd send him home into a collision at the plate, and the next day he'd be taping his ankle and leg, never saying a thing. He never wanted anyone to know he was hurting.

Dawson was the same way. All those years playing on artificial turf in Montreal destroyed his knees. By the time he came to the Cubs in 1987, he was playing on hollow knees. Still, he led the league that year in both homers (49) and RBIs (137), and became the only player in history to win an MVP Award for a last-place club.

"The Hawk" was hurt a lot of 1989 and hit only .252 with 21 homers in 118 games. Most of his big hitting came at the end of the year—"crunch time." People don't know how bad his knees were. He'd tape them up to take bp, come into the clubhouse, un-tape them, and take treatment on them from the trainer, then tape them up all over again for the game. By the end of his career, there was no cartilage at all left in his knees. He was a very special person. If there was one thing about the 1989 season I have regrets about it was the playoffs against the Giants. Not because we lost, but because Andre tried so hard and just couldn't help us. It killed me seeing him come up to bat so many times with men on base and just not be able to get a base hit. He had hit homers and doubles every day down the stretch to help us get to the playoffs—that was pressure. But he just hit one of those unexplainable slumps in the playoffs.

Between Dawson and Sandberg, you couldn't find two more quiet leaders. You barely got a "hello" from them. But if a guy hoots and hollers and can't play a lick, does that make him a leader? Dawson and Sandberg led by sheer example.

In September we took command of the '89 race in the NL East, with 18 wins in our last 29 games. The Cardinals made one last-gasp challenge, winning 11 of 15 at one point in the middle of September. We were scheduled to finish the season in St. Louis, and I didn't want us to be in the position of having to win even one of those three games to clinch the division title. My concerns were put to rest with four games remaining when we beat the Expos 3–2 in Montreal behind Maddux, and the Cardinals lost their second straight game in Pittsburgh.

We finished 93–69, a far cry from what I had envisioned way back in Mesa, and took the division by six games. Without any question, that clinching night in Montreal was my biggest thrill ever in baseball. Frey came into the clubhouse after the game, grabbed me and screamed, "Screw 'em! Screw 'em all! We did it!"

Later, Frey took Peter Durso, Ned Colletti, and myself up to his suite at the hotel, and we stayed up all night telling stories, drinking beer, and reliving the greatest season of my career. There may not have been any champagne or tickertape parades, but I celebrated like I've never celebrated anything in baseball before or after.

After the season, I was named Manager of the Year, a wonderful honor that was nevertheless nothing more than a testimony to the players I had. They called the '89 Cubs "the Boys of Zimmer," and my players made me a real big celebrity in Chicago. How big? I was doing commercials for both a diet center and a fried chicken chain. You don't get much bigger than that. I had all the bases covered.

The one "down" in that wonderful season was losing my mom, Lorraine. She'd been very ill all season, but she said to me, "I'm not going to die until you win a championship." After we lost in the play-offs, she passed away.

I wish the 1989 season had an encore after the pennant race was won. Unfortunately, like every other season going all the way back to 1945, a Cubs World Series was not to be. My old pal Roger Craig and his Giants beat us four games to one in a series that became almost a private hitting forum for Grace and Will Clark.

Between the two of them, Grace and Clark had 24 hits, all of them solid, in the five games. Grace went 11-for-17 with three doubles, a homer, and eight RBIs for us, while Clark was 13-for-20 with three doubles, two homers, and eight RBIs for the Giants.

We were pounded 11–3 in the first game as Clark went 4-for-4 with both his homers and six RBIs. In the second game, it was Grace's turn to retaliate, going 3-for-4 with a pair of doubles and four RBIs in leading us to a 9–5 win. We lost Game 3, 5–4, when Lancaster gave up a two-run homer to Robby Thompson in the seventh inning. Game 4 was decided when I allowed my lefthanded reliever Steve Wilson to pitch to Kevin Mitchell with runners at second and third in the eighth inning and a 4–3 lead. There were two lefthanded hitters coming up after Mitchell, and I didn't want to leave Wilson with no margin for error by walking Mitch intentionally to load the bases. So with Mitchell waiting to hit, I went out to the mound and told Wilson what I wanted.

"Pitch him inside," I said, "and don't leave anything out over the plate. If we walk him, we walk him, but keep the ball inside."

Wilson did the best job he could and so did Mitchell, who fought off 11 pitches before finally getting the one he wanted, out over the plate. As I watched Mitchell's homer sail over the left field fence for a 6–4 Giants lead, I couldn't fault Wilson. It was just one of those things where he got beat by a professional hitter. You could only tip your cap to Mitchell for a great at bat.

The last game was equally tough. The game was tied 1–1 in the eighth inning and Bielecki had pitched brilliantly for us. With two out in the eighth, he suddenly lost his control and walked three straight batters, bringing Clark to the plate. I brought in Williams, who immediately got ahead 0–2 on Clark. But like Mitchell the game before, Clark battled back, taking a ball, then fouling off three straight pitches before getting a fastball out over the plate—which he smashed through the middle for a two-run single.

I was criticized afterward for staying too long with Bielecki and, in hindsight, maybe I did. There are maybe four or five times during the course of a season where you've got a guy warmed up in the bullpen and you ask your pitcher how he feels. The other 150 times you go out to the mound knowing what you're going to do and the pitcher isn't going to change your mind.

I went out to Bielecki after the second walk and said, "How do you feel?"

"I feel as strong as I was in the first inning," he insisted.

If he'd said anything else, he would have been gone. Up to that point he'd pitched so great and I said to myself, "What's one more hitter?"

Bad as I felt about losing the NLCS and not being able to take it one more level, I felt especially heartsick for Dawson, who had a terribly frustrating series that culminated with him striking out with the bases loaded in the ninth inning of Game 5. I know one thing: There isn't anyone else I would have wanted up there for us in that situation. "Hawk" was such a warrior and, as I said before, one of the greatest players—and people—I ever managed. I couldn't believe it when some reporter actually asked me why I didn't pinch hit for him!

Even though everything imaginable went right for the Cubs in 1989, I could not have foreseen us falling off so badly in 1990. But just as in 1985 under Frey, our pitching simply fell apart on us.

Sutcliffe, who we had hoped would be able to come back from his shoulder problems, didn't throw a pitch for us until August 29. Mike Harkey, a rookie for whom we had high expectations after injuries in 1989 had postponed his arrival, was sidelined twice for extensive periods with shoulder tendinitis. Shawn Boskie, another rookie we had counted on, went down with an elbow injury on August 4, and Maddux and Bielecki simply had off years.

The bullpen was equally decimated, especially after Williams stumbled and tore up his knee and had to undergo surgery. Lancaster's magic act in '89 became a disappearing act in 1990, when we again had to send him to the minors because of ineffectiveness. He did come back in September to save a couple of games as my closer replacement for Williams. Two other long relievers I had banked on, Bill Long and Jeff Pico, also succumbed to injuries.

We were never in the race in 1990, finishing 77–85 in fourth place, 18 games out. The only bright spots were Sandberg, who hit 40 homers and became the first National League second baseman since Rogers Hornsby in 1925 to win the home run title; and Dawson, who defied all his critics who thought he was finished by hitting .310 with 27 homers and 100 RBIs.

After the season, Frey and I agreed we had three primary needs: a new closer, since we didn't know if Mitch was ever going to be the same again after his knee surgery, another starting pitcher, and a power-hitting outfielder. That winter we filled all three needs in the free-agent market—or so we thought. We signed reliever Dave Smith, who had saved 23 games for the Astros in 1990, lefthander Danny Jackson, a 23-game winner two years earlier, and George Bell, the American League MVP for Toronto in 1987. The combined cost for the Tribune Co., which owned the Cubs, was nearly $30 million.

As the spring got going and we started playing exhibition games, a young third baseman named Gary Scott quickly caught everybody's eye. This kid put on some show, hitting and fielding. Halfway through spring training, it was a no-brainer. He was my third baseman. The only question was where he'd hit in the lineup.

In a way, Scott's total reversal of form when the season started mirrored the entire ballclub. All of a sudden he couldn't hit anything, and he wasn't making the plays at third. I couldn't believe I was looking at the same guy I'd seen all spring. Finally, after 31 games, he was hitting .165 and we had to send him back to Iowa.

Neither Smith, Jackson, nor Bell lived up to expectations either. Smith and Jackson had arm injuries and couldn't pitch, and Bell didn't hit. After a six-game winning streak in early April, we lost eight of the next 10, and a reporter asked me: "How do you feel sitting here with no contract for next year?"

I said, "That'll take care of itself. Bell's gonna hit, Dave Smith is gonna start saving games, and Jackson's gonna win his share before it's all over."

Now the reporter went to Don Grenesko, the Tribune-appointed club president, who responded: "Zimmer's got a contract for this year and we'll evaluate him at the All-Star break."

When I read that, I hit the roof. I went to Frey and said, "I want to talk to this guy Grenesko."

"I wouldn't do that," Frey cautioned. "Let it lie. You'll cool off tomorrow."

The next day, however, I hadn't cooled off at all. I told Frey again, I wanted to speak to Grenesko.

"Just leave it alone," Frey pleaded. "The guy knows nothing about baseball. Why go in there and ask for trouble?"

"Because I have to live my own life," I said.

Frey was afraid I was going to go in to Grenesko and raise hell. I wasn't going to do that. All I wanted was to get a clarification from him that I wasn't on some sort of trial until the All-Star break. Just the same, Frey decided to go with me.

In the meeting with Grenesko, I never raised my voice. What I said was, "I don't think your comments helped our club."

His response was, "Well, I didn't know you were going to take it so personal."

I said, "What does it mean, after being here for two years and after all I've accomplished, that I'm going to be evaluated at the All-Star break?"

He didn't really have an answer for that, and after we left his office, Jimmy said to me, "This could cost you your job, you know."

Grenesko went back to the Tribune Co. and called the chairman, Stanton Cook, and the president, Andy McKenna. They should have been able to hear my side of the story, but they never did. The next day, Grenesko came out in the press saying I made all these demands. All I said to him was: "Let me know by June 30 whether you still want me to manage this team." He made it sound like I had demanded a new contract, something that never even came up.

It made him look good, which was horseshit in my opinion. I never knocked anybody after being fired, but I did with Grenesko—and I will continue doing so for the rest of my life. He wanted Jim Essian, our Triple-A manager at Iowa, to manage the club. He just didn't know how to do it, so he put out a bunch of bullshit to make me look bad.

The day after all this flap hit the papers, we were in New York for an off day, prior to a three-game series with the Mets. It would have been an easy day to fire me, but nothing happened. Tuesday, May 22, I went to Shea Stadium early by myself and was sitting at my desk making out the lineup when Frey walked in with Grenesko behind him. Jimmy was grimacing so I knew this was it.

Grenesko began: "We're going to make a change..."

I let him have his say and got up from my desk.

"All I can do is wish the Cubs good luck," I said, and walked out the door.

I was back in my hotel room at the Grand Hyatt, packing my bags to go home, when the phone rang. It was a couple of the Chicago writers, Joe Goddard and Barry Rozner.

"C'mon up," I said. "I'm fired."

When they got to the room I was on the phone with Soot, trying to explain what was going on.

"There's a couple of writers here who came to say goodbye," I said, but she still wasn't understanding why I was calling her from my hotel room when I should have been at the ballpark. Finally, I hollered, "Honey! Don't you know what I'm saying? I've been fired! I'm coming home!"

There was a bunch of mini-bottles of liquor, chocolates, and a big bowl of fruit on the table in the middle of the room. I told the writers to take all the stuff with them. I chuckled as I watched them walking out of the room, their arms full of fruit, chocolates, and booze bottles.

Not long after I got fired, a story appeared in *Penthouse* magazine, linking me to a noted bookmaker in St. Petersburg, and detailing all these huge bets I was supposed to have made on football and basketball games. This was around the same time baseball was investigating Pete Rose for all of his betting activity, and now I was being dragged into it.

The bookmaker in question was Dino Margaritis, and I never denied to baseball officials that he was a friend of mine in St. Petersburg. I'd see Dino at the dog track and he was a great guy. We had lots of fun together. We'd played golf and even had dinner together a few times. The guy who sold the story to *Penthouse*—I never even knew his name—was always hanging around the dog track, and must have done a lot of business with Dino. All I know is, Dino seemed to always be taking care of this guy, until one day he cut him off. Now the guy apparently needed a new source of money and decided to go to the big magazines to sell his story. He knew I was friends with Dino and that the best way to get back at Dino would be to expose him as doing illegal betting business with some prominent sports figures. Nobody knew who Dino was, but everybody knew who Zimmer was, and that was the only way this guy could make a buck for his story.

Was I making bets on basketball and football? The answer was yes, but not anywhere remotely close to the kind of bets this guy accused me of in *Penthouse*. In addition, the guy suggested in the article that the reason I was fired by the Cubs was because of my betting. That was absolutely false.

Before the article came out, I had been summoned to a meeting with baseball commissioner Fay Vincent and his top security aides, Kevin Hallinan and John Dowd. When Vincent asked me if I had been betting on basketball and football games, I didn't deny it to him. They then told me whom I bet with, and I didn't deny that either. I've got to say, Vincent, Hallinan, and Dowd were great with me. They told me some things they had heard, and I told them that was wrong. This guy had me betting $5,000 a game in the *Penthouse* story, which was pure fantasy. I didn't have that much money in the bank! The most I bet on games was $50 or $100.

After listening to my testimony, Vincent looked at me and said with a shrug: "I know there's all kinds of betting going on with baseball people. I can't stop it, but I can slow it down. I'm saying to you: No more illegal betting."

I haven't bet on football or basketball games since. Vincent did me a favor. He saved me a lot of money, and now I don't have to get even on Monday nights anymore. As for the guy who sold the story to *Penthouse*, he disappeared from St. Pete and nobody has seen him since. He tried to make a big thing out of something that wound up being dismissed and forgotten in a day and a half.

It was a sad trip home for me to Treasure Island after my firing. I loved Chicago. I probably have more fans there than any other place in the world. I figured, even if I didn't have the showdown with Gresko, how much longer was he going to wait anyway? You'd think a CEO who hired you would be tickled to death after winning a division title. But people who knew him told me he just got tired of me getting the credit for 1989.

I left the Cubs with nothing but great memories. Having Grace, Girardi, Walton, and Maddux at the start of their careers, and Dawson and Sandberg in the prime of theirs was a blessing for me. The first lights at Wrigley and all the great people I worked with there—Colletti, Durso, Yosh Kawano—and Dallas Green, too. Dallas and I had our differences, but he was a baseball man and I respect him for that.

As for Frey, Gresko got him too after the season. Frey managed the Royals to the World Series in 1980 and was fired a year later. He then wins two division titles in five years for the Cubs and gets fired twice. And you don't think baseball's a crazy game?

One time when I was at Sportsman's Park in Chicago I ran into Stormy Bidwell, the owner of the track.

"I'd like to buy you and your wife dinner at Kelly Mondelli's," Bidwell said.

I wasn't sure why he was so insistent, but I agreed to meet him there a couple of days later. When I got to the restaurant, there was this huge table set up for Bidwell, a bunch of his friends, and Aldo Botallo, a great pal of mine who owned a cab company in Chicago. At the end of the dinner, Bidwell presented me this beautiful set of jockey silks in Cubs colors, encased in glass. To this day, it sits in the middle of my living room—a prominent and lasting symbol of what the Cubs and Chicago meant to me.

11

A Red Sox Redux and a "Rockie" Retirement

T his is probably as good a place as any to take a brief "detour" to the racetrack.

If there is one other place on earth where I've spent more time than on a baseball field, it's the racetrack. In fact, if you asked me where I've spent the most time, I'd say it was probably a dead heat. On so many occasions I've been able to enjoy the best of both worlds by going to the track with friends from baseball. I only wish dogs and horses were as easy to handicap and evaluate as ballplayers. I'd be a wealthy man today in every way.

A lot of funny things have happened to me at the racetrack—some of them not so funny at the time—and being that this is my life story, it wouldn't be complete without a few track tales.

My earliest experiences with betting horses were when I was a rookie with the Dodgers. In spring training at Vero Beach, there was this little old guy who'd come by the barracks where we slept, walking his dog every morning. I heard somebody say he was a bookmaker, and that we could place bets with him. Lee Scott, the Dodgers' traveling secretary, would bet $2 a horse with him, and there were four or five other players who were all betting with this guy. They'd make their bets, and the next day he'd come by to either pay them off or collect.

One morning the guy came by the barracks with his dog, and keeled over dead. Now through the years this story has gotten exaggerated and changed to include me in it. I would like to state for the record here: It wasn't me. This is how it happened: The guy was lying there dead, and somebody who'd won on the previous day's bets went over to the body and removed his winnings from the old man's pocket. I don't know who it was, but I swear it wasn't me. The incident happened after I got traded to the Cubs.

It took me a long time to realize that bookies who hung around ballparks and ballplayers usually weren't to be trusted. When I was playing winter ball in Havana with Ed Roebuck in 1951, we used to go to Caliente, Cuba's grand old racetrack. One day I was standing near the betting window when this little Cuban guy about my age approached me.

"Stick with me," he said, "I can make you some money. Any time you want to make a bet in the states I can get that down for you, too."

Well, from that day on I'd pick up the Racing Form and the *Miami Herald* at the Nationale Hotel, and pick my horses at Garden State and Hialeah and give my bets to him. Then every morning he'd come by the place I was staying, and to let me know he was there he'd whistle outside my window. It got to a point where Soot started getting really aggravated.

"There's the whistler," she'd say. "I guess it's time to get up."

This went on for a couple of weeks, and I'd make a few bucks and lose a few bucks with the whistler. Then one Saturday morning, I gave him between $50-$80 worth of bets on races at Hialeah. The next morning Roebuck and I were driving to the ballpark and stopped at the Hotel Nationale where Eddie got out to pick up the newspapers. As we headed to the park, I had him check out the race results at Hialeah. I asked him who won the first race and he gave me the horse. "That's me!" I said. Same thing for the second race. Then I told him to pull over.

"I got to do some checking," I said. Sure enough, I'd hit like five races for $880. I knew the whistler didn't come by on Sundays because there was no racing, so I couldn't wait till Monday morning. At 9 A.M. on Monday I was awake waiting for the whistler, just like always—only he wasn't there. I waited and waited all that morning, and 50 years later I'm still waiting for my $880. He waited for the right time, when I finally hit it big, and took off on me. I'll never forget Soot that morning. She said, "I'm sure glad we didn't have to listen to that whistler today." What could I say to her?

Never trust your money with a horse player. I can attest to that. In 1965 with the Washington Senators, Frank Howard had finished up the season with a bad elbow. The day after the season he went into the hospital to get it operated on, but before he did, he asked me if I'd stay at his house until he got out. I called Soot, who was expecting me to come home to Treasure Island, and she said, "Sure, what's a couple of more days?"

So Brant Alyea—another outfielder on the Senators—and I moved into Howard's house while he was in the hospital. Right after the operation I went to visit him. There he was, big Hondo, his arm elevated in this cast as he called me over to him.

"Popeye," he said, "I need you to do me a favor. I got my check here and I need you to go down to the Windsor Park Hotel and give it to the manager there, Johnny Vie, to get it cashed. Then I need you take out $150 for me and put the rest of it into a cashier's check to send to my wife."

No problem, I said. What I hadn't told him was that Alyea and I had been to Charles Town racetrack in West Virginia the previous two nights and had tapped out. So now I took Howard's check down to the Windsor Park. I got it cashed when Alyea said to me, "We can go to Charles Town now and get even."

"Great," I said, "but what if we blow out again?"

After thinking it over for a few minutes I decided, what the hell, let's go. We went to Charles Town with Frank Howard's $700 and proceeded to lose it all in the first five races. The next day, I went to the hospital and the moment I walked in the room the look on my face must have tipped Hondo off. He knew me too well and he said, "Ohhhhh noooo, Popeye, please don't tell me one of your stories!"

I said, "Here is the story, Hondo. I cashed your check, but I don't have your $150 or the money for your wife. On the way to the bank I made a slight detour."

"Ahhhhh Popeye!" he screamed.

"Don't worry," I said. "I will get the money to your wife."

I had to make a quick transaction, which was to call a good friend in Cincinnati, who bailed me out. I learned my lesson the hard way. That was the last time I lost someone else's money at the track.

Probably my most embarrassing day at the track occurred on the last Saturday night of the 1956 season. Being that it was the end of the season, our families had all gone home, and before our game that day Podres and I went in to get our checks from Lee Scott. We then gave the checks to John Griffin, the clubhouse man, who cashed them for us. After the game Podres and I were sitting around our apartment having a couple of beers when he said to me, "What's say we go to Roosevelt?"

Podres had this big white Chrysler, and the two of us hopped into it and headed out the Belt Parkway to Roosevelt. In those days there was a ten-cent toll on the Belt Parkway, about two miles before you got to the track. We got out there in time for the first race and decided to watch all the races from the bar. After about four races had been run, Podres looked at me and asked, "How you doing?"

"I don't have a winner," I replied.

"Me neither," he said.

Now two more races went by and Podres asked me again. "Any winners yet?"

"Nope," I said.

"Well that makes two of us."

Finally, it was the ninth race and we're paid up at the bar. I reached into my pocket for the last couple of bucks I had and left it on the bar for the bartender. I hadn't cashed a single ticket, and I knew I was totally tapped out.

We got in the car and headed back out onto the Belt Parkway where we came to the toll. I started fumbling around in my pockets, but I knew I didn't have a cent on me. I said to Podres, "I've got only twenty-dollar bills."

He was fumbling around in his pockets too, and he said to me, "Let me have one of those twenties."

Well, now I've got to tell him that I don't have a dime on me, and it suddenly becomes clear that he doesn't either. It was almost comical if it wasn't so embarrassing. Podres pulled up to the tollgate, rolled down his window, took out his empty wallet and said to the clerk, "Sir, take a look here. I'm Johnny Podres with the Dodgers and this is Don Zimmer. Would you believe we don't have a dime for the toll? We left everything we had at Roosevelt!"

"I know who you guys are," the clerk said, and with that he took a dime out of his pocket and tossed it in the bucket for us. As we drove off Podres said, "I want to pull over and just have a good cry."

I know a lot of people frown on going to the horse track, but that's my enjoyment. I don't drink, I don't smoke, and I don't go to the movies. I go to the track and it's my money, my business. I don't bother anybody. One time, though, I was at Sportsman's Park in Chicago and I decided to get a haircut from the barber they have right there at the track. I was sitting in the barber chair reading the Racing Form, minding my own business, when out of the corner of my eye I saw this disheveled-looking guy staggering through the door.

I said to myself, "Uh-oh, what's this SOB doing. He's not gonna even make it through the door."

Suddenly the guy lurches against the door, straightens up and glares at me.

"You getting a haircut?" he slurred.

I nodded.

"Well, I'll tell you something, buddy," he said. "Man oh man you are goddamn *ugly!*"

The guy was loaded, but he wasn't bashful about his opinions.

"You are *really* ugly!" he continued. "You ain't even got any hair to cut!"

Finally I'd had enough.

"You know, pal," I said, "you ain't exactly Clark Gable yourself!"

I've come to understand the racetrack is not a place you go if you're looking for respect.

For only the second time since my professional baseball career began, I found myself home for the summer after my firing from the Cubs in 1991. It was kind of nice having time with my family and doing the things I'd never gotten to do when I was playing, managing, and coaching. But as the summer wore on, I started to really miss baseball, and I wondered if I was ever going to work in it again.

I didn't hear from anyone in baseball the rest of the summer, not that I expected to in the middle of the season. But then, shortly after the season ended, I got a call from my old third baseman, Butch Hobson, who had just been named manager of the Red Sox. Butch had worked his way up, paying his dues as a minor league manager, but because of his inexperience he wanted me to help him out as his bench coach. At the time, "bench coach" was a fairly new concept in baseball, and people have often asked me, "What the hell does a bench coach do, anyway?"

I tell them, "A bench coach's job is really quite simple. He sits next to the manager, and when a hit-and-run or a steal works for the team, he pokes the manager for the benefit of the TV cameras so it looks like it was his suggestion. And if a play doesn't work, he gets up and walks away to the water cooler so he's nowhere in sight when they pan again to the manager."

For most of my playing career—with the exception of the Cubs' goofy college of coaches experiment—managers had three coaches, one to coach the pitchers and the other two to handle the bases. Usually one of the base coaches doubled as a batting coach, but that was it. Now most staffs are comprised of as many as six coaches, with separate batting, bullpen, and bench coaches. I can't imagine Charlie Dressen ever feeling a need for a bench coach, but I will say this: I know I've helped the managers I've served as bench coach with suggestions during the games. They really do serve a purpose. How can it not be a good thing for a manager to have an extra pair of eyes during a game?

So when Butch called, I didn't hesitate in accepting. What a great thing, I thought: going back to Boston and Fenway Park. My daughter, Donna, her husband, and my granddaughter were living in New Hampshire, not far from Boston, and I'd be working for a young manager who played for me. I looked at this as an opportunity to finish my career in Boston. What better place to retire? If only it had turned out that way.

When I got to spring training in Winter Haven, I got the feeling Butch was having some problems. It didn't help either that the team he was taking over wasn't very good. One of his key players, Jack Clark, was bothered by assorted injuries all spring and wound up having a miserable season in which he hit .210 with just five homers. Butch had counted on him to be a big middle-of-the-order run-producer. Two other veterans expected to provide a lot of offense, Mike Greenwell and Ellis Burks, were also sidelined for extended periods of time.

The Red Sox got off to a good start in 1992 and were actually four games over .500 and 2 ½ games out of first place on May 28. Then it all began to fall apart. A seven-game losing streak in June dropped them under .500, and after the All-Star break they went 12–18 in August and 11–17 in September to settle into last place.

As the season wore on, there were a couple of incidents that disturbed me about Butch. He was drinking a lot and doing a lot of off-the-field carousing. There was one incident on an airplane flight in which I felt Butch really embarrassed and undercut himself with his players. He'd had a few too many drinks with his pitching coach Rich Gale, whom I wasn't real fond of, and asked me if I thought it was okay for him to take the microphone and tell some jokes.

I told him: "I wouldn't do anything like that without first asking the captain."

The captain apparently told him it was okay with him, and the next thing I knew, Butch was on the microphone telling a lot of dirty jokes. They were so raunchy that one of the flight attendants in the back came rushing up to the cockpit in tears. I tried to tell Butch, "You're drinking away there with your buddy and you say and do things you wouldn't ordinarily do," but it was too late.

With his veteran players getting hurt, Butch turned to a bunch of the young players he'd managed in the minor leagues. When you manage guys in the minor leagues, it's easy to fall in love with them, and that's what Butch did with Scott Cooper, a big third baseman, and Bob Zupcic, a big righthanded-hitting center fielder. In both cases, they weren't the players Butch thought they were.

Cooper had been a third baseman in the minors who was moved to first by Butch. He had no speed and very little power. He hit .317 that year, but I always felt he was playing a little better than he should have. He lasted three more seasons in Boston and was out of baseball by 1995, having hit a total of 30 homers.

Zupcic was a big kid who hit homer after homer over the Green Monster during batting practice at Fenway. To me, he was the classic example of the kind of hitter who should just be left alone to hit the way he hits best. There's no such thing as a pull hitter anymore, because all batting coaches want to teach righthanded hitters to hit the ball to right-center and right field, and lefthanded hitters to hit to left-center and left field. Richie Hebner is a real good friend of mine and one batting coach who tried to emphasize pulling the ball and letting it fly. But people don't want to hear that, and as a result he kept getting fired.

I remember when Whitey Herzog was managing at Kansas City in the early '70s and had primarily a speed team of players like Hal McRae, U.L. Washington, and Willie Wilson. It was built around speed because they played on turf. Then one day they finally got a guy who hit the ball into the seats, a big lefthanded hitter named Clint Hurdle. But the batting coach for the Royals, Charlie Lau, had Hurdle hitting the ball between third base and shortstop. That's what I heard was among the things that led to Herzog and Lau having a falling out.

I thought Zupcic could last only one way in the major leagues, and that was to hit the ball to left and hit home runs. He couldn't make it hitting the ball to right. Nevertheless, that was the style they insisted on teaching him, and he was out of the big leagues by 1994.

The one thing about baseball, if you're going to survive in this game evaluating ballplayers, you're never going to be right all the time, but you'd better be right the majority of the time. If I'm 50–50 in my opinion on ballplayers, I'm no good for you. That's why I've always believed teams should have everybody on tape when they're sitting around making evaluations. When you're talking about $4 million ballplayers and higher, you'd better not be making too many mistakes.

That said, I've certainly been wrong about some players. In '92 Mo Vaughn was in his first full season with the Red Sox, and I've got to say I didn't think he was going to be a hitter in the big leagues. He was big and strong, but he just looked like he had a lot of holes. Thank goodness nobody asked me about him. And, by the way, if they asked me now I'd say you'd have to be crazy not to want this guy on your ballclub.

Another guy I was dead wrong about was Robbie Alomar. I watched him when he played against the Red Sox for the Blue Jays in 1992. I thought he was going to be a decent hitter, but he didn't look like a good second baseman to me. Today, he's only one of the best second basemen in the game. Like I said, you're never going to be 100 percent judging players. I'd like to think, however, I'm at least 80 percent, or else I wouldn't have been able to last as long as I have in this game.

One day during the second half of the '92 season, I was standing by the batting cage when I heard Haywood Sullivan calling to me from the box seats next to the Red Sox dugout. Haywood was still running the ballclub, and I could see he wasn't happy.

"What do you think of how our boy is handling the club?" he asked me.

I was afraid Haywood was getting ready to fire Hobson, and I wanted to do my best to prevent that from happening.

"I think he's shown improvement," I said. "I really think you ought to give him at least to the end of the season to prove himself."

"I don't know . . ." Sully said.

"Look," I persisted, "he's had a lot of injuries to deal with and he's still learning. I think he'll be all right given time."

I believed in Butch Hobson, primarily because I knew what kind of player he'd been for me, going out there every day with that bad elbow and gutting it out. He was an ex-quarterback for Bear Bryant at Alabama and I felt he could lead a ballclub. Unfortunately, his life was a mess. A few years later it was revealed he'd had a drug problem, and Butch admitted he'd partied his life away. To this day I can't tell you if he ever took drugs. I just know I wasn't comfortable being around the Red Sox that year, and I didn't want any more part of it. A couple of times I tried to talk to him about straightening himself out. I told him this could be a dream job for him and that he could last seven or eight years in Boston and that I wanted to work with him. Toward the end of the season, though, I could see I wasn't getting through to him, so I let Butch know I wasn't coming back. He had a pretty good idea and never asked me why.

Hobson lasted until the end of 1994 as Red Sox manager, and after he was fired, all the stuff about the drugs came out. He's since taken great steps to turn his life around. Despite everything that happened in 1992, I love Butch Hobson. He's a good person and a great competitor, who for whatever reason just let his life get untracked for awhile.

Once again a season had ended with my facing the prospect of having no job for the next year. I got home to Treasure Island and didn't get any phone calls. After the World Series ended, I decided to go to Las Vegas for a couple of days with Vince Genovese, a good friend from Fort Worth. I instructed Soot not to tell anybody where I was. The second night I was in Vegas I got a call from Soot, who told me that Bob Gebhard, the general manager of the expansion

Colorado Rockies, was trying to get a hold of me. The Rockies had yet to play a game, and Gebhard was in Arizona, checking out the Fall League and interviewing manager candidates. After missing connections with him a couple of times, I was laying in my room in Vegas, relaxing, when the phone rang.

"Don," he said, "Bob Gebhard here. I'm in the process of interviewing managers and I've talked to five candidates. The last guy I interviewed, Don Baylor, said that if he got the job he'd like to have you as his bench coach. I asked him how he knew you, and he told me you'd been together with the Yankees in '83. Anyway, if Baylor is hired, would you come with him?"

I really believe he had already made up his mind to hire Baylor and that he was asking me, thinking I'd say no. Instead, I told him I'd be thrilled to work with Baylor. I was also excited about the prospect of going to a new city, Denver, and working for a brand new franchise. It figured to be yet another new experience for me.

The one drawback to this new experience, I quickly discovered, was the fact that the Rockies trained in Tucson, a two-hour drive from Phoenix and Scottsdale where all the other teams in Arizona trained.

We got to Tucson and there must have been 75 players in camp, nearly 40 of them pitchers. It became quickly apparent we were going to have to play a ton of split-squad games in order to properly evaluate all these pitchers. The problem was, as the only team training in Tucson, it was going to be necessary to send at least one squad every day on the two-hour trip to Phoenix. As Baylor's right-hand man, I got the honor of managing the "B" squads. That spring, Brad Mills, the Triple-A manager, and I made all the road trips, and I can attest to knowing every cactus plant and ostrich farm by heart on that two-hour bus ride through the desert.

Late in the spring, we were all together on a bus ride back from Phoenix. Baylor was sitting in the first row and I was in the row right behind him. Across the aisle from me was the team trainer. About 20 miles out of Tucson, my right eye suddenly started burning like crazy. It felt like a jalapeno pepper. I got a hanky out of my pocket and rubbed it, and it seemed to subside a little. Then about 10 miles later, as we were approaching the outskirts of Tucson, I looked out the front of the bus and I was seeing three highways. I tried to talk and my lips felt like they were all blown up. I couldn't get any words out. Baylor turned around and hollered over to the team trainer to help me. I didn't know what was going on.

Right about then, we went down an off ramp into Tucson where, lucky for me, there was a hospital right there. They pulled into the hospital and had me checked in. I was in intensive care for three days while the doctors gave me a battery of tests and stuck me with all kinds of needles. There were two Asian doctors working on me and they were just great. After the first day, they told me I'd had a mini-stroke, something called a T.I.A., in which some vein in the lower part of my head had gotten weak.

Once I was coherent again, one of the doctors asked me if I smoked. I told him I didn't.

"What about chewing tobacco?" he asked.

"Only since I was 18," I replied.

"Well," he said, "I'd suggest you cut it out. Tobacco can affect your blood vessels."

I haven't had a chew of tobacco since. They told me that in 20 percent of cases like mine, the patient has a recurring stroke within 6–8 months. It's been eight years and I've been fine. For that, I thank those doctors. I don't know what would have happened if my seizure had happened in the middle of the desert.

For the first few days after I got back to camp, I was taking different medications, and my equilibrium was all screwed up. I was walking around like a drunk. Aside from almost dying again, it really was a fun spring. Just about every night, Baylor, Ron Hassey (another of his coaches who had been a catcher with the Yankees in '86 when I was there), and I would all go out to dinner together with our wives. Hassey lived in Tucson and knew all the good restaurants. We all got along great, and despite the bus rides I was really enjoying myself.

When we got to Denver for the start of the season, I couldn't believe the wacky weather. I'd wake up some mornings and it would be snowing like hell, and by game time the sun would be out and it would be 60 degrees. Go figure.

As expected of an expansion team, the Rockies finished last in '93 with a 67–95 record, but there were some encouraging performances and, overall, everybody felt pretty good about the direction the club was heading. Andres Galarraga, a big happy-go-lucky first baseman with an infectious smile and a personality to go with it, became the first expansion player to win a batting title, hitting .370. I never realized what a great first baseman he was until I watched him throughout that year. I hit ground balls to him before every game, and for a big guy he was a wizard over there. Everything was fun for him. Charlie Hayes, who I'd hook up with again later on the '96 Yankees, set three expansion-team records with 175 hits, 98 RBIs, and 45 doubles. And Dante Bichette set an expansion-team record by scoring 93 runs.

The first-year Rockies also set an all-time attendance record that'll probably never be beaten. They drew 4,483,350 to Mile High Stadium, which because it also housed the NFL Broncos could seat over 80,000. The thought of a team drawing over four million was unbelievable to me, especially when you consider the Dodgers barely drew over two million in their first couple of seasons in Los Angeles, playing in the 100,000-seat Coliseum.

Naturally, because of the thin air and the high altitude in Denver, people tended to downplay the offensive records the Rockies set. At the same time, the pitchers have always seemed to be psyched out pitching there because of it. I'm not saying there's no truth to the ball carrying there and not breaking for pitchers, but what are you going to do? My suggestion to Baylor was to get these pitchers straightened out in the head. We know the ball doesn't sink, I said, but if you throw the ball down and away consistently enough you're going to get your share of outs. If you throw four high sliders in someone's eyes they ought to be home runs—in Denver or anyplace else.

I'm not denying the curves don't break in Denver the way they do back east. I'm just saying pitchers have to make adjustments there. Find a way to throw the ball low and away.

On August 12, 1994, baseball went on strike, and for the first time in history they canceled the World Series. Not that the Rockies were going to the World Series. Before the players walked out, the Rockies showed a marked improvement over '93, finishing 53–64 in third place. Galarraga had another big season, hitting .319 with 31 homers before breaking his hand July 28, when he was hit by a pitch. The guy who really baffled me was Howard Johnson, who had been signed as a free agent during the offseason. If ever there was a player I thought would thrive in Colorado it was Johnson, even though he was coming off two subpar seasons with the Mets in which he'd been hurt a lot. In '91, he'd led the National League in homers (38) and RBIs (117) and was one of the best players in the game.

I can't recall if I was asked about Johnson, but I would have soundly recommended him after seeing him play against me during my years with the Cubs. I also would have been wrong. He just couldn't play any more. He started the season as our third baseman, but wound up pinch hitting by the time the season ended. In 93 games, he hit .211 with 10 homers. His career just died and there was really no explanation for it. I felt bad for him, because he was a good guy.

It was also during the '94 season when I began to detect my relationship with Baylor wasn't the same as it had been in '93. We'd always sit next to each other on the bench, and I knew Baylor needed me. He'd never managed a game in his life or made out a lineup card. He chose me to help him because he needed someone to help him. There's so much to managing you've got to get used to—double switches, talking to pitchers, when to run, etc.—if you've never done it before. One time early on, I had to stop him from going out to talk to a pitcher after the pitching coach had already been out there. He'd forgotten the "second visit" rule and he'd have had to take the pitcher out of the game.

Anyway, I got a sense late in 1994 that things were drifting away. In spring training of 1995 it became even more evident. It seemed there was bad blood between Gebhard and Hassey, and Baylor was allowing himself to get in the middle of it. Everybody knew I was friends with Gebhard, but I try to stay clear of ballclub politics, and I didn't realize there were sides forming here. I did tell Baylor once that he shouldn't let Hassey turn him against Gebhard, because Gebhard hired him.

During the calisthenics in spring training, Baylor and I always sat next to each other and discussed the plans for the day. But that spring it changed. I'd find myself sitting alone while Baylor and Hassey were sitting together at the other end of the bench. I had also been in charge of working all the double-steal plays and the baserunning, but toward the end of the spring I came out to the park and found Hassey working them. I said to myself, "What's happening here?" It didn't take an Einstein to figure it out.

Things really kind of came to a head during a series against the

Braves in June. We had a player on the club, Jim Tatum, who had bounced around the minor leagues for a long time before finally getting a chance in the majors. He was a utility guy who could catch, play first, third, or the outfield. He'd had some family problems, but he'd persevered and I took a liking to him—which Hassey knew. Before one of the games against the Braves, Baylor and the coaches had been told that Tatum and a pitcher, Lance Painter, were being sent down to the minors right afterward. I was sitting on the bench, watching a bunch of writers gathered around Painter. I couldn't hear what they were talking to him about, but I suspected maybe they'd heard he was being sent out.

The game began, and in the sixth inning Baylor sent Tatum up to pinch hit. After the inning, Tatum went into the clubhouse and nobody saw him for the rest of the game. Later, Gebhard came down from his office to send Tatum out and couldn't find him. The clubhouse man told Gebhard that Tatum had dressed immediately after he got done pinch hitting and went home. Apparently someone had told him he was being sent to the minors, and he was really upset.

While all this was going on, Hassey came up to me and said, "You're close to Tatum. Did you tell him?"

That really stung me, to be accused of betraying a confidence from the front office.

"What kind of a man do you think I am?" I said, seething. "That's the general manager's and manager's business. It's absolutely horseshit that you would ask me that!"

By then it was obvious to me I had been needed for two years, but not any longer. Hassey had brainwashed Baylor and his wife against Gebhard, and it was obvious they looked at me as a Gebhard ally, and therefore someone not to be trusted. I went back to our place in Denver and told Soot, "That's it. I'm quitting."

Soot said, "You shouldn't quit, at least don't use that word. It makes it look bad for someone. Why stir things up any more than they have to be?"

So I decided to go in and tell Gebhard I was retiring June 6, in the fifth inning.

"I don't get it," Gebhard said. "Why in the middle of the game?"

"Because I don't want no fanfare," I explained.

Now I had to tell Baylor. Naturally, he wanted to know why.

I would only tell him: "I've got to live my life the way I want to live it."

"Well, why the fifth inning?" he asked.

"What if you win the game on June 6," I explained, "and I'm in the clubhouse packing all my bags when everyone comes in afterward? The media will be all over me, and I don't ever want to be in a position where I'm gonna take anything away from the ballclub."

Gebhard had told me he wanted to have a day for me, which was the last thing I wanted. When June 6 came, the Rockies ironically were playing the Cardinals, managed by Joe Torre. In the fifth inning of the game, I got up from the bench, walked past Baylor, tapped him on the knee and said, "Good luck the rest of the way, pal." When I got to the clubhouse, Gebhard was in there with Cardinals general manager Walt Jocketty. I shook hands with both of them, headed out the door and went home.

Afterward, I told people the fun had gone out of the game for me. In truth, it had in the months leading up to my decision to leave. But I wasn't ready to retire. I just didn't want to work someplace where I really wasn't needed anymore. Baylor didn't need me, and I sure as hell didn't need him. It was as simple as that. We never had any harsh words and there weren't any bad feelings. After I left, somebody in Chicago actually wrote that Baylor and I had squared off! For me to fight Baylor, I'd have to be absolutely nuts. He'd kill me in about 20 seconds.

We never had an argument the entire time I worked for him. To this day, I have nothing but respect for Don Baylor, and I think he feels the same way toward me. A prime example of that perhaps is a conversation I had with him after he'd been named manager of the Cubs in November 1999. The Yankees had a minor league pitching coach named Oscar Acosta who they let go, supposedly because he was too tough. I had seen him work with the pitchers in spring training, and I was impressed with the way he conducted himself. I had also heard good things about him from other people in the Yankees organization who'd worked with him through the years. After he got fired, Acosta called me.

"I know you know Don Baylor," he said. "Would it be asking too much if you could contact him and ask him about a job in the Cubs organization?"

I told him I'd be happy to do it. I called Baylor and told him about Acosta. I told him he was a tough SOB who took no bullshit, but had done a good job with pitchers every place he'd been in the Yankees organization. It just so happened, Baylor said he still hadn't hired a pitching coach for himself. The more I told him about Acosta, the more interested he got.

"If you don't have anyone else in mind," I said, "take this guy. But don't just take him on my recommendation. Call Joe Torre."

Torre never knew I had recommended Acosta to Baylor, but apparently when he got called he said the same thing. Hire the guy. Three days later, Acosta called me and sounded like he was about to cry.

"I can't thank you enough," he said. "Baylor hired me to be his pitching coach."

Late in the 2000 season, I called Joe Girardi, our catcher with the Yankees from 1996–99 who had gone over to the Cubs as a free agent, and asked him about Acosta.

"He's a real special guy," Girardi said. "The pitchers love him."

Things like that make you feel real good—when you can recommend someone, and that someone gets a break and works out well. It was the same thing with Buddy Bell in Colorado keeping Clint Hurdle as his batting coach. Bell, who is a good friend of mine, took over as Rockies manager after the 1999 season and was putting together a whole new coaching staff. He happened to call me to ask me for some suggestions about coaches and I told him, "If nothing else, keep Clint Hurdle."

Hurdle had been the Rockies' minor league hitting coach when I was there. From what I saw, he was real good with the hitters. Every year Baylor had a different batting coach, but it was never Hurdle. All the while he was being passed up, Hurdle never complained. He just did his job. That showed me something. Finally in Baylor's last year, he brought up Hurdle, who's been there ever since. About the greatest reward you can have in baseball is to be able to help someone.

I went home June 6, knowing there was little chance of any other job opening the rest of the season, and once again I was looking at a rare summer home. When I told Baylor I wanted to live my life the way I wanted to, part of that meant being with my family for a change.

My daughter Donna lives in Windham, New Hampshire, and is

sort of the unofficial fundraiser for athletic facilities in her town. I've tried to help her along by donating for auction a lot of the baseball stuff I've picked up through the years. A big part of my daughter's zeal to help and improve the athletic programs in the town is her own daughter—my granddaughter, Whitney, who happens to be one heck of an athlete. Donna had been bragging on Whitney all the time to Soot and me, but I was never sure whether it was just a case of a parent being naturally biased about her kid. So I asked her to send me a schedule of Whitney's basketball games. I noticed there were three games scheduled in one week and told Soot we were flying up to New Hampshire to watch some girls' basketball. I've got to say my daughter was right. Whitney could really play. She was also a shortstop and a windmill style pitcher on her softball team that won the New Hampshire Little League finals, and she plays field hockey, which I've never seen. I had always hoped I could pass on my athletic genes, but I never thought it would include the female side of the family!

My son Tommy, who's been a scout for the Giants for 21 years, lives right in St. Pete, and it was a joy to get to see his two kids, the identical twins, Ron and Lane, play baseball that summer. Ron is a first baseman and he's really learned how to play the position. I've told him he picks the ball out of the dirt the way Gil Hodges used to do it. Lane is a shortstop/second baseman who's had to overcome a serious injury in which he broke a bone in his elbow throwing one time. He had to have a bone chip screwed back on, and as a result, he doesn't have the smoothest throw, but he's learned to compensate. They're both good ballplayers and great kids, who I don't think have ever had a cross word with each other. They're more than just brothers—they're best friends.

Tommy was a good ballplayer when he was a kid, good enough to get scholarship offers to both Florida State and Manatee Junior College. He chose Manatee because there would be no restrictions as to when he could get drafted and turn pro. He was an infielder who converted to catcher, and it was as a catcher that the Cardinals drafted him. He didn't get any bonus to speak of. He just wanted a chance to play. He rose in the St. Louis system all the way to Double A with their Arkansas team in the Texas League that featured, among others, Garry Templeton, Jerry Mumphrey, and Larry Herndon, all of whom went on to decent careers in the big leagues.

Right after that year, Tommy got released and went immediately into managing. He was really too young, though, as most of his players were older than he was. After a couple of years of managing, he was let go by the Pirates organization and it looked like he might have to get a job out of baseball. That's when the Giants called and offered him a scouting job in Florida in which he'd be in charge of the whole state for amateur talent. He wanted to stay in uniform, but I told him this could turn out to be a perfect job in that he was still very much in baseball and could be around his three boys, not away half the year.

Tommy's other son, Beau, wasn't into baseball the way everyone else was in the family. Instead, when he was in grade school he got a job on this local TV show in St. Pete for kids. It was on every Saturday morning and he became a regular on it. That led to him going to Lakewood High School where they had a special course for TV journalism. All through high school, he was involved as a sports commentator on the school's TV news show, and he got some big interviews. He went from there to the University of Florida, and for two summers he was an intern for Dan Rather's "48 Hours" show at CBS in New York.

I also got to spend time with my sister, Erma Johnson, and her husband, Harold. After my wife, Erma has been my biggest fan, having followed my career closely since we were kids, through all the cities and all the adventures.

I really enjoyed that summer at home, but in my heart I wasn't ready to retire after leaving the Rockies. As the summer went by without any teams calling me, a friend of mine said, "Why don't you sign up for Social Security?"

It had never occurred to me, so I did. All of a sudden, two weeks later a couple of checks arrived in the mail, one for me and one for Soot. I said, "This ain't too bad!"

Barely a week after I cashed them, I got a phone call from Joe Torre.

12

I'm a Yankee Doodle Dandy

When I picked up the phone and heard Joe Torre introduce himself on the other end, just one thing went through my mind: This man is calling me to ask me about some ballplayer. I had known Joe through the years, having managed against him when he was both a player and a manager. There was a mutual respect, and I always liked Joe, but other than that, we didn't know each other that well. So I was naturally a little curious at how he began the conversation.

"How's your health?" he asked.

"Fine," I said. "I'm feeling great."

"How's retirement treating you?"

"Pretty good," I replied. "It's been nice being home, and just the other day I cashed my first Social Security check."

"No kidding?" he said. "The reason I'm calling is because I need a bench coach here in New York, and I'd like you to come with me."

Now, I knew my pal Billy Connors was working for the Yankees as a minor league pitching instructor, and I immediately began thinking either he or Steinbrenner had to have put Torre up to this. I couldn't figure out any other reason why he'd called to choose me.

"Are you aware that Steinbrenner and I are friends?" I asked.

"Not really," Torre said.

"Well, is this really your choice or has somebody else mentioned my name?" I persisted.

Torre insisted the choice had been all his, but in my heart I couldn't believe him. I had to find out how this all came about, so I asked him if I could take a day to think about it.

"Take a week," Torre said. "Two weeks if you want."

"No," I said, "I'll get back to you right away. I don't want to leave you hanging."

As soon as I hung up with Torre, I called Billy Connors, who I knew sat in on all the meetings Steinbrenner had with the Yankee staff. I told Billy that Joe Torre had called me to offer me the job as his bench coach.

"You were in all the meetings," I said, "where did my name come in?"

"All I know is," Connors related, "George told Torre he could have a bench coach if he wanted, and Joe said, 'I'd like Zimmer'—to which George said: 'You're kidding! He's one of my pals!'"

Naturally, when I heard that, I was flattered. I called Torre back the next day and told him I'd be delighted to end my retirement and go to work for him. The next thing I did was to go down to the Social Security office and tell them not to send me any more checks. I was working again. I've prided myself in the fact that I've never made a dime outside of baseball my entire life, and until I officially retire, that's the way I want it.

In August 2000 Torre was talking about our relationship and how it all started. He told this funny story about how I was the first Mets third baseman, and that after I was traded, they went through something like 60 third basemen over the next 20 years, one of which was Torre. "When I got to third base with the Mets," Joe said, "I found a note under the bag that said: 'If you ever get to be a major league manager and need a bench coach, call Don Zimmer'."

How did he know the note was for *him*?

Anyway, I needed only two weeks of spring training to conclude that Joe Torre and I were going to have a very special relationship. The way he talked to everybody, communicated, I just knew there was never going to be a problem. This guy was someone who just knew how to deal with people.

Right off in spring training, the Yankees suffered a key injury when Tony Fernandez broke his elbow. Fernandez was being counted on to play second base for sure, or shortstop if Derek Jeter proved he needed more time in the minors. At least as far as Joe and his coaching staff were concerned, Jeter showed us enough early on to convince us he should be the Yankee shortstop for 1996. There were a few dissenters, Clyde King for one.

King was one of Steinbrenner's spring training "advisors" who arrived at camp three weeks into it when the games began. He was assigned mostly to scouting other teams in Florida, but when Steinbrenner gathered the staff to evaluate the Yankees, King said something about Jeter needing to improve on his footwork. Because of that, there was this unfair question most of the spring as to whether Jeter was going to win the job. There was no question in Torre's mind, of course, and that's all that mattered.

I love George Steinbrenner. He's been a great friend to me and my family. We've had our beefs with each other. We always will, because it's both our natures to speak our minds. George is probably the greatest baseball owner there's ever been in terms of doing and spending what it takes to produce a winner for his fans. The fans of New York are the luckiest fans in the world. I've had to laugh when the New York media would rip George for his outbursts or his excesses.

At the same time, if there's one thing about George that's aggravated me over the years it's his willingness to value the judgements of people who barely see and know his ballclub, more than the people who see the players every day. In the spring of 2000 Al Rosen, who hadn't been around baseball for seven years, was invited to camp by George and happened to be watching a game in which Clay Bellinger made an error at third base. Rosen told George that Bellinger couldn't play third, and from that day on, Bellinger was a marked man with the Boss.

I admit it. I'm an underdog guy. A champion of the scrapper-type players who might not have the natural ability but who make up for it in their approach to the game. Bellinger was that kind of player, having bounced around in the minor leagues for 10 years before getting invited to his first big league camp with the Yankees in 1996. Let me say right up front: My son Tommy signed Bellinger out of Rollins College in Florida for the Giants in 1989. But that isn't the reason I liked him. Believe me, if you recommend a player to people on the basis of personal relationships when you know in your heart that player can't play, you won't last long in baseball.

From the time I saw Bellinger in that first camp, I felt he had the right kind of baseball instincts to help us when the time came. It didn't come until three years later, when because of injuries we needed an extra man, and Bellinger came up from Columbus and filled in at third base and the outfield. Then in the spring of 2000 he was in camp vying for a spot on the roster as the 25th man. He can catch, play the outfield, second, and third base—but if I had to pick his best position it would be third.

Rosen was long gone from the scene when Bellinger was pressed into duty in 2000, playing third base for Scott Brosius, second base for Chuck Knoblauch, and center field for Bernie Williams. People don't realize what a good job Bellinger did for us. No matter where Joe played him, he did a credible job. And tell me: How hard do you think it was for him to step in and have to play center field in Yankee Stadium for Williams?

I wasn't about to say anything to George about Bellinger, but in my mind it's not right for him to pay so much attention to the opinions of people who don't know his players.

Another player I always felt wasn't nearly appreciated enough by George was Joe Girardi, and we got into a few beefs over him too. It was purely coincidental that for Girardi's first 11 years in the big leagues, I was with him for 10 of them—first with the Cubs, then with the Rockies, and finally with the Yankees. When the Yankees traded a minor league pitcher named Mike DeJean to the Rockies for Girardi shortly after Torre had hired me in the fall of 1995, it was also purely coincidence. I didn't have anything to do with the trade and wasn't asked anything about Girardi until after they'd already acquired him.

Later that winter, Joe asked me for a rundown on Girardi, and my reply was: "He'll hit you .270; he's unselfish, a manager's player, he can throw, and he's got decent speed, especially for a catcher."
Joe said: "That's my opinion too."

In spring of 1996 the three players under the biggest microscope were Jeter, who at 21 was trying to win the shortstop job; Tino Martinez, who was being asked to replace Don Mattingly at first; and

Girardi, who was brought in to replace fan favorite Mike Stanley at catcher. Both Tino and Girardi got off to slow starts and heard their share of boos at first, but by the end of the season all three of those guys could look back in satisfaction at having played major roles in the first Yankees world championship in 18 years. Jeter hit .314 and was named Rookie of the Year, Martinez hit 25 homers and led the team in RBIs with 117, and Girardi took charge of the pitching while hitting a career-high .294.

Girardi also stole 13 bases that year and quickly showed himself to be the best hit-and-run man we had on the ballclub. In a game against Kansas City in April, Torre ordered a double steal in which Girardi stole home on the front end of it. Not since Jake Gibbs in 1968 had a Yankee catcher stolen home.

But right off, Joe knew this wasn't your conventional Yankees team of lefthanded power. We talked about it when we left Florida. I said to Joe, "I think we're going to have to do a lot of improvising here and manufacture runs." And it was fun. Joe had them hitting and running, squeezing, safety squeezing, double stealing, while on all the radio talk shows they were saying we weren't doing things the Yankee way, that we were playing National League ball. Well, Joe and I may have had our roots in the National League, but baseball is baseball, and we were just doing the things the personnel dictated we do. And like my 1989 Cubs, the 1996 Yankees executed all year long.

I can't remember how many times Joe called a safety squeeze with Girardi on third base, and Girardi would get us that extra run. Still, Girardi could never seem to get the Boss's approval. Maybe it was because George got spoiled with Thurman Munson back in the '70s and felt that no catcher could measure up to him.

One night in spring training, Steinbrenner invited me and my wife out to dinner with him at the dog track. Naturally, our conversation quickly got around to baseball and the ballclub. When Girardi's name came up, George said to me, "Oh, Girardi's your friend. My people don't think he can do anything." Well, there it was again. Other people who weren't around the club every day were giving their opinions on a player, and George was taking their opinions over ours.

I just said, "Okay, if that's what your people think, then just give him away. Release him. All I know is, the guy's a winner. He was a rookie catcher when I won with the Cubs in 1989. He was Colorado's catcher when they made the playoffs in '95, and he's been the catcher on nothing but winning teams here. I don't think that's no accident."

After that, we left it alone, agreeing to disagree, as George and I have done a lot. Now, a few weeks later, just before we broke camp, we had this staff meeting. Everybody was there—from Brian Cashman, the GM, to all the Tampa people, the scouts, and Joe and his staff. The room was so crowded I was sitting on the floor. George went around the room asking for opinions on the team when the catching situation was brought up.

The general opinion was that Jorge Posada was going to be the catcher of the future, and everyone was saying what a great player he was going to be. I wasn't disagreeing with any of this. Here was a young catcher who could switch hit, hit with power, throw good. There was no question he was going to make a ton of money in this game. He deserved all the high marks he was getting.

All the time, George wasn't saying a thing. Then Girardi's name came up and George spoke up.

"He won't be with us next year," he said.

Now, I'd had enough. I got up from the floor and said, "George, it's a shame you have it in for Joe Girardi. I know you like tough people, and I can assure you there's no one in this room as tough as Joe Girardi. I remember you saying that 'your people' don't think Girardi can do anything. Here's their opportunity to speak up."

Gene Michael, the head of scouting, and Mark Newman, the VP of the player development department in Tampa, both got up and said some more things about what a good player Posada was, and I spoke up again.

"It's just too bad," I said, "that you think so little of a guy who's done so much for this ballclub."

It turned out, 1998 wasn't Girardi's last year with the club after all. He was brought back for 1999, primarily because Joe Torre wanted him back and recognized how important he was to the team. I had told George in our argument about Girardi not to take my word if he thought I was prejudiced for the guy. I told him to ask Torre (a former catcher, by the way) and Mel Stottlemyre how important Girardi was in handling the pitchers. They're the ones who worked closest with him every day.

In 2000, with Girardi now having left as a free agent to go back to the Cubs, George could have asked Glenallen Hill about him. Hill had just come over to the Yankees from the Cubs, and one day I asked his opinion on Girardi.

"The absolute glue of that team," Hill told me, not having any idea of how I felt about Girardi.

During the 1998 and '99 seasons you'd see Girardi every day sitting down with Posada, going over hitters and the fine points of catching. It was as if Girardi wanted Posada to take his job tomorrow. He knew his days were numbered with the club, yet here he was doing his best to groom his successor. How often do you see that? That's how unselfish Joe Girardi is. He's as fine a person as I've ever met in baseball.

The 1996 season was a bizarre year. I wasn't aware the Yankees hadn't won a World Series since 1978. I only remembered them winning all the time back then. Nor was I aware that Joe Torre had never been to a World Series. No sooner had we gotten into the season than Joe's brother Frank went into the hospital to have a heart transplant. Then when the team was in Cleveland in June for a day-night Saturday doubleheader, Joe got a call between games that his other older brother, Rocco, had died of a heart attack. When he told me, all I could think about was the day I was managing the Red Sox and Bill Crowley had come to tell me my dad had died. Joe was devastated, but like me, he stayed and managed the second game with all his grief, and went home the next day.

Another catastrophe to confront us that season was David Cone being diagnosed with an aneurysm in his pitching arm in early May. He underwent surgery, and no one really expected him back that season—if ever. But he returned to pitch September 2, when we had already built up a four-game lead, and he threw seven no-hit innings against the Oakland A's. I remember being in a restaurant called Johnny's Downtown in Cleveland, sitting at the bar with Torre and Jose Cardenal, our first base/outfield coach, waiting for our table, when a guy next to me introduced himself as a doctor.

"I hope I'm wrong," he said, "but your pitcher, David Cone, will never throw another pitch."

He was a nice guy, and he was sincere and meant well. I wish I'd have gotten his card to send him a note after Cone's gem in Oakland. But I'm sure the guy was thrilled to death for David, like we all were.

Three months into the 1996 season, the team changed. On July 4 Darryl Strawberry, who had been signed earlier off the St. Paul team in the independent Northern League, joined us from Columbus. Later that month Joe had finally had enough of Ruben Sierra, who was constantly complaining about how he was being played and doing nothing to back it up. On July 31 Sierra was traded to the Tigers for Cecil Fielder. Now all of a sudden we had some real big boppers, and we didn't have to steal as much anymore. I remember one time in a game, Fielder was on third and Tino was on first, and I turned to Joe and said, "What do you think? Double steal here?"

Joe looked at me and said, "You really are a wacko, aren't you?"

Still, we'd pick our spots to keep our running game from totally shutting down.

Another indispensable part of that 1996 world championship team was John Wetteland, our closer, although I must say first impressions are misleading. The first time I saw John Wetteland, he came skating into the clubhouse on roller blades with elbow and kneepads. I said to myself, "What the hell is this? This guy is a real kook."

Of course, as the season played out, Wetteland and Mariano Rivera emerged as one of the greatest 1-2 relief punches in the history of baseball. Wetteland led the league in saves with 43, while Rivera appeared in 61 games as the seventh- and eighth-inning set-up man and struck out 130 batters in 107 ⅓ innings! The man was unhittable, and would continue that way in the years to come when he succeeded Wetteland as the closer.

Wetteland, too, was a very special person. Like Girardi with Posada, Wetteland tutored Rivera and all the other relievers, knowing that they'd likely be taking his place on the club. He was like a mother hen to them in the bullpen and epitomized the unselfish attitude of that 1996 team. He's a great friend to this day, and I was saddened when he had to leave as a free agent for Texas after the '96 season.

Just a few more words about Rivera here: When I first saw him that '96 season, coming in game after game and blowing away batters with just one pitch—a hard, rising fastball—I said to myself, "How long can this last? Sooner or later, good fastball hitters are going to start knocking this guy around." When Wetteland left, none of us were sure if Rivera was going to be able to handle the closer's job. We were surer of his disposition for it than we were of his one-pitch arsenal.

About the only adjustment he made was that he perfected his cut fastball. He has a slider and a change, but he throws them about four times a year. Any man who is able to do what he's done with just one pitch is truly gifted.

It didn't take long for me to realize this was something special I'd become part of in 1996. This was a group of unselfish players and that attitude came from the top. They responded to Joe, and he in turn knew how to get through to each and every one of them. Jeter, the rookie, kind of set the tone when from day one he always referred to Joe as "Mr. Torre." To this day, he still does.

With that cast of characters—Jeter, Bernie, Paul O'Neill, Strawberry, Fielder, Andy Pettitte, Cone, Wetteland, Rivera et al—we won the American League East by four games over the Orioles, then had to play them again as the Wild Card in the ALCS. As I said, a lot of spooky and bizarre things happened that season, not the least of which was a fan reaching over and interfering with what was ruled a home run for Jeter in Game 1 against the O's.

I couldn't see what happened from my vantage point in the dugout. I never saw the fan reach over and grab the ball before the Orioles' right fielder Tony Tarasco could time his leap to catch it. All I saw was the umpire, Richie Garcia, running out and waving his right hand to signal a home run. The next day, looking at the replay, I'd have to say the fan interfered. No question. But if it wasn't a playoff game we wouldn't even be talking about this. Just like Bill Buckner's error in the '86 World Series against the Mets, or the Larry Barnett interference call in the '75 World Series—these are things that happen all the time in the course of ballgames. The World Series or playoffs just magnify them, and Buckner is going to have to live with his boot the rest of his life.

A lot of people tried to say the Yankees got a lucky break there and that's what turned around the series. If you ask me, that's just baseball. There are always going to be things like that, and in order to get to the World Series, we still had to beat the Orioles three more times—which we did in the next four games.

The World Series was Joe Torre's crowning achievement. He'd waited his entire career to get there and when he did, he savored every minute of it. After the Braves won the first game, a 12–1 blowout, George came down to Joe's office, very distraught.

"You play all year and then you go down the drain in the World Series," he said.

"I don't see it that way, Boss," Joe replied. "We just had a bad game, that's all. We may lose tomorrow too, but then we're going back to my town where we'll win three straight and come back home here and wrap it up."

"Are you nuts?" George said.

Joe just laughed. I couldn't believe what he said either, but by this time, after everything else that had happened during the course of this season, I wasn't about to doubt the confidence and conviction of Joe Torre. Joe had played in Atlanta and was one of the few Braves managers to ever win anything there before Bobby Cox came over from Toronto in the '90s. Joe knew this Yankee team better than anyone; knew their mental makeup and their inner resolve not to accept defeat. As it turned out, his prediction to George was right on the mark. We did lose the next day, and then we went down to Atlanta and swept all three games before coming home to New York and wrapping up the Series in six.

I'd have to say Game 4 was the turning point—and Joe's managing masterpiece. Kenny Rogers, our starting pitcher, put us in a quick 5–0 hole by the third inning and we were down 6–0 going into the sixth, when we cut the deficit in half. Cox brought Mike Bielecki, one of my old Cubs, into the game at that point, and he shut us down into the eighth when Mark Wohlers, the Braves' closer, took over.

Wohlers had had an even better year than Wetteland as far as putting games away, but he was immediately greeted with back-to-back singles by Charlie Hayes and Strawberry. That brought up Jim Leyritz, who was no stranger to postseason heroics, having hit a game-winning home run for the Yankees in the second game of the 1995 Division Series against Seattle. For some reason, Wohlers tried getting Leyritz out with a slider instead of his No. 1 "out pitch," his 100 mile-per-hour fastball, and Leyritz hit it into the left field seats for a game-tying three-run homer.

Now the game went into extra innings, and Joe started manipulating players and pitching matchups. In the top of the 10th, Tim Raines walked with two outs and Jeter singled. With Andy Fox (who had assumed the cleanup spot in the lineup when Joe sent him in to run for Fielder a couple of innings earlier) on deck, Cox elected to walk Bernie Williams intentionally, loading the bases. It was the right move to make, but Joe had saved one last trump card on his bench in Wade Boggs. Boggs had not been a great clutch hitter that season, but Joe knew as a six-time batting champion he had a great eye, and this was the perfect opportunity to utilize it. Sure enough, Boggs drew the walk that got us the go-ahead run, then an error by first baseman Ryan Klesko led to an insurance run.

In the bottom of the inning, Joe still had a couple of more moves to make. There was no question Wetteland was coming in to save it, but with Fox, Fielder, and Tino Martinez all having been used up, we didn't have a first baseman! That's when Hayes came over to Joe and said he could play first.

"Have you ever played it before?" Joe asked.

"Yeah, once earlier this season when I was with Pittsburgh," Hayes said.

Joe looked at me, I suppose for reassurance since I'd been with Hayes in Colorado. I just shrugged.

As Hayes trotted out to first, Joe said to me, "We kind of do things by the seat of our pants here, don't we?"

Here it was in the bottom of the 10th inning of a World Series game and we're both sitting there laughing.

That's the way it's been with Joe and me. We have a very close relationship and we've had a hell of a lot of fun, both with each other and at each other's expense. I won't soon forget the costly advice he gave me about not letting umpires have the last word. We were playing the Twins in the Metrodome in June of '96 when there was a controversial play involving Bernie Williams on the basepaths. All I knew was, when Joe came back to the dugout after arguing he told me that the first base umpire, Jim Hendry, had thrown *me* out of the game.

"Me?" I said. "Why me?"

"I don't know," Joe said. "I guess he thinks you're the one who was getting on him the most. But as long as you're getting tossed, why don't you go out there and get your money's worth."

So I went out there and did my own screaming at Hendry, but all it did was assure me of getting fined.

Almost a year later we were playing the Marlins in an interleague series in Miami, when in the first game of a doubleheader, the home plate umpire Greg Bonin was missing a lot of pitches. We were all getting on him when he pointed to the dugout. Joe went out to argue, and once again he came back and said to me, "He's throwing you out."

Well, here I went again, charging out to Bonin, screaming that a 3–0 pitch to Fielder had been a foot outside. I'm carrying on, waving my arms wildly, getting all hot when Bonin says: "Are you on drugs!"

That really did it! I've been called a lot of things in baseball but nobody's ever accused me of taking drugs—even if some of my managing moves might have led people to think that. In my opinion, Bonin had stepped way over the line, and now I really lit into him. I was still hot after the game and told the writers that if I had to do it all over again I might have punched Bonin for what he said. I also said if I was fined by the league, I was quitting baseball.

Of course, all the while this is going on, Torre's in his office laughing. As we went back out to the field for the start of the second game, I said to him, "Sure, you were the one who told me to go out there and get my money's worth. I do that and the man says I'm on drugs. Thanks a lot, pal."

Joe did a lot of things that '96 season not many managers would dare to do. Even though Tino was our leading RBI man, Joe would pinch hit for him when he wasn't swinging good. And for Game 5 of the World Series, Joe decided, with the exception of Strawberry, to bench all his lefthanded hitters—Tino, Boggs, and O'Neill—against Braves righthander John Smoltz. It was purely a hunch move, going against the book, but the righthanded hitters had all been swinging well and the lefties weren't.

O'Neill was the last of them Joe called in before the game. I was at my locker in the clubhouse when O'Neill came out of Joe's office.

I could see Paul was absolutely crushed. Joe had explained his reasoning to me for wanting to leave the righthanders, Fielder, Hayes, and Raines, in the lineup against Smoltz, and I'd agreed with him. Still, the look on O'Neill's face made me feel that maybe we should reconsider. So I went in to Joe's office and said: "O'Neill's really down."

"I know," Joe said. Then, sensing what I was thinking, he added, "Let's put him back in there for Raines."

I went back out to the clubhouse and called O'Neill over. "Go back in there and see the boss," I said. "There's been a change."

It turned out to be another inspired decision on Joe's part.

In that final game, O'Neill got us started on our 3–2 win by doubling off Maddux in the third inning and coming around with the first run on a triple by Girardi. And it was O'Neill who finished our Game 5, 1–0 victory with his defense. One of the reasons Joe had initially decided not to play O'Neill that game was because Paul's leg was really bothering him. A hamstring strain had him gimping around like an old man. I'd pretty much forgotten about that until two outs in the ninth inning, when Luis Polonia pinch hit for Terry Pendleton, representing the Braves' final out, and battled Wetteland by fouling off six straight fastballs.

On the next pitch, Polonia finally hit a ball fair, a fly to right-center. O'Neill, who right before had been moved two steps to his right by our outfield coach, Jose Cardenal, went charging to his right and out for it, stumbling as he went. You could see him straining with every ounce of energy he had left as he extended his arm and caught the ball in front of the warning track.

There could not have been a more fitting person or a more fitting way for the Yankees to win the world championship. O'Neill epitomized the determined, never-say-die attitude of that team. A year later he would epitomize it again—only this time in a losing cause—in the ninth inning of the Yankees' Game 5 loss to the Indians in the Division Series. With two out he just missed hitting a homer to right-center, and slid in safely with a double. It was to be our last gasp, as Bernie followed by making the final out.

Paul O'Neill will always be one of my all-time favorites. I feel bad for him, though, because the man is never going to have fun in baseball. He's so intense. It hurts me to see what he puts himself through.

The first time I saw him in spring training in '96, I was standing by the batting cage while he was taking BP. I'm watching and I'm saying, 'This guy's a nut!' If he didn't hit the ball right on the button, he was slamming his bat against the batting cage. As the season went along, we talked more and more, a lot about our common home, Cincinnati, and we soon became good friends.

I'd watch him go through a period where he'd be hitting everything right on the nose and they're all outs. He'd be breaking bats, screaming and hollering, not bothering anyone really, except himself. After a third straight line-drive out in a game, O'Neill came back into the dugout and everybody was watching. As he walked past Joe, Mel Stottlemyre, and me, he looked at me and noticed I was grinning.

"What the hell is so damn funny?" he barked.

"*You* are," I shot back.

Our relationship just got better after that.

Another time that season, O'Neill got jammed on a pitch and came back to the dugout muttering about quitting. The next day I saw him talking to Girardi next to their lockers. So I walked over and said: "Can I talk to you, Paul? Joe, you come here too."

I wanted to make sure I had a witness to what I was going to say. O'Neill was looking at me quizzically as I continued my little sermon.

"This man," I said, looking at O'Neill, "said he was quitting and going home to Cincinnati last night. I have a friend in Cincinnati, Jack Roth, who has a concrete block company and I can probably get him a job there. The pay is $300 a week."

From that day on, every time O'Neill threatened to quit—and he was usually good for it two or three times a month—I'd say, "I'll call my friend in the morning."

During the 1999 season, Jack Roth sold his business. I told O'Neill, "I can't help you anymore, pal."

This doesn't apply to the people who see O'Neill day in and day out, but this man is a lot better all-around player than he's sometimes given credit for. He's an excellent outfielder, with a strong, accurate arm. He's not what you'd consider a great speed guy, but he can steal a base. As a hitter, he's a perfectionist. I know when he struggled mightily with the bat over the last six weeks of the 2000 season and into the first round of the playoffs, most people wanted to write him off as being through at 37. He'd had a hip injury, and it didn't look as if he was ever going to be the same hitter because of it. He had only one extra-base hit after September 6 and people would say to me, "It's too bad about O'Neill. He's hurt." To that, I'd answer, "Not true. He *was* hurt, but he's not anymore. He's just all screwed up with his timing and mechanics."

That was born out in the playoffs. I could see Paul was starting to come out of it when he got a couple of hits in Game 5 of the Division Series against the A's. By the time we got to the World Series against the Mets, he was the old O'Neill again. The 10-pitch walk he worked Mets closer Armando Benitez for in the ninth inning of Game 1 was one of the most important at bats of the whole Series. He wound up hitting .474 with a couple of triples against the Mets, and could have very easily been the Series MVP were it not for Jeter hitting .409 with two big homers.

O'Neill loves playing in New York, loves being a Yankee, and that makes him special to the people of New York. It's also no accident he's won five World Series rings. The man's a winner. A nutcase perfectionist maybe, but a winner. I wasn't buying the stories about the Yankees not bringing him back for 2001. Everybody is finished one day in this game, but in my mind O'Neill sure wasn't. Paul O'Neill will let us know when he's done. He can't stand hanging on.

Repeating that magical 1996 season, we knew, was going to be next to impossible. Too many dramatic events had all worked in our favor. The 1997 Yankees had the same positive, selfless makeup, just not the same breaks.

Tino wound up hitting 44 homers and was second in the AL with 141 RBIs, and Pettitte had a near–Cy Young season going 18–7 with a 2.88 ERA. But the Yankees just never could catch the Orioles during the regular season. Injuries had as much to do with that as anything. David Cone was the best pitcher in the league for the first four and a half months of the season. Then he hurt his shoulder and was pretty much of no use to the club in September and October. Bernie had two stays on the disabled list with hamstring problems, and Strawberry's season was ruined by a knee injury.

We managed to make the '97 postseason as the Wild Card team, but made an early exit in the Division Series against Cleveland. His shoulder still bothering him, Cone lasted just 3 ⅓ innings in the first game (which we came back to win). The series turned in the fourth game when Rivera gave up a game-tying homer to Sandy Alomar in the eighth inning. It was to be the last time in a long time Rivera would fail in a big game.

The '97 season had barely ended for the Yankees and George Steinbrenner, as is his way, was already hard at work with his staff deciding on what improvements needed to be made to get the team back to the World Series. More than anything, what was needed was a healthy return to form from Cone and Strawberry, but George wasn't leaving anything to chance.

On November 7 the Yankees traded Kenny Rogers, a good pitcher who simply couldn't pitch in New York, to the Athletics for third baseman Scott Brosius. The word on Brosius was he was an excellent defensive player who could also play second, but had mysteriously had a season-long batting slump in which his average dropped from .304 in '96 to .203 in '97. The newspapers called it a mutual salary-dump deal. It turned out for the Yankees to be a "salary steal" deal, as Brosius hit .300 in 1998 and provided the best third base play they'd seen since Graig Nettles.

A month later, as a hedge in case Strawberry couldn't come back, George signed Chili Davis, a switch-hitting designated hitter with a reputation for being a strong, positive force in the clubhouse. He proved to be all of that.

Then, just before spring training, George and his staff made their final big offseason move by sending four top minor league prospects to the Twins for second baseman Chuck Knoblauch. If there was one thing we hadn't had on the '96 or '97 clubs, it was a bonafide lead-off hitter who could set the table for Jeter, O'Neill, Williams, and Tino and also steal bases. Now we had one.

I've never liked being asked to compare teams and players, simply because I don't think you can really do it. When people ask me if Jeter is the best shortstop I ever saw, I can't answer that, simply because Pee Wee, for instance, was a totally different player. Pee Wee was as great a shortstop as I ever saw—for his era.

Nevertheless, I'd have to say that 1998 Yankees team was the best I've ever been around. Once again, it was a total team effort that produced such a remarkable season. There was no one MVP—just a lot of MVPs for given periods of the season. I guess the closest to an overall MVP season was Jeter's. He hit .324, stole 30 bases, and began to flex his muscles as a source of power for us with 19 homers and 84 RBIs. I've never hid the fact that Jeter was one of my pet projects early on and one of my real favorites, despite the constant pranks he's always playing on me.

When I managed, I instructed my infielders to go full blast for any pop flies hit to the outfield and not to assume the outfielder is going to get it. I wanted them instilled with the idea of tracking the ball until they hear the outfielder shout "I got it." This was one of the things I worked with Jeter on, especially that first year, '96, when he was a rookie still feeling his way.

"You take charge out there," I told him. "Don't wait to be run off the ball."

Jeter is about the most coachable player you could ever want. He never takes offense to any suggestions Willie Randolph or I might make to him. One time in 1996 he was getting ready to go up to the plate, and as he walked past me in the dugout, he stopped, took my hat off, and rubbed the top of my head. Then he went up and got a base hit. From that day on, he's been rubbing my head before every at bat. Sometimes he'll rub my stomach, too. And if I need a haircut, he'll rub the top of my head and shriek, "Oh my! You got to get it tightened up, Zim!"

Oh yeah, he's a beauty, that Jeter. He and his buddy Posada are always doing things to me. Now he's got my grandkids all telling me, "You got to get it tightened up, Pops!"

Through the years in baseball, I've seen a lot of guys change with success. In Jeter's case, he hasn't changed one iota in the five years he's been in New York. This is another special guy, and it's a credit to his upbringing that all the success, money, and adulation he's gotten as a celebrity ballplayer in New York never went to his head. One other thing that says a lot about what kind of player Jeter has been: Has anyone kept track of how many second basemen he's had to play with and tried to get used to? Before Knoblauch came along in 1998, there were at least a half-dozen, and the parade got even longer in 2000 when Knoblauch missed half the season with his arm injury.

If Jeter came the closest to being our MVP position player in '98, the pitching, which Joe has always rightfully maintained really drove the team, had a number of MVPs. I suppose you have to start with David Wells, who was nearly unbeatable at 18–4, plus a perfect 4–0 in the postseason. Overall, the Yankees were 25–5 in the games Wells started that season. And on the subject of perfect, there was also that 4–0 gem of a game he pitched May 17 against the Twins. What made it even more remarkable was that Wells went to the same Point Loma High School in San Diego as did the last man to pitch a perfect game in Yankee Stadium—Don Larsen!

Larsen and Wells, it turns out, had a *lot* in common. They were both incorrigible free spirits. When Larsen was with the Yankees, I heard he drove Casey Stengel crazy with his off-field antics, although old Casey, who liked to tip a few cocktails himself, had a soft spot for him. As one story goes, one time in spring training Larsen drove his car into a mailbox at 5:30 in the morning. When the reporters asked Casey about it the next day, all he said was: "So the man was either out too late or too early. Who's to say?"

I liked David Wells, even though he did a few things I didn't approve of. Steinbrenner signed him as a free agent after the '96 season, despite his reputation for not staying in shape and being a bit of a roustabout off the field. Then that winter, before he ever threw a pitch for the Yankees, he got involved in a bar room fight in San Diego and broke a bone in his hand. Between the healing hand injury and his excess weight, Wells was behind all the other pitchers most of that '97 spring. To his credit, he got himself ready by Opening Day and won 16 games for us, although not without further incident.

In a game against the Indians at Yankee Stadium in June, Wells decided he was going to pitch while wearing this old cap that had once been Babe Ruth's. He'd apparently picked the thing up in an auction for $35,000. When he came back to the dugout after the first inning, Joe spotted the musty old cap and ordered him to take it off.

Wells' weight became an issue again in 1998 when in a game in Texas he was handed a 9–0 lead in the second inning and frittered it away until Joe had to lift him in the third with the score 9–7. Afterward Joe had words with him and plainly suggested the reason Wells couldn't hold the lead in that 95-degree weather was because he needed to lose weight.

Then in September of that year, Wells gave us more cause for concern as to whether he had the stability and proper concentration to do the job in the postseason. In a game against the Orioles, which the Yankees wound up winning 15–5, Wells showed up Jeter and outfielders Chad Curtis and Ricky Ledee by glaring at them when a pop fly dropped among them in left-center. Once again, Joe had to admonish him for his childish behavior, and while nobody said anything publicly, it took awhile before the other players forgave him.

In a way, Boomer was just a big child. He'd do and say dumb things like that, without thinking, and immediately come to regret them. We got into a couple of shouting matches. During the games, a few of the players had a habit of going up into the clubhouse and lying around. On days he wasn't pitching, Boomer was a frequent clubhouse lounger. One particularly cold night, I happened to go up to the clubhouse during the game for a cup of coffee, and Boomer was lying on the couch, arguing with another player and one of the clubhouse guys.

Now, if I see something going on that I feel could affect the ballclub, morale-wise, I would definitely tell Joe. But one thing I'm not is a spy. I don't know how many times I've seen guys late for stretching before the game—a $100 fine—and never said anything. Just the same, on this night, Boomer was obviously in one of his bad moods and decided to make something of me coming into the clubhouse during the game.

"I've heard enough about you, too," he said. "That you go and squeal to the manager about us being up here in the clubhouse."

I looked at him and I could feel my blood starting to boil.

"I didn't come in here to rat on you," I said. "I'm embarrassed you would even think that."

Now he immediately got up and put his arm around me.

"Oh, Zim," he said. "I was just kidding."

I knew he wasn't, but it was no big deal as far as I was concerned.

Every time Wells would be pitching, though, there would be this constant battle with Joe when it came time to take him out of the game. We'd be in the eighth inning, Boomer would come in and Joe would ask Mel: "How many pitches?" Mel would tell him and Joe would say, "Okay, that's it." But when Mel went down to tell Wells he was done, Boomer would scream, "Oh that's bullshit. I ain't coming out!" and Joe would have to get up and tell him, "That's it!"

One particular time when this happened, Rivera was warming up in the bullpen, and Wells looked at me and yelled, "*You* told Joe to take me out!"

"You big asshole," I said. "Don't get on me! Do what the manager says to do!"

To this day, though, Boomer and I are friends. He reminds me a lot of my old Dodger teammate, Billy Loes, who had a goofy personality and was a free spirit just like Wells. On the mound Loes, also like Wells, knew what he was doing. In a way, Boomer and I are a lot alike too. The bottom line for both of us is we're trying to win ballgames. I'm not here to be a spy for Joe Torre. I'm here to help him try and win ballgames.

Another MVP pitcher for the Yankees in 1998 didn't join us until June. That was "El Duque"—Orlando Hernandez, the Cuban refugee who reportedly had escaped Castro's Communism on a rickety raft. It's a story I would have to believe, if only because of the fearlessness and toughness of character El Duque demonstrated right from the get-go as a major leaguer. There was a spiritual side of him too, as I found out from an article by Jack O'Connell of the *Hartford Courant*, which someone showed me. In the story, El Duque talked about the impact New York's Cardinal O'Connor had on him and his family. O'Connor baptized El Duque and his wife at St. Patrick's Cathedral after they got married in February 2000. He had apparently earlier enlisted the Cardinal's assistance in bringing his two daughters to the U.S. from Cuba. "I think it was God who got him involved," El Duque said.

Although Cone had his first 20-win season in 10 years, and Wells won 18, our pitching didn't really solidify until El Duque joined the rotation and went on to go 12–4 with a 3.13 ERA the rest of the way. His unorthodox high-kick motion was something hitters hadn't seen before, and it was almost impossible to pick the ball up on him.

If you ask me, El Duque pitched the most important game of the 1998 season for the Yankees. That was Game 4 of the ALCS against Cleveland. We were down two games to one in the series, and you could just sense the momentum shifting over to the Indians, whose confidence had been boosted with wins in Games 2 and 3. Then in Game 4 El Duque completely shut them down on three hits over seven innings, and the bullpen finished the 4–0 win.

All was well again for us. The Indians didn't score a run off our bullpen the rest of the series, and went down in six. El Duque followed that up with one last superb effort over the Padres in the World Series. By midseason 1999, with Wells having been traded and Cone beginning to experience the ravages of age and wear on his shoulder, El Duque had emerged as the unofficial ace of our staff.

Everything was world class about the 1998 Yankees, including the brawl they had with the Orioles on May 19. It got started the way most brawls in baseball get started—with Tino Martinez getting hit in the back by a pitch from Orioles reliever Armando Benitez, following a home run by Bernie Williams. There was no doubt in anyone's mind it was a deliberate act on Benitez's part, and Tino was justifiably miffed at getting drilled right in the back by a 98 mile-per-hour fastball. The home plate umpire Drew Coble immediately ejected Benitez, but Darryl Strawberry and Chad Curtis had already begun leading the charge out of the Yankee dugout.

The next thing I knew there was mayhem all over the field, and inexplicably I found myself right in the middle of it. With all the things that have happened to my head, the last thing I need to be doing is participating in a brawl, whether as a peacemaker or not. I happen to feel these things wouldn't happen nearly so much if baseball instituted a rule in which suspensions would be automatic for any players leaving the dugout or bullpen. Believe me, you'd see a lot more managers on the top step of the dugout restraining players from rushing out to mix it up. At the same time, if a catcher and four umpires can't break up a fight between a hitter and a pitcher, then something's wrong.

Anyway, here I was, out there with everybody else, as fists were flying and players were piling up on top of each other. Then it started to get really scary as the whole mass of brawling players began gravitating toward the Baltimore dugout. I was afraid someone was going to break his neck falling into the dugout. At one point Strawberry reached over the top of everyone with that 6-foot-6 frame of his and cold-cocked Benitez. I saw Baltimore pitcher Scott Erickson rushing in from left field, and I grabbed him and shouted, "What are you gonna do in there? Stay out of there. Do you want to break your arm?"

It was right about then that Elrod Hendricks, the Orioles' long-time bullpen coach, spotted me and said: "Zim! What the hell are *you* doing out here? Are you nuts? You're too old for this!"

I did feel foolish, especially considering it was probably the worst, most violent baseball brawl I'd ever seen. It's a miracle no one got seriously hurt, given all the heavyweight hitting going on, and the fact it spilled into the dugout like it did. The next day, even Steinbrenner got involved, stating he'd be willing to go three rounds with Orioles owner Peter Angelos to settle the matter. I cracked up when I read that. What a dandy, that George!

I mentioned Strawberry and how he had led the charge to pay back Benitez for what he had done to Tino. Darryl came to us in 1996 with a ton of baggage and a very questionable reputation since his early peak seasons with the Mets. He'd had drug problems, tax problems, marital problems, you name it, and he'd managed to play himself off the Dodgers and Giants and finally out of baseball altogether, until Steinbrenner rescued him in June 1995.

I know Joe was leery of him. We all were. As it turned out, however, he was a great teammate and never gave Joe an ounce of trouble. At least while he was with the team. Away from the field, of course, he gave Joe a lot of heartache.

I'm not sure where we would have been without Darryl's contribution in 1996. I remember watching him in awe when he first joined the team, hitting ball after ball into the upper deck in right field in his first batting practice.

"This guy is truly amazing," I said.

It was always something special watching him hit with such raw and natural power with that buggy-whip swing of his. I don't think people realize how much we missed him in '97 when he was hurt all year, and in 2000 when he was suspended again for drugs. In '96 and '98, he was one of Joe's most dangerous weapons just sitting there on the bench. That was because other managers were forced to leave pitchers in longer than they wanted, or make other moves they might not ordinarily have made, just to avoid having to deal with Darryl. In that regard, he was instrumental in winning so many games without ever coming to the plate!

When we got to Texas for the start of the divisional playoffs in 1998, everyone was in a state of shock upon learning Darryl had been diagnosed with colon cancer. All I could think was: *What more can go wrong for this poor guy?*

From a personal standpoint, you could not have been around a better guy than Darryl Strawberry. What hurts is knowing what's happened to him off the field. I guess the hook of those drugs is something so powerful it's hard to comprehend. I can only say that's not the Darryl Strawberry I knew.

After such a perfect season as 1998, everyone was pretty much of the same mind not to make any drastic changes, and let essentially the same cast come back and defend its crown. The only question was Bernie, who was eligible for free agency, and that was resolved when he re-signed in November for a seven-year, $87.5 million contract. I won't even get into the money players are making in baseball today, except to say: Was it really that long ago I was arguing with Buzzie over a couple thousand dollars and he was subtracting his $50 race track loans to me from his contract offers? Needless to say, the money a single player is making today would have bought an entire ballclub 10 years ago.

We had been in spring training barely two weeks when, on March 10, all the good feeling and celebratory hangover from '98 evaporated the moment Joe called me into his office and told me he'd been diagnosed with prostate cancer. As he was explaining all his options to me, I was both numb and dumfounded. I just listened to him, not really comprehending what he was telling me. At the same time, I had just had arthroscopic surgery on my right knee, and I was barely able to walk.

I had a room at the Holiday Inn Express hotel, a mile down the road from the ballpark in Tampa. I was staying there instead of at home in Treasure Island, because it was easier for me to get to the ballpark early in the morning for treatment on my knee. That afternoon after Joe told me about his situation, I was lying in my bed at the hotel with two pillows under my leg to elevate the knee and an ice pack on it to keep the swelling down. All of a sudden, there was this heavy knock at the door. Soot went to the window and peaked out.

"I don't believe *this*," she said. "It's your boss!"

She opened the door and in stormed Steinbrenner.

"Get your ass out of this bed!" he bellowed. "You've got to run this ballclub now!"

Here I was lying on my side like an invalid. George was trying to make light of my situation, but I also knew he was serious. I was Joe's right-hand man and, bum knee or not, it was my duty to take over the club for him. Still, I made up my mind: If I was going to run the Yankees, I wasn't walking into the ballpark on crutches. That was the first bad move I made.

Those first couple of weeks, I was hobbling all over camp. It was no fun, thinking about Joe and trying to do my job with this aching, bad leg. Everybody tried to help me and, for that, I'm grateful to this day. Gary Tuck, one of our spring training coordinators, was especially helpful with the paperwork in putting all the squads together and assigning all the players to their proper designations for the workouts. All the while, I would periodically talk to Joe and he'd tell me: "Don't worry about how I'd do it. Do what you want."

If it was my team, I would have done it my way, but it wasn't my team. It was Joe's, and I wanted to keep things as much the same as they were under him if I could. But after about 10 days, it became clear to some people I was miserable, primarily because I was trying to be Joe Torre when I wasn't. Then Girardi came up to me one day and said: "Be yourself, Zim. That's the only way this can work."

I said, "Well, I don't know how long I'm going to have to do this, but from here on out, I *will* be myself!"

I thought spring training went pretty well under the circumstances, and then came the famous last Thursday before we broke camp to fly to California, when Hideki Irabu was pitching his final tuneup for the No. 5 starter's job. Irabu, a barrel-chested, righthanded Japanese import, had been one of Steinbrenner's personal "trophy players" after being acquired in a trade with the Padres the year before. He'd been a star in the Japanese leagues, and the Boss pulled out all the stops to acquire him, eventually giving up Ruben Rivera, the one-time prize prospect of the entire Yankees farm system. He then gave Irabu a four-year contract worth $12.8 million.

But after a good start in 1998 Irabu slumped off the second half, and Joe didn't use him at all in the postseason. Like Wells, Irabu had a problem with his weight, but coming into that start on the final

Thursday of the spring, he had pitched good enough to convince all of us he should be the No. 5 starter again. There was one thing, however, with which Irabu seemed to have a problem, and that was getting over to first base in time for relay throws.

His fastball had routinely registered in the 94–95 range that day against the Indians, but in the ninth inning, pitching in relief of El Duque, Irabu was late covering first base on a grounder by a Cleveland rookie named Jolbert Cabrera. After the game, George threw a fit and ripped into Irabu, calling him a "fat toad."

Until then, I'd made up my mind Irabu was pitching the second game of that first two-game series in Oakland when the No. 5 spot in the rotation came up. Now he hadn't covered first and got knocked around a little, and George was in a fury. I was the last person to get into the clubhouse that day, and by that time, George had already made his "fat toad" statement to the press. I walked in and all this commotion was going on. I asked the coaches, "What the hell is happening here?"

They explained that George had said this, and now all the writers were running all over the clubhouse getting comments.

"Oh, shit," I said.

I looked around the clubhouse and saw Irabu and his interpreter standing by the coaches' room door. They wanted Mel Stottlemyre. I said to them, "Come with me," and I took the two of them and Mel into Torre's office and shut the door.

Irabu and the interpreter, George Rose, were sitting down while Mel and I were standing.

"His confidence is shot," the interpreter said. "He doesn't think he can pitch here anymore. He doesn't want to pitch."

I can't believe what I'm hearing. Nevertheless, I tried to reassure him. Meanwhile, everyone outside—the media and probably the players too—assumed we were in there raising hell with Irabu. The fact was, nothing could have been further from the truth. Instead, we were trying desperately to smooth everything over. But Irabu was really down and he didn't want to go to California.

I'm thinking, *What can we do here?*

Finally I said to the interpreter, while pointing to Irabu: "Let me tell you something. This man is a very important man on this ballclub. We need him to start so we can keep [Ramiro] Mendoza in the bullpen. Tell him right now he's our No. 5 starter and that he's pitching in Oakland."

Rose relayed it to Irabu, who shook his head.

"He doesn't want to pitch in Oakland," Rose reiterated. "He says he's just not ready mentally to do that."

"Okay," I said. "Let's try this. He goes to California with us and we'll send him down to the bullpen. I won't expect him to come into a game in the middle of an inning. What I will do is use him to start an inning if need be and be sure to give him plenty of time to get ready."

After listening to Rose relay that, Irabu again shook his head.

"No," Rose said, "he's just not going to pitch."

Throughout all of this, not once did Mel or I raise our voice, frustrating as it was getting. I later found out that Irabu had just bought a house in Florida and he wanted to stay there awhile longer.

After about a half-hour of this, George came into the room to apologize to Irabu for the incident. I told Rose to take Irabu outside. After they left, I explained to George what had happened over the past half-hour, that Irabu was refusing to pitch. He couldn't believe it. How could anyone?

Now George was steaming. I asked him, "Do you have to pay this guy? He refuses to start! He refuses to pitch!"

"I don't know," George mumbled, leaving the clubhouse.

At this point there was a knock on the door and in comes a pizza man with two boxes for the coaches. Everyone was still waiting around to leave for California! At last, word came from upstairs that Irabu would be staying in Florida. As we were flying to the West Coast, I turned to Mel and said, "Number one, tell Mendoza he's pitching in Oakland. And before we get to the hotel, I'll bet I'll be told to pitch Irabu in that spot. But no matter what, Mendoza is the guy."

The Sunday before we were to open the season, we had a workout in Oakland. I got to the ballpark and the first thing the press all asked me was: "Who's pitching Tuesday?"

"Mendoza," I said.

"Well, we heard George wants Irabu," they said.

This is where it began to look as if George and I were in a war.

As I had predicted to Mel, George had obviously told the writers he wanted Irabu to pitch.

This went back and forth, back and forth, with the writers continuing to ask me who was pitching and me continuing to tell them "Mendoza." It got to be a running joke with everyone laughing. All the while, the writers were assuming George was having his people call me to relay his desire to have Irabu pitch Tuesday.

I didn't want to hang Irabu out to dry. I wasn't trying to go to war with George, but if I was going to manage this team, I didn't want someone telling me I had to start a man who had refused to pitch. Throughout it all, I never talked to George, much to the media's disbelief.

After we'd won the first game in Oakland, a box with a dozen roses showed up in my office in the visitors' clubhouse.

"I knew George would come through," I said to the writers. In fact, the roses were from one of Joe's good friends in Atlanta.

Tuesday morning, I was sitting at my desk when the writers all came in.

"So Mendoza is really starting today?" they said.

"Now you got it," I said.

And, as I promised them, Mendoza *did* start—and pitched eight brilliant shutout innings against the Athletics. Then for the ninth I gave everybody what they wanted. I brought in Irabu and he pitched a perfect inning to complete the 4–0 win. When the media came in afterward, I sat there straight-faced and said, "I never said Irabu wasn't going to pitch. All I said was that Mendoza *was.*"

Even though we got off to a 7–1 start, which helped ease the pain in my leg, the idea of running the club because Joe was sick, plus the pain I was in, took all the fun out of it. I didn't enjoy it at all. By May 1 we were 15–7 and in first place, but I was far from comfortable. Then we lost six out of seven, and there were rumors Joe was coming back when the team went to Boston May 18. On the final game of our homestand, Pettitte beat the White Sox 2–1. We'd been told the day before that George wanted to have a meeting after that last game, so before I went to the park, I told Soot I'd be late getting home.

We went up to George's office following the game and everybody was there—Brian Cashman, all the coaches, and of course Joe, who was sitting to the right of George. George immediately started in raising hell, as he had a right to do.

"I feel like I'm getting cheated here," he said, "the way this team is playing."

I'm listening to this and I'm not feeling well to begin with. My leg was aching, and I really didn't care to hear how lousy the team was going or how lousy a job I was doing. Then George said, "If there's anyone in this room who honestly thinks they've done the best job they could, they're excused."

With that, I got up and walked out.

I couldn't think of anything I might have done better or differently. It all happened so quick I just kept right on walking out the front door of the stadium, got in my car and went home.

"I thought you said you were going to be late?" said Soot when I walked in the door.

"I was excused," I said.

"What do you mean excused?"

I explained to her what happened and she chuckled.

At about 11 P.M. Joe called.

"Geez," he said, laughing, "that all happened so fast, I didn't know what to say!"

Joe went on to tell me that when George started in on the pitching, Mel got up and said, "I knew I should have left when Zim left!"

That's when George stood up and hollered: "Wait a minute! You guys are ganging up on me!"

You have to understand George to work for him; and, believe me, it's a lot easier to understand him when you work downstairs on the field rather than in the front office. He puts all his money into his team and he expects to win. Every day. And when the team slumps, he gets angry and wants answers. It does no good to try and tell him that sometimes there are no easy answers for why a team goes into a slump.

There were times during the period I took over for Joe that I thought George might fire me over a difference we had, but it was always forgotten the next day. I think one of the reasons George and I have gotten along so well through all our beefs is because he knows I'm never going to give him a lot of bull. I'll always tell him what I think and I don't care whether he agrees with me or not.

I was relieved when we got to Boston and Joe took over again. I was trying to do a job for both Joe and George, but it wasn't my team. My boss had cancer and had far more important things to worry about than me and the ballclub. I was just happy to give the team back to him in first place. The whole time, meanwhile, I never spoke directly to George. The first day in Boston we happened to run into each other in the visiting clubhouse. I'd heard that George had said he sensed "bad feelings" between myself and him. When he saw me, he said, "Thanks for running the club." That was it. Later he told Billy Connors he thought I'd be more enthused.

So many things happened off the field that 1999 season, and looking back it's a wonder the team was able to play through it all while trying to defend their championship. It's really a credit to the players: They were able to keep their focus on the business at hand and not let all the distractions bother them.

Most of the distractions were tragedies, the most directly affecting, of course, being Joe's cancer. Two days before Joe revealed his illness to the team, Joe DiMaggio died in Hollywood, Florida, after a six-month battle with cancer at 84. The players didn't really know DiMaggio personally. He'd come by the clubhouse on Oldtimer's Day games and other big occasions when he'd be throwing out the first ball. But he didn't really mingle with the new Yankees. That was his way.

I got to know DiMaggio fairly well the year I was in San Francisco coaching for Roger Craig. I'd see him at Bay Meadows racetrack where he would have lunch a couple of times a week. He had a friend who would pick him up and drive him there, and a few times his friend would pick me up, too. I had lunch with Joe frequently that summer, and we shared a lot of good baseball stories.

About seven or eight years later, I was doing an autograph show at Hofstra University. Joe was doing the same show. I was signing in the morning from 11 to one, and he had the afternoon shift, from one to three. Knowing he was going to be there, I brought three baseballs from Florida with me to ask him to sign for my three grandchildren. When my time was up, I went into a room to sign some more things for the show promoter, Steve Hisler. I had a three o'clock flight, so I gave the baseballs to Hisler and asked him if he would have DiMaggio sign them for me.

"No problem, Zim," he said.

A couple of minutes later, Hisler came back and said, "Joe says he'll sign them after his session."

Okay, I said to myself. I guess that's that. I certainly wasn't going to miss my flight waiting around for DiMaggio to sign the three baseballs. As I headed out to the airport, I knew one thing: I was never going to ask him again.

The next year, DiMaggio was throwing out the first ball on Opening Day at Yankee Stadium when he saw me in the clubhouse.

"Do I owe you something?" he asked.

"No, Joe," I said.

In the big picture, I'm just a nobody. I've known a lot better ballplayers than I ever was who were turned down by Joe DiMaggio. As far as I was concerned, if he didn't want to do something for me that would have taken him 20 seconds, then I sure as hell didn't want him to do it now.

Another Yankee and baseball legend with whom I have a totally different relationship is Yogi Berra. Although we were opponents in those Yankees–Dodgers World Series in the '50s, Yogi and I became good friends when we were coaches together under Billy Martin in 1983. When I say good friends, I mean really good friends. During the winter, Yogi will call me once a week. The phone will ring and on the other end I'll hear, "How ya doin', kid?" Yogi calls everybody "kid."

After that 1983 season, I went home to look for a new job. That December, when Martin popped a marshmallow salesman in Minneapolis, Yogi was named to replace him as manager. Inevitably, George got impatient with the team not winning and fired Yogi 16 games into the 1985 season. It was a very bitter firing from Yogi's standpoint— not just because George gave him only 16 games in 1985 (10 of which he was without the services of Rickey Henderson), but because instead of telling Yogi himself, George had his GM at the time, Clyde King, do it. From that day on, George and Yogi never spoke, and through the years it became the most famous feud in baseball.

It was hard on a lot of people like myself who were friends with both of them, but I didn't consider myself a Yankee and I was never going to get involved. I just figured if it's meant to be healed, it will be. Then over the winter before the 1999 season, Suzyn Waldman, the Yankees' reporter for WFAN radio in New York, quietly arranged a meeting between George and Yogi at the Berra museum in Montclair, New Jersey. Numerous other people had tried to get George and Yogi to reconcile through the years, with no success. I have to believe it was just time. In any case, it was a tremendous thing knowing that Yogi would be coming back to Yankee Stadium after a 14-year absence. I know I felt like a kid on Christmas morning when Yogi called to say it was "over."

To mark the occasion, George set aside July 18 as "Yogi Berra Day" at the Stadium. It was a hot, sultry Sunday afternoon with 41,930 people in the ballpark to pay tribute to Yogi. Don Larsen, whose perfect game Yogi caught in the 1956 World Series, came back too, and the two of them reenacted the famous final pitch of that game.

Then David Cone went out and pitched his own perfect game!

I've got to say, even after all those years at Ebbets Field, being around those storied Dodger teams, nothing can compare to the incredible string of magic moments that have occurred at Yankee Stadium. I can't believe my good fortune to have been a part of so many of them. This was just another one.

David Cone has the heart of a lion. I've seen him battle through so many adversities, reinventing himself so many times to keep his career going. Three years earlier, they'd found that aneurysm in his shoulder and there were serious doubts if he'd ever pitch again. Now, here he was throwing one of the greatest games ever pitched, setting down the Montreal Expos, batter after batter, with complete domination. So dominant was Cone that he needed just 88 pitches—nine less than Larsen in '56, to complete his 6–0, 10-strikeout masterpiece.

I'm sitting there watching this, a year after I'd watched Wells pitch *his* perfect game, and I know Larsen's even in the ballpark this time, and I'm saying to myself, "Is this really happening?" You tell me if there isn't something magical just being around Yogi Berra.

Once again I was in the right place at the right time. Since Larsen hadn't been at Wells' perfecto, I can say I was the only person to be uniform at Larsen's, Wells', *and* Cone's perfect games. I wouldn't even want to begin trying to figure out the odds of that. Even more unbelievable, I was also there in 1983 when Dave Righetti pitched his July 4 no-hitter at Yankee Stadium against the Red Sox. After that one,

Steinbrenner bought commemorative wristwatches for everyone on the team. I was in the dugout again and my wife, Soot, was in the seats at Yankee Stadium, wearing the wristwatch from the Righetti no-hitter when Dwight Gooden pitched *his* no-hitter against Seattle, May 14, 1996. That's three perfect games and two no-hitters at Yankee Stadium for which I've been in uniform with a view from the dugout!

The more I think about it, maybe there's something about *me* that's magical! Actually, I know it's got to be Yogi. Joe always said, any time Yogi was in the ballpark, he felt like he couldn't lose. That's just the way it is about one of the finest, most genuine human beings I've ever known.

From the joy and triumph of Cone's perfect game, the roller coaster of emotions in '99 provided more tragedy when, on Saturday night, August 14, I got a call from Gene Kirby informing me that Pee Wee had died of cancer in Louisville. Pee Wee was 81, and though I knew he was in terrible shape, it was still a shock. Gene Kirby, who lives near me in Treasure Island, had worked with Pee Wee on the old NBC Saturday afternoon broadcasts in the '60s, and Dottie Reese, Pee Wee's widow, wanted us to be pallbearers.

The last time I'd seen Pee Wee was the previous winter. He had a winter home in Venice, about an hour and a half south of St. Pete. Soot and I drove down to have dinner with Pee Wee and Dottie and their friends, Norm Iler and his wife. At the time, Pee Wee was extremely weak from the cancer and could barely walk. I had my own problems, limping around on my bad knee that needed the operation. We went to this nearby restaurant called the Crab Trap II.

The restaurant had a set of stairs going into it, and as Dottie and the Ilers went ahead, Pee Wee and I lagged behind. Going up the stairs Pee Wee had his arm around me for support, and I was holding onto the banister, just trying to stay on my feet. They were all at the table as the two of us came hobbling across the restaurant, holding on to each other for support. At that point, Pee Wee hollered over to Dottie for everyone to hear, "Hey, Dottie? You ever see two old broken down shortstops like this?" The whole place burst out laughing.

I knew how bad a shape Pee Wee was in, but I didn't want to believe he was never going to get well again. When he died, all I could feel was emptiness. He'd been a part of my life my entire 51 years in baseball. He treated me like a son when I first came up to the

Dodgers, but the truth was, we were like brothers. It was a devastating loss.

I think of Pee Wee all the time, none more so than in 2000 when David Cone was going through his struggles. Coney, who had always managed to find a way to overcome sore arms and just plain slumps, was becoming increasingly frustrated at not being able to get anybody out anymore. I don't know if it was any consolation, but I recalled for him the time Pee Wee and I had been out golfing a few years ago. Pee Wee was 77 and his body was already breaking down from the cancer. But he'd been a great golfer all his life, regularly shooting in the 70s, and now he could barely hit the ball fifty yards.

"Look at that!" he complained. "I can't hardly hit the damn ball out of my shadow!"

"Look at *us*!" I countered. "Thank God we're *on* the golf course, still playing! It doesn't matter how far you can hit the ball anymore. The joy and satisfaction is just *being* here!"

I look at Coney, knowing all he's overcome, and I say it's a tribute to him just that he's still out there.

It seemed death was around every corner in 1999. Besides DiMaggio and Pee Wee, Paul O'Neill, Scott Brosius, and Luis Sojo all lost their fathers that year. Closer to home, I lost my brother Harold on July 21. Then on September 9 Catfish Hunter died of ALS—Lou Gehrig's disease. He was only 53. I didn't know Catfish that well, except to see him when he came to spring training. It was only from others that I knew what a great man he was. The last time any of us saw him was in spring training when I was running the team for Joe. The previous winter Catfish had revealed that he had ALS, and George felt it would be good for him to come to spring training and be around the team for a couple of days.

I'll never forget lying in the trainer's room, getting treatment for my knee, and seeing Gene Monahan rubbing Catfish's limp arms down, knowing he had no chance. Monahan loved Catfish. They'd been close going all the way back to the mid-'70s when Catfish joined the Yankees. After Catfish left the room, smiling and uncomplaining as always, Monahan, who always maintains a tough outer demeanor, had tears in his eyes.

As I said, it was remarkable the Yankees were able to play through all that tragedy and turmoil in '99, not to mention the impossible task of having to live up to the previous season. Besides all the deaths and Joe's cancer, Strawberry got suspended again in April for violating his probation in Tampa. It wasn't until August when he rejoined us. And still the Yankees managed to win 98 games and take the division by four games over the late-charging Red Sox.

Once again we met the Rangers in the first round of the play-offs, and once again it was no contest. The hex we had over Texas was one of baseball's great mysteries. They had a helluva team, with good righthanded hitters like Juan Gonzalez and Ivan Rodriguez to poten-tially counteract our lefthanded pitching. It just didn't figure we'd beat them as much and as easily as we did. It got to a point where they knew in their hearts they couldn't beat us. I know that feeling. I was on the Dodgers when the Yankees regularly beat us in the World Series in the '50s. Believe me, you don't know how big that Dodger win in the '55 Series was to all of us, to get that monkey off our backs. I think we'd have all been scarred for life if not for Podres pitching his 2–0 shutout in Game 7.

In 2000 when Texas came to town for the first time, Joe and I were standing around the batting cage as Rangers manager Johnny Oates approached us.

"I just want to tell you, I'm sick and tired of congratulating you two guys," he said.

I can understand.

Beating the Wild Card Red Sox in the ALCS wasn't nearly so easy, even if it did take only five games. After winning the first two games in New York, the Red Sox clobbered Roger Clemens, 13–1, in Game 3. That seemed to rejuvenate everyone in Boston, and it was important when we came right back and pounded them 9–2 behind Pettitte in Game 4. Afterward, I was reminded how Pettitte was almost dealt to the Phillies at the July 31 trading deadline. Pettitte had got-ten off to a slow start and George wanted to make some changes. But pitching is the name of the game—especially ours—and both Joe and Mel were adamantly opposed to trading Pettitte.

They say in baseball some of the best trades are the ones you don't make. I'll never know how close we came to trading Pettitte, but if we had, it probably would have cost us winning it all again. I can't imagine how we could have gotten equal value for him.

It looked like we were going to wrap it up fairly handily when

El Duque took a 4–0 lead into the eighth inning of Game 5. The Red Sox, however, had one last gasp in them; and had they been able to pull it off, it could have meant a big momentum shift in the series.

When Jason Varitek homered and Nomar Garciaparra doubled to start the eighth for Boston, Joe lifted El Duque and brought in lefty Mike Stanton to face the lefthanded Troy O'Leary. That didn't work, as Stanton walked O'Leary. Now, Joe brought in Jeff Nelson, who retired Mike Stanley on a flyout. With another lefty hitter, Brian Daubach, due up, Joe replaced Nelson with his other lefty reliever, Allen Watson. Red Sox manager Jimy Williams countered that move by sending up righty Butch Huskey, who drew another walk.

All of a sudden we were facing a bases-loaded, one-out situation and the very real possibility of blowing the clincher we thought we had won. It was here, six months after I'd started him over Irabu in that game in Oakland, that Ramiro Mendoza had what I feel was his defining moment as a Yankee. I don't know how many times during the course of the previous two years Mendoza would have a bad outing—and Joe would have to call George and talk him out of sending the kid to Columbus. There's just something about Mendoza. He can start, relieve, he's got a good sinker and curveball, and he's been a very valuable part of the team. He was sorely missed in 2000, especially when Nelson and Stanton were going through all their problems in August and September.

So after the Daubach walk, Joe brought Mendoza into the game with obviously no margin for error. Mendoza responded by striking out Scott Hatteberg and retiring Trot Nixon on a foul pop to Brosius. What is it Warner Wolf, the longtime TV sportscaster in New York says? You could have turned your TV sets off right there. It was on to Atlanta for another World Series confrontation with the Braves.

This World Series, however, wasn't nearly as challenging as '96. I suppose we can thank the Mets for doing their best to wear the Braves out in a grueling six-game NLCS. We got great pitching from El Duque and Cone in Games 1 and 2 in Atlanta, then came home and completed a second straight World Series sweep in New York. That gave Joe Torre a record 12 straight World Series wins for a manager!

Over the winter, a lot of the key players on the two straight championship teams moved on. Chili Davis retired, Girardi and Sojo were let go as free agents, Chad Curtis was traded to Texas, and then in March, Darryl was found to have failed another drug test and was suspended again, this time for the whole year. As for me, I was nearly gone too.

After putting it off and putting it off, I finally decided to get a knee replacement operation. For nine out of 10 people these operations are fairly routine, and their new knees are as good or better than the old ones. I was the unlucky one it didn't work on.

When I reported to spring training, I could hardly walk. Instead of giving me the mobility I hadn't had in years, the knee hurt worse than ever. After a couple of days, I told Joe I didn't think I could make it.

"Don't worry," he said. "There's plenty of time and plenty of help here. Just be here with me."

I agreed to stay, but it was embarrassing watching Willie Randolph have to perform so many of my duties for me. I was both useless and hurting. Then on the third or fourth day, George got me a golf cart to get around to all the fields. That was great, but it was embarrassing, too.

Meanwhile, we had only one staff meeting the entire spring, none with Steinbrenner. With about five days left, Brian Cashman called us all in. His first word was, "How do you like the team?"

Nobody answered. Finally, I spoke up and said it wasn't the same team.

Cash almost seemed to take offense.

"What do you mean?" he asked.

I replied: "We don't have Straw, Chili, Girardi, Sojo, and Curtis. I'm not saying it's not a good team. It's just not the *same* team. Plus, our fifth starter [Ed Yarnall] has already failed."

"We've got Mendoza," Cashman said.

"That isn't where we need him," I said. "We've won because we've had him in the bullpen."

I didn't want to tell Cash how I really felt—which was that this was going to be a tough year. One day, Lee Mazzilli, who had replaced Jose Cardenal as our first base coach, and I were talking about what the team needed. He was thrilled to be part of it and looking forward to going to the World Series.

"This ain't gonna be any automatic cinch this year," I said.

It wasn't until halfway through the season that Cashman, who wanted to give this team every chance, came around to the same thinking and swung into action. I'm not sure if the Yankees finish first again if Cashman doesn't get David Justice, Glenallen Hill, Denny Neagle, Jose Vizcaino, not to mention bringing Sojo back. We were staggering into July. Then Justice came over from Cleveland and hit 12 homers with 38 RBIs in his first 45 games for us, and Hill was picked up from the Cubs and hit 10 homers in his first 51 at bats. Between the two of them, they filled the huge middle-of-the-order power void left by the loss of Chili and Darryl.

Vizcaino, who Cash got from the Dodgers for Jim Leyritz, proved to be an especially important acquisition because of Knoblauch's injury. He couldn't replace what Knoblauch gave us at the top of the order—nobody could—but he gave us a sure-handed second baseman and helped solidify our defense up the middle. Looking back on that conversation I had with Cashman in the spring, I didn't even know we were going to be without Knoblauch most of the year—and that may have been the biggest loss of all.

Because Knoblauch had this throwing malady, when he went out in late July complaining of a sore elbow, the front office was skeptical. They cited all the medical reports that couldn't find anything wrong with him. People speculated it was all in his head because he was afraid to play second base and make a crucial throwing error.

Knoblauch's inability to play in the field caused Joe considerable problems when we got to the World Series. But first we had to get there; and the way we collapsed down the stretch gave me serious doubts about that. My initial doubts about this team had been lessened when Justice, Hill, and Vizcaino came over and provided the quick shot in the arm they did. But then, with no apparent reason, as we were closing in on clinching the division title, everything that could go wrong went wrong.

From September 14–30 we lost 15 out of 18 games and were outscored 148–59! It was by far the worst streak of baseball by the Yankees in the five years Joe had been managing them, and about the worst streak I'd ever been associated with. I wondered if we'd ever come out of it. Actually, we hadn't had a consistent winning streak all season in which the pitching and hitting all clicked together, but this was a case in which they all went bad together! People kept saying we were going to make the playoffs anyway. My response to that was, "Who are we gonna beat?" I'd never seen anything like this. In '78 with the Red Sox we simply stopped hitting. This 2000 Yankee team stopped doing everything. It wasn't pretty. If you tried you couldn't be so horseshit.

At the same time, the Red Sox—under my pal Jimy Williams—were taking advantage of our futility, managing to hang in there. Barely. They were still mathematically alive in the AL East race up until September 28. I think it's remarkable the Red Sox were even in contention after the way their general manager, Dan Duquette, totally undermined Jimy in the heat of the pennant race. All season long, Jimy was finding himself in the position of trying to keep his hot-tempered center fielder, Carl Everett, under control. Everett simply wasn't a good guy, judging from the way he carried on. At least that's the way people like myself viewed him from afar. He seemed to be a constant disruption, threatening and screaming at umpires, coaches, teammates, writers, and ultimately Jimy. Earlier in the season he'd been suspended 10 games for nearly head-butting umpire Ron Kulpa, and on the day he was reinstated he got into a shouting match with Jimy. He seemed to need some kind of help. Instead Duquette babied him at the expense of undercutting his manager's authority and creating disunity on the ballclub.

In the middle of a critical five-game series with the Indians in late September, Everett, who was limited to pinch-hitting duty because of a hamstring injury, showed up late to the ballpark for the first game of a day-night doubleheader. Jimy had assumed Everett was okay to play because he hadn't come out early for treatment, and he'd written his name in the lineup. But when Everett finally showed up he said he was unable to play, forcing Jimy to replace him with his backup center fielder Darren Lewis. There was a confrontation between Everett and Lewis in the clubhouse right after that. But when Jimy pointed out how nuts it was for a player to be showing up late for a game in the final days of a pennant race, Duquette, incredibly, sided with Everett, saying: "The bottom line is how you perform on the field."

Anybody in baseball should have been outraged. Jimy merely said, "If I was the general manager I would certainly back the manager. If you can't back him you probably need to get rid of him."

What should have happened, if you ask me, was for the Red Sox to get rid of Duquette. In 52 years in baseball, I'd never seen a general manager do such an underhanded thing to a manager. To publicly back a player—a player who was clearly in the wrong—over the manager was disgraceful. I was especially disappointed in John Harrington, the Red Sox CEO, for saying and doing nothing in Jimy's defense.

Harrington and I were good friends, going back to when I worked in Boston. We hung out together, went to dinner and the racetrack. But I've lost all respect for him now. Jimy Williams is a good and decent baseball man, hard working, dedicated, and an excellent manager. He certainly didn't deserve that kind of treatment from his bosses. Even after I got fired in Boston I always rooted for the Red Sox, except when they were playing a team I was with. But as long as Duquette is running the Red Sox, I hope they lose every game they play. As far as I'm concerned, he and Everett deserved each other.

Meanwhile, bad as the Yankees were going (we finished the season with just 87 wins, the fewest of any of the 2000 playoff teams), I knew we were better than this, and I just had to hang my hat on that. I have to admit, though, I wasn't real enthused about our chances going into the playoffs, first against Oakland. The A's were a young, energetic, and confident ballclub, and they weren't intimidated by us. They had a lineup full of good hitters, especially their first baseman, the AL MVP Jason Giambi, and they had two young pitchers in Tim Hudson and Barry Zito who are going to be among the best in the game for years to come. We knew we had our work cut out for us.

Joe decided that, this being a five-game series, he was going to go with only three starting pitchers. Neagle, after winning his first couple of games for us, had struggled most of September, and Joe felt we had a better chance of getting through the first round going with a three-man rotation of Pettitte, Clemens, and El Duque. They were all proven pressure-game starters. They just weren't used to pitching on three days' rest.

In addition, Joe had a dilemma with his bench after a late-summer waiver claim added Jose Canseco to it. Now we had Hill, lefthanded-hitting Luis Polonia (who was signed on for his third tour of duty with the Yankees in early August), and Canseco all wanting playing time at DH. Joe handled that by calling a meeting with all three of them and promising he'd find a way to get them all at bats. A lot of managers would have just let them sit and wait, but Joe believed in letting them all know they were part of the team and would be worked into it as best he could.

We took a 2–1 lead in the best-of-five Division Series against Oakland, and hoped to wrap it up in four games at home. But Clemens had an off night in Game 4 and we got smashed, 11–1, forcing a Game 5—and an all-night plane trip back to Oakland. That was about the worst trip I ever had to take, and I'd even told a few writers before Game 4 that if I *did* have to take it I'd probably retire right there and then. But what I noticed on that long flight back West was a team clearly angry—but not moaning—about their fate. I just sensed they were determined to take care of business the next night.

Before the fourth game, Knoblauch had decided to pass up infield practice, telling reporters he saw no point in it if he wasn't going to play. I don't know to this day what Joe said to him on the plane ride back to Oakland. I only know Knoblauch was back in the leadoff spot in the lineup—at DH—and ignited the six-run first inning that carried us to a 7–5 win in that Game 5.

Pettitte didn't have it, showing the ill effects of pitching on three days' rest. But fortunately Mike Stanton, Jeff Nelson, and Mariano Rivera did, throwing 5 ⅓ scoreless innings of relief to get us to the ALCS.

In my opinion, Stanton more than anyone else epitomized the Jeckyl & Hyde personality of the 2000 Yankees. In the month of August he suddenly couldn't get anybody out. I suspect his arm was hurting, but he never used that as an excuse. It got so bad that George blasted him in the papers, and Joe had to stop using him in his normal setup role of protecting leads in the seventh and eighth innings. He started straightening himself out in September, during the team's bad streak, but we went into the playoffs not really sure of which Stanton we were going to have. Then in Game 5 of the Division Series against Oakland, Pettitte was out of gas in the fourth inning, and Joe had no recourse but to bring Stanton on with two out, runners at first and second, and two runs already in.

Stanton got Eric Chavez to ground out to leave those two runners stranded, and that started him on a tremendous streak of dominant, shutout relief pitching in the postseason. He didn't pitch in the ALCS against Seattle, but Joe used him in four games in the World Series. In those appearances Stanton was just about perfect. He faced 14 batters in the Series and retired all of 'em—seven by strikeouts. It kind of got overlooked, the job he did, but to use a term more associated with the Mets, he was amazin'. You could've made just as strong a case for him as for anyone to be the World Series hero.

All of a sudden, after winning that Game 5 against the A's, I was feeling better about this team. The way they responded to being written off and roughed up in the Oakland series made me think there might be another World Series run in them after all. Still, I knew Seattle would be a formidable opponent, if only because they'd handled us pretty well during the regular season. One thing Joe had concluded from the Oakland series was that we had to return to a four-man rotation, which meant Neagle would pitch Game 1 against the Mariners.

He didn't pitch badly. Freddy Garcia, the young, hard-throwing Mariner righty, simply was better that night. Garcia struck out 13 in pitching Seattle to a 3–2 win and a 1–0 lead in the series. And we were well on our way to being down 0–2 after the first two games at home with Mariners lefty John Halama taking a 1–0 lead into the eighth. That's when we suddenly broke out, scoring seven runs on eight hits, the brunt of the damage coming off lefty reliever Arthur Rhodes. I know Mariners manager Lou Piniella had relied on Rhodes all season long, especially against lefthanded hitters, and justifiably so. It just wasn't a good idea against us. Teams wanted to pitch lefthanders against us because they didn't realize our lefthanded hitters could hit them.

A prime example of that was when we went into Baltimore late in the 2000 season. The Orioles were winning the game fairly handily—as was the case with most of the opposing teams during that awful stretch—when their manager, Mike Hargrove, brought lefthanded reliever Buddy Groom into the game. Groom was trying to become only the second pitcher in history to achieve five straight seasons of 70 or more appearances. The reason for this achievement was his ability to get selected lefthanders out. Just not ours. Going into the 2000 season Tino Martinez was 8-for-17 against Groom and Paul O'Neill was a phenomenal 10-for-14.

Our lefties had the same kind of success against Rhodes, who had a career ERA of 7.14 against the Yankees going into the 2000 postseason. What we also had going for us, though, were the extensive scouting reports prepared by Gene Michael and his staff. I've never seen as thorough and detailed reports as Michael and his scouts provided us for the postseasons from 1996–2000. In the case of Rhodes, we knew he was essentially a fastball/slider pitcher, and that when he got ahead he'd throw his slider. If he was behind, though, nine times out of 10 he'd throw his fastball. Piniella brought him in again in the seventh inning of Game 6 to face David Justice. There were two on and the Mariners were leading, 4–3. Rhodes fell behind in the count, 3–1, and threw Justice a fastball, which was slammed into the upper deck in right to help send us to the World Series.

I guess I don't have to state here how important *this* World Series was. A *Subway Series*. Anybody who'd been following George Steinbrenner for the past quarter-century knew how obsessed he was with winning—and how even *more* obsessed he was about the Mets. It went all the way back to 20 years earlier, when the only time the Yankees and Mets ever met was in meaningless spring training games. They were meaningless to everybody but George, and his managers—whether it was Billy Martin, Lou Piniella, Bob Lemon, or whoever—dreaded those spring training games against the Mets because they had to play them as if it were the World Series.

Well now it *was* the Mets in the World Series, and as you might imagine, George was consumed with beating them. In the workout at Yankee Stadium before the first game, he was on the field checking all the conditions with his security people. During Game 1 he spent most of his time in the Yankee clubhouse, watching it on TV with Mel Stottlemyre.

Among all the things that weren't right about the Yankees during the 2000 season, the most serious was Mel being diagnosed with cancer of the blood plasma in April. We're talking about a very special person here, whose importance to the Yankees is immeasurable. Mel continued to work with the pitchers throughout the season, around his chemotherapy treatments. You'd have never known what he was going through. He was a rock. When it was finally time for him to undergo what they called a stem-cell transplant, he left the team in September.

After we got the through the playoffs, Mel was able to return to the ballpark on a limited basis. He had to stay in the clubhouse, away from crowds, because he was so susceptible to infection. He didn't go to the games at Shea at all. After the final game I went into Joe's office in the visiting clubhouse and asked Rick Cerrone, the Yankees' media relations director, for Mel's phone number.

When Mel answered the phone, he sounded ecstatic.

"Is this something?" I said.

"Unbelievable," Mel replied. "I wish I could have been there for the guys. They're some group, huh? I'm really proud of them."

Later on that night, I found out that Mel's brother had died earlier in the day of a brain tumor. Because of his own condition Mel couldn't even go to the funeral. He never said a word about it on the phone because he didn't want to ruin the night for the rest of us. That's what kind of a person he is.

I've always said you can't predict anything in baseball, but it figured this Yankees–Mets World Series was going to be a low-scoring proposition. There was just too much good pitching on both sides. Game 1 bore that out. For seven innings it was a duel between Al Leiter and Andy Pettitte, two really tough lefties. We were trailing, 3–2, going into the ninth when Bobby Valentine brought in his closer, Armando Benitez.

After Posada led off by flying out deep to center, it was O'Neill who had the most important plate appearance of the Series by drawing an 11-pitch walk. I'm watching this, seeing O'Neill foul off pitch after pitch, and I'm saying to myself, "This is what this team has been all about for five years now. Working the opposing pitcher deep into the count, being patient, figuring out a way to win." Due up next was Scott Brosius, who hadn't been swinging the bat particularly well. Joe decided he was going to pinch hit. Looking down at Canseco and Hill, he said to me, "What do you think, Canseco?"

"How about Polonia?" I said.

Joe smiled. He figured exactly as I did: Polonia, a lefthanded hitter, had a much better chance of making contact here against Benitez, and all we wanted was a base hit to keep the rally going.

Sure enough, Polonia singled into right field and Vizcaino got the second of his four hits in the game to load the bases. Coming into the Series, Vizcaino hadn't hit a ball good in about 45 days, but Joe decided to start him at second on a hunch he might be able to hit Leiter. We then tied it on Knoblauch's sacrifice fly, but the game went into extra innings and immediately became one of the all-time Series classics, in fact the longest game in history—4 hours 51 minutes.

We left the bases loaded in the 10th and two more on in the 11th, and by now the suspense was becoming almost unbearable. At least our bullpen was making it easier, with Rivera and then Stanton retiring 11 straight Mets from the ninth to the 12th.

Against righty Turk Wendell—Valentine's fifth reliever of the night—we staged the winning rally in the 12th on singles by Tino and Posada, and finally another two-out single by Vizcaino. The next day Ozzie Smith, who was working the Series as a TV commentator, was joking about how all of Joe's moves seemed to work out right.

"I can't get over how smart Joe got since he managed me in St. Louis," Smith said. "Like yesterday morning. He woke up, saw a ray of light coming through the windows, raised his hands and said, 'VIZ-CA-INO!'"

"Yeah," Joe laughed, after it was all over. "I'm so smart I started Vizcaino again in the fifth game against Leiter and he went hitless. Instead it's Luis Sojo, his replacement, who got the winning hit."

We won the second game of the Series too, although with all the hullabaloo over Roger Clemens and Mike Piazza you'd have never known it. Clemens pitched a gem of a game, blowing away the Mets on two hits and nine strikeouts over eight shutout innings. But his effort got buried by an incident in the first inning, when Clemens broke Piazza's bat with a fastball and wound up fielding a large piece of it as it whistled past him on the mound.

Nobody seemed to know where the ball had gone (it was in our dugout), least of all Piazza, who had started to first. I know Clemens didn't see Piazza when he threw the bat piece in his direction. Nevertheless, the media jumped all over it, and that's all anyone wanted to talk about after the game. Of course, Fox TV had done a pretty good job of fueling the controversy by showing the Clemens–Piazza beaning incident from a couple of months earlier about 70 times leading up to and during the game.

Let me say a few things about this.

First of all, is Piazza the only guy who ever got hit in the head with a baseball? There's only one man who knows if that ball was thrown at his head purposely and that's Roger Clemens. But I don't believe there's a human being in professional baseball who would throw a ball *hoping* to hit a man in the head. I was disappointed in Piazza coming out and saying Clemens threw at him on purpose. What's Clemens supposed to do? Throw the ball over the plate so Piazza can keep hitting home runs off him, or make him feel uncomfortable? I've been hit in the head twice—and without the benefit of a protective helmet. The problem you have in baseball today is that hitters don't know how to get out of the way of pitches because pitchers are afraid to pitch inside anymore. That more than anything else is why you have all these 5.00 earned run averages.

As for the bat-throwing incident, do you think Clemens was going to throw that bat at Piazza if he was standing at home plate? He had no idea Piazza was in the first base path. If he were deliberately throwing the bat at Piazza, he would have hit him. Clemens has been made a villain in all of this because he pitches inside. I think that's unfair. I'm just glad he's been on my side.

We lost the third game despite another tremendous postseason pitching effort by El Duque. That ended a streak of 14 consecutive World Series wins, and I have to believe no team will ever break that record. For one thing, it's quite an achievement just to *be* in 14 consecutive World Series games. Even more amazing was this: By winning the 2000 World Series in five games, it gave Joe Torre's Yankee teams 16 wins in 17 World Series games after they lost the first two to the Braves in 1996. And in those 16 wins, the Yankees were behind six times in the seventh inning or later!

Before that third game against the Mets, Steinbrenner was already in the visiting clubhouse at Shea Stadium at 4 P.M., pacing around with that stern look on his face. I was out in the dugout when first Billy Connors and then Tony Cloninger came out. They'd been ordered by Steinbrenner to get off their stools and let the players sit down on them. The Boss was extremely unhappy over the accommodations in the visitor's clubhouse and he decided to do something about them. The next day a Ryder truck pulled up to the press gate at Shea Stadium, and the attendants proceeded to unload all of the furniture from our clubhouse at Yankee Stadium.

You've got to give George credit, though. The comforts of home served the players well, and with another shut-the-door job by the bullpen, Joe was able to piece together a 3–2 Game 4 win. Neagle started and again pitched okay, except for a two-run homer to Piazza in the third. After retiring the first two Mets in the fifth on flyouts to left, Neagle was one out away from being in position to get the win. But Joe had decided long before Piazza came to bat again that Neagle wasn't going to pitch to him. As Piazza began strolling to the plate and Joe walked to the mound, waving to the bullpen, the crowd was in shock.

Not only was he taking Neagle out of the game, he was replacing him with *David Cone*, who had pitched only one inning (against the Mariners in the ALCS) in three weeks. Cone had just a terrible 2000 season in which all his tricks of the trade betrayed him, leaving Joe no choice but to take him out of the rotation in September. There was some debate about putting him on the postseason roster, but Joe's loyalty to him and Cone's experience won out in the end. Joe would use him in long relief, or in situations just like this one with Piazza.

Neagle, I'm sure, was pissed. But he had to know this was how we operated here. As Jeter had often said: On this Yankee team, you checked your egos at the door. And wouldn't you know, Cone got Piazza on a harmless inning-ending pop-up to second. It may not have been the biggest out of Cone's career, but I'm sure it will be the one he most remembers. It turned out Joe had to pinch hit for Cone the next inning, so that was the extent of his World Series contribution. Believe me, though, it was big, and I'm just glad Cone got to feel he had a part in it. It turned out to be his final appearance as a Yankee.

Neagle also left the Yankees as a free agent after the season. I'm not sure how he was going to fit in on that team anyway. They say lefthanders can be a little strange, and this guy surely was. Among the quirky rituals he had was his habit of going into the clubhouse and getting himself a water bottle between innings of his starts. He'd then come out with a bottle, take a couple of sips out of it, spit them out, and set the bottle down on the bench. Between every inning it was the same thing, and the longer Neagle stayed in the game the more near-full water bottles there were lined up on the bench. One time somebody—I think it might've been Knoblauch—decided to knock over all the bottles, and it really screwed up Neagle's mind. But what can I say? The man got $50 million from the Colorado Rockies. I've got to tip my cap to him.

Joe needed five pitchers to hold the Mets to two runs in that game, and I believe we had to make more decisions in those five World Series games than we did in two months. Another decision in Game 4 that didn't work out so well was when Joe sent Canseco up to pinch hit for Cone in the sixth. Canseco had become another "forgotten man" on the club, having been left off the roster for the first two rounds of the postseason, and this was to be his only at bat in the World Series.

I don't think I ever rooted harder for a guy to get a base hit than I did for Canseco in that situation, mainly because of what he's been through recently. Until he came over to the Yankees on waivers from Tampa Bay, he was a regular his whole career—often one of the best power hitters in the game. Now he'd been sitting around for three weeks without swinging a bat. Unfortunately, he was unable to shake off the rust and looked at three strikes.

The final game of the 2000 World Series was also one for the ages, as far as I'm concerned. Once again, Pettitte and Leiter faced off, and this time they were even better. Bernie Williams finally broke out of his 0-for-15 Subway Series slump with a homer in the third to put us up 1–0, and Jeter later tied the score 2–2 with another solo homer in the sixth. Otherwise, Leiter completely dominated. Pettitte was right there with him. After battling with his control early, Pettitte made some great pitches when he had to, getting Benny Agbayani on an inning-ending groundout with runners on second and third in the sixth, and striking out both Todd Zeile and Robin Ventura to leave another stranded in the seventh.

It all came down to the ninth inning. Leiter struck out Tino and O'Neill to start it, then walked Posada after thinking he'd struck him out on the 2–2 pitch. This was the second-biggest plate appearance of the Series. Similar to O'Neill in Game 1, Posada used up nine pitches for his walk.

This time Joe elected not to hit for Brosius, and Scott—who, it should not be forgotten, had been the World Series MVP in 1998—

rewarded his faith with a base hit to left. Now Joe had to hit for Mike Stanton, who had pitched yet another scoreless inning of postseason relief in the eighth.

At the same time, Valentine had a decision to make. Leiter was up to something like 140 pitches, and later, the second-guessers would all be screaming he should have taken him out at that point. I know what I was thinking. I was *praying* Valentine would take Leiter out because this guy was a warrior in the same mold as O'Neill. I'd have gladly taken our chances against any reliever Valentine might bring in.

Joe sent Luis Sojo up to hit against Leiter, and Sojo bounced a ball through the middle for the go-ahead run. Brosius also scored when the relay from center field hit him and skipped away from Piazza. John Franco relieved Leiter right after that. As Leiter left the mound, all of Shea Stadium stood and gave him a standing ovation. I was over in the corner of our dugout, and, thankfully, the cameras didn't catch me tipping my cap to this man. I thought it was only fitting, considering the way the season had gone for us, that Piazza—like the Mariners' Edgar Martinez in the ALCS—should be at the plate for the final out, representing the tying run. When he flied to deep center Joe let out a scream, and, for a moment, until we saw Bernie settle in under it, we both thought he'd tied it up.

After the game, amid all the champagne spraying in our clubhouse, Claire Smith, the columnist for the *Philadelphia Inquirer*, came over to me for my comments on the whole turn of events.

I told Claire: "We have the happy side of it right here, but in my heart, I really feel for Al Leiter. He pitched one helluva ballgame tonight. It's a crime for people to be second-guessing Bobby Valentine for leaving him in so long. He'd knocked the bat out of Brosius's hands three times before in the game!"

I wanted to go over to the Mets' clubhouse and see Leiter and Valentine, but it just didn't seem appropriate. They were both hurting. But Leiter is some kind of pitcher. He reminds me of a lion in a cage the way he stalks around the mound. And Bobby Valentine is one good baseball man.

In my opinion, Joe Torre did his best job of managing in 2000. As I said, we didn't have near the deep and talented team we'd had the other championship years, and while we were able to fill some major holes, particularly with the trades for Justice, Hill, and Vizcaino and the re-acquisition of Sojo, there were serious problems that never got resolved. We missed Ramiro Mendoza in middle relief and as a spot starter, especially when Cone struggled as he did. And we had to go through the entire postseason with a grab bag at second base when we were forced to use Knoblauch in a DH role.

The only person who really knows if Chuck Knoblauch was genuinely hurt and not just mentally unable to go out there in the field is Chuck Knoblauch. If there's one thing I learned as a manager, it's to take a player's word about an injury. When I was with the Cubs we had a pitcher, Scott Sanderson, who complained of having a back injury. He'd pitch five innings and immediately look to the dugout to get him out of there. Players on both our team and the opposition noticed it, and said he just waited until he had done enough to get a win.

All I know is right after Jim Frey and I got fired in Chicago, Sanderson went into the hospital and got a back operation.

Of course, I'm a fine one to talk about wanting to come out of there. It seemed like every other day in 2000 I wanted out. I came very close to going home at the All-Star break. My knee—which was filled with calcium deposits the like of which the doctors had never seen—was killing me, and I wondered if I'd be better off getting off the road and retiring to Treasure Island. But every time I'd go to Joe, he'd say, "What's the point of going home? You're going to hurt just as much there."

And whenever I found myself complaining about my knee, I'd think about that day on the golf course with Pee Wee.

I was in pain, but I was still there, after 52 years and seven decades; still drawing my only paycheck from baseball. I look back at all the baseball people I've been privileged to call friends—people from all walks of the game, from owners like George Steinbrenner, Walter O'Malley, Gene Autry, and Danny Kaye; executives like Buzzie Bavasi, Haywood Sullivan, and Dick O'Connell; legends like Yogi Berra, Pee Wee Reese, Jackie Robinson, Roy Campanella, Sandy Koufax, and Duke Snider; other great players like Don Drysdale, Gil Hodges, Johnny Podres, Frank Howard, Carl Erskine, Clem Labine, Andre Dawson, Ryne Sandberg, and Jim Rice; managers like Joe Torre, Jim

Leyland, Jimy Williams, Tommy Lasorda, and Gene Mauch; fellow "lifers" like Jim Frey, John Vukovich, Joe Pignatano, and Gene Kirby; to the broadcasters like Vin Scully, and all the writers who listened to all my bullshit—and I feel I've been truly blessed. For a lifetime .235 hitter, I've had one hell of a life.

INDEX